Archives & Manuscripts:

Administration of Photographic Collections

Mary Lynn Ritzenthaler
Gerald J. Munoff
Margery S. Long

THE SOCIETY *of*
AMERICAN ARCHIVISTS

BASIC MANUAL SERIES

Chicago, 1984

7th Printing 2002

ISBN #0-931828-61-9
Library of Congress catalog card #84-51384

A number of registered trademarks are used in the text. Kodak, Kodachrome, Kodacolor, Ektachrome, Ektacolor, Pana-tomic X, Type C, and Type R are registered trademarks of the Eastman Kodak Company. Polaroid, Polaroid-Land, and Polacolor are registered trademarks of the Polaroid Corporation. Agfacolor is a registered trademark of Agfa-Gevaert, Inc.

Foreword

Photographs in archival holdings offer unique documentary information and at the same time pose singular problems in their organization and care. To assist archivists in identifying and defining the issues, the Society sponsored a series of workshops on the administration of photographic collections. This manual grew out of these presentations and will serve as a guide to managing photographs in an archival manner.

The Society is pleased to offer *Archives & Manuscripts: Administration of Photographic Collections* as the latest publication in its *Basic Manual Series*. This series provides sound information on such archival functions as appraisal, arrangement and description, reference and access, security, and surveys, as well as on the special topics of conservation, automated access, public programs, exhibits, and reprography.

We gratefully acknowledge the support of the National Endowment for the Humanities, which helped to make this publication possible.

David B. Gracy II
President

Contents

Introduction

Mary Lynn Ritzenthaler

This manual is directed toward archivists, manuscript curators, librarians, picture specialists, and others who work with historical photographs. Its primary focus is on photographs that have documentary value as historical resource materials for research, publication, and exhibition. Most often such photographic records are found in archival and manuscript repositories, libraries, and historical societies and museums. Such institutional collections vary widely in size, subject focus, and use, but share many common problems. Whereas many repositories contain special treasures—examples of scarce historical processes or unique images of great research value—typical archival collections also contain masses of photographs that in themselves do not have great value as individual images. Rather, such massive accumulations gain their significance as they relate to an entire collection, either of other photographs or of pertinent manuscript and archival materials. Photographs that are valued solely as fine art are largely outside the scope of this manual.

The manual addresses all aspects of managing historical photographic collections, from appraisal and accessioning through research use and exhibition. The manual is written from an archival perspective, stressing the principle of provenance and the development of systems to organize, access, and preserve entire collections, rather than individual images. Photographs have not always been recognized as important resource materials within archival repositories; thus, they have been relegated to secondary status and in many cases have never been described or recorded in guides or finding aids. Although photographs have increasingly been used for research, archival practice regarding their organization and management is far from standardized. The manual serves as an initial step toward this end. Dynamic, rather than static, concepts are presented in the realization that these will change over time as repositories, as well as the archival profession in general, refine their approach to photographic materials.

Optimum practice for managing photographs is presented, with the realization that repositories cannot necessarily achieve ideal conditions immediately. The manual thus offers guidance in setting priorities and making sound decisions based on the scope, character, monetary value, and research potential of the photographic materials. In this context, the institutional goals and priorities that will affect the manner in which photographs are stored, used, and handled must be evaluated. With all of these factors in mind, it is possible to make reasonable and balanced—if sometimes difficult—decisions regarding the management of photographic collections.

Although the manual is introductory, the authors assume that readers have an understanding of basic archival principles and practices. Building upon this framework, the authors address issues and concepts that are integral to administering a photographic collection, including access, arrangement and description, and appraisal and collecting policies. Legal issues, which are closely intertwined with collecting photographic materials and making them available for research use and publication, are covered in the manual as well. Since technical knowledge of the history of photographic materials is required to properly identify, store, date, and interpret images, a brief technical history of photography is included, along with aids for identifying major processes. Preservation procedures that apply to entire collections, rather than individual items, are emphasized. Proper storage and handling rather than chemical treatments are thus recommended, as are practical means of solving access and storage problems. Copying photographic materials, which is an important preservation tool and a very necessary aspect of reference service, is also addressed to complete the range of concerns that must be considered.

While archival systems designed to handle photographs at the group rather than the item level are generally advocated, in many instances optimum practice mandates that photographs be evaluated individually during a number of archival procedures, such as appraisal, identification, and devising appropriate storage systems. Despite the apparent conflict between group vs. item-level handling, the governing approach or concept is the group approach. Thus, appraisal decisions represent cumulative evaluations based upon looking at many individual photographs and considering individual items in the context of the overall group. Descriptions in finding aids integrate knowledge gained from looking at many single images and describing them collectively. Also, preservation and storage policies are carried out on groups of photographs that have the same individual requirements. As will be discussed throughout the manual, archival management of photographic collections requires developing broad integrated systems to manage unique materials.

The history of photography involves an extensive number of technical processes and innovations. This manual focuses on the photographic materials produced by major processes that are likely to be found in historical collections, rather than the fascinating but obscure derivations from major trends. Black-and-white still photographs form the core of most archival collections, and are the primary focus of this manual. Color processes, most of which are inherently unstable, are considered primarily from the perspectives of storage and preservation through image reproduction, although other archival activities, such as appraisal and exhibition, are of special concern when dealing with color images. Optical disk and laser technology are still in their infancy, but, like microreproduction, have applications for photographic collections, especially in the areas of preservation and access. Information is presented on these as well as other developing technologies that show promise for enhancing use and management of photographic collections.

Archivists responsible for photographic collections should develop a comprehensive understanding of photographic materials, from the perspective of their content as well as their technological development and physical form. Photographs often evoke an emotional response in the viewer, but archivists must also respond to photographs intellectually and be aware of the wide range of information to be gained from the photographic record. Some of this information will supplement and support the written record, and some will be unique to the photographic medium. It is also important to understand the limitations imposed by the point of view of the photographer and the technical capabilities of given periods and processes. Historical methodology similar to that applied to evaluate textual records must be applied to photographs to test their authenticity and research potential. For example, images must be scrutinized to determine whether they are originals or copies, as this can affect identification and dating. It is equally important to remain skeptical, rather than to accept photographs as what they purport or appear to be, until all data has been tested. Thus, it is necessary to verify the truthfulness of the images as well as the accuracy of captions or written notations that date or identify them. The process of verification is a responsibility shared by the archivist and the researcher, but it is of great archival importance when creating collection descriptions and writing captions for photographs used in exhibits and publications.

While photographs should generate excitement and open new avenues of research and methodological approaches, archivists should not feel intimidated or overwhelmed by them. Not all images have the same value or deserve the same treatment or handling, and archivists must be able to differentiate among good and bad photographs as well as those that contain a great deal of information and those that are repetitious and redundant. Appraisal criteria similar to those applied to textual records when making acquisition and disposal decisions must be developed for photographic materials.

In order to adequately administer photographic collections, archivists must become "visually literate." This literacy can be acquired in part by looking at many images and evaluating their informational content as well as their technical quality. Archivists should not fall victim to thinking of photographs merely as pretty pictures or illustrations, but should think of them as historical documents of unique value that must be evaluated on their own terms.

1 Photographs in Archival Collections
Margery S. Long

Written archives date back to the ancient world. The photographic record, by comparison, is very young. It began in France in 1826, when Nicéphore Niepce placed a camera loaded with a light-sensitized pewter plate in an attic window. After being exposed to the sun for eight hours, the plate contained the image of his courtyard. Niepce called it a heliograph, using the Greek words for sun and writing.[1]

In the years since Niepce's invention, photography has become a vital, familiar part of life and a universal form of communication. Journalists use photographs to inform and entertain their readers. Meteorologists use satellite photographs to plot and predict the weather. Urban planners, oceanographers, environmentalists, and developers of natural resources consult aerial photographs when making decisions on projects. Physicians depend on the X ray and photomicrography in research and diagnosis. Television newscasters inform their audiences of world events through photographic images. Photography helps people to understand their world and affects almost every aspect of their lives. The widespread use of photography is now accompanied by a burgeoning interest in the historical photographic record that has accumulated in archives, historical agencies, museums, and private collections over the relatively short life span of photography. There is a new, growing respect for the importance of photography as a link with and a record of the past.

The Photographic Record

Photographs have not always been regarded as important historical sources. Lady Elizabeth Eastlake, in her 1857 essay, "Photography," admonished the art world to cease thinking of photography as the usurper of artists and realize its own importance. "Photography's...business is to give evidence of facts, as minutely and impartially as only an unreasoning machine can give. Photography...is sworn witness to everything presented to her view...facts which are neither the province of art nor of description, but of that new form of communication between man and man...."[2]

Oliver Wendell Holmes, an ardent amateur photographer, was so impressed with photography that he called it "the mirror with a memory." In 1859 he wrote that there would "soon be such an enormous collection of forms that they will have to be classified and arranged in vast libraries, as books are now...We do now distinctly propose the creation of a comprehensive and systematic stereographic library, where all men can find the special forms they particularly desire to see as artists, or as scholars, or as mechanics, or in any other capacity."[3] In 1888 George E. Francis addressed the American Antiquarian Society with a request that it begin a "systematic and comprehensive photographic record of our country and our time."[4] For the most part, these pleas for a photographic library went unheeded.

Eventually librarians did form picture files of engravings, lithographs, and clippings from magazines and newspapers, as well as photographs, as a reference service for their patrons. They arranged the pictures in the same subject classifications as books and other published materials. The subject classifications chosen were determined by the librarian's knowledge and interpretation of the meaning of the pictures and any identifying information that accompanied them. The terms used for the subject files were taken from standard library classification systems and subject heading lists.[5] Such practices continue today in many libraries and even in some special collections departments formed to handle manuscript and non-print materials.

Archivists and historians did not always recognize photographs as primary source materials. In the formative years of archives, only written records were regarded as archival and deserving of preservation. Pictorial materials, if they were retained at all, often were removed from the collections of records and manuscripts and assembled in general picture files; the principle of provenance was seldom applied to them. Some archivists designated photographs "miscellaneous ephemera" or "memorabilia" and relegated them to the last boxes in manuscript and archival collections. Some photographs were not even noted in finding aids, but were left in their original location, intermingled with manuscripts, documents, and correspondence. Since photographs often had no identifying information written on them, such undisturbed positions in archival collections were fortunate. Often the only clue to indentification for some photographs is their location in files, reports, or dia-

[1]Beaumont Newhall, *The History of Photography* (Boston: Little, Brown and Company, 1982), 13–16; Robert Taft, *Photography and the American Scene, 1839–1889* (New York: Macmillan, 1938), 3–5; and Peter Pollack, *The Picture History of Photography from the Earliest Beginnings to the Present Day* (New York: Harry N. Abrams, Inc., 1969), 16–41.

[2]Lady Elizabeth Eastlake, "Photography," reprinted in *Photography: Essays & Images,* Beaumont Newhall, ed. (Boston: New York Graphic Society, 1980), 94. First published in *Quarterly Review* 101 (April 1857): 442–68.

[3]Oliver Wendell Holmes, "The Stereoscope and the Stereograph," *Atlantic Monthly,* 3 (June 1859): 738–48. reprinted in Newhall, *Photography: Essays & Images,* 60.

[4]George E. Francis, "Photography As An Aid to Local History," *Proceedings of the American Antiquarian Society* (April 1888): 282.

[5]Melvil Dewey, *Dewey Decimal Classification and Relative Index,* first published 1876. Charles A. Cutter, *Rules for a Dictionary Catalog,* Boston Atheneum, first published 1876. U. S. Library of Congress, *Subject Headings Used in the Dictionary Catalogs of the Library of Congress,* first published in 1897. Minnie Earl Sears, *Sears List of Subject Headings,* first published in 1923.

ries, or their proximity to a letter describing the events or naming the persons shown in the photographs.

The photographic record steadily accumulated in size and content as archives and historical agencies acquired collections of archival materials. Today the archival collections of photographs are as diverse in subject and size as the institutions that house them. An historical society, large or small, usually collects photographs that emphasize the history and culture of a specific geographic or political region. The archival collection of a religious group or denomination often includes a visual history. Business archives document the history of commerce or industry and their products. Institutional archives, such as those of colleges, universities, or social agencies, also build visual histories of their parent institutions and often develop a topical collection as well. These topical collections document a wide range of subjects, such as women, social welfare, immigrants, labor, railroads, mining, ethnic groups, performing arts, literature, and photography itself. Government archives contain photographs from the agencies and departments within the jurisdiction of the local, state, or federal government they represent.

Photographs from Historical, Aesthetic, and Sociological Perspectives

Long before Niepce made his discovery in France, many scientists and artists in other countries had attempted to capture the elusive image of reality. Not until 1839, when Louis Jacques Mandé Daguerre, who had formed a part-nership with Niepce, revealed his process, had a practical method been achieved to create a sharp, clear, permanent image. It did not take Americans long to learn this new technology. By 1845 every good-sized town and city in the United States had a daguerreotype studio and traveling photographers were taking their wagons and cameras through the countryside and villages.

Photography had a profound influence on American society and served as a direct aid to cultural nationalism. Americans were trying to free themselves from the ties to England and Europe and develop customs, traditions, and a culture that would unite the expanding country. To develop this nationalism, the public needed accurate visual information about the landscape, scenes of life in urban and rural society, and pictures of great men and women of the age. Photography provided such clear views of American life that the viewer had a feeling of actually experiencing the scenes and events. Photography allowed provincial Americans to see people and places that they would never encounter in their ordinary lives, and it helped them adjust to the transition from an insulated agrarian society to the more integrated society of the industrial revolution. Photography helped to educate and encourage artistic taste in the newly forming middle class of craftsmen and tradespeople, who had money to spend and a desire to imitate the social graces and tastes of the moneyed and landed classes. Members of the middle class wanted to immortalize themselves in a portrait as the upper classes did with paintings: the middle-class portrait was the photograph.

Figure 1-1. The reception area of a typical daguerreotypist's studio was elaborately furnished and displayed the photographer's artistry for sale. "Interior view of Meade Brothers' Daguerreotype Gallery, Broadway, New York." *Gleason's Pictorial Drawing-Room Companion*, February 1853, Vol. IV, No. 6.

Figure 1-2. In the 1860s family parlor tables held albums containing cartes de visites, cabinet cards, and tintypes, as well as a collection of stereographs to view in the hand stereoscope. *Howard Collection, University Archives, Wayne State University.*

A visit to the portrait photographer's studio was an occasion (see figure 1-1). People dressed in their best and most stylish clothes for the sitting. The studio reinforced the aura of special occasion with an atmosphere of grandeur. Because of the need for large skylights to provide strong natural light, the studio was usually on the top floor of a building. The reception area was as large and elaborately furnished as the photographer could afford. Displayed on the ornate walls and tables was a daguerrean gallery of the photographer's artistry for sale: portraits of prominent persons and scenic views of local and faraway places, which clients viewed while they waited their turn to be photographed in the "operating room" at the rear of the studio. After the sitting, the dageurreotype was developed and placed in a fancy case.

In the 1850s photography grew rapidly as a result of refinements of the known processes and the development of new ones. The collodion process introduced two new portrait forms, the ambrotype and the tintype. Because they were cheaper than the daguerreotype, they brought photography into the lives of an even broader level of American society. The most important use of the collodion process became the wet plate negative, which, for the first time, made possible duplicate paper copies of a photograph. The development of the albumen process for paper prints in 1850 eventually made the older process obsolete. The albumen paper prints were mounted on cards of various sizes, including cartes de visite (a French term meaning visiting cards), cabinet cards, and stereographs, and were very inexpensive.[6]

Personal photograph collections were common in the 1860s. On parlor tables, families had collections of cased photographs and albums containing tintypes, cartes de visite and cabinet cards depicting family members, landscapes, travel and architectural views, and portraits of famous statesmen, military leaders, and celebrities in literature, music, and the theatre (see figure 1-2). Collections of stereographs reproduced many of the same images, as well as views of the wonders of the world, scenes illustrating news events, Civil War views, and scenes of family life and humor, and were standard parlor entertainment for family and friends. Many of these family collections are now in archival repositories, preserving a rich social and cultural record of an era.

[6]William C. Darrah, *Cartes de Visite in Nineteenth Century Photography* (Gettysburg, Pa.: William C. Darrah, 1981), 19.

Lantern slides, positive transparent images on glass, were another form of photograph developed in the nineteenth century to entertain and educate. These glass slides were usually presented by traveling lecturer-projectionists in narrated "magic lantern" shows in meeting halls in towns and cities throughout the country. Sets of lantern slides in orig-

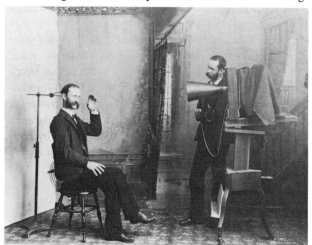

Figure 1-3. A cast iron stand with an adjustable clamp to hold the subject's head steady during long exposure times was frequently used in taking portrait photographs. The camera also was secured on an adjustable stand. "The Photographer" by A.H. Wheeler, 1893. *Photograph courtesy of the Library of Congress.*

inal slotted wood cases along with their scripts and advertisements for the shows offer documentation for the study of nineteenth-century social history. As artifacts, these materials are also of interest to students of photographic history and material culture.

Aesthetics

The fact that most early daguerreotypes, ambrotypes, tintypes, and card photographs are portraits reflects the high demand for personal likenesses and the relative immobility of the picture taking process. Exposures were long and subjects had to remain perfectly still. Thus, outdoor scenes, landscapes, and street scenes appeared deserted, since people present when the exposure began either walked out of the scene and did not register in the image at all or became a blur before the exposure was completed. As technology improved and exposure times shortened, photographers learned that in taking long shots looking down streets, people and vehicles moving toward or away from the camera registered less of a blur than traffic that crossed before the camera lens. Cameras were mounted on elaborate stands to keep them steady during long exposures. Until magnesium flash lighting was developed in 1878, there was not enough light available in the interior of homes, buildings, or factories to take photographs indoors, except in the specially skylighted photographic studios.

Composition, lighting, and the conventions of posing not dictated by technical limitations were borrowed directly from portrait painting. The subjects of nineteenth-century photographs are shown in serious, formal poses, sometimes with the chin resting on a hand to help steady the head during the long exposures. A cast-iron stand with a headrest was a common piece of studio equipment (see figure 1-3). Open smiles were difficult to maintain during long exposures. Also, since teeth were not as well cared for as they are today, the sitter did not want to reveal them to the camera; smiling poses are a twentieth-century convention.

Women are shown wearing their very best—dresses of the latest fashion, fancy bonnets or precisely coiled or curled hair, and jewelry (see figure 1-4). If they did not own any jewelry, the photographer could paint on touches of gold in the finished photograph. Men were almost always attired in their best suits, rarely in the garb of their profession or trade. Cartes de visite and cabinet card photographs of the 1860s and later reflect the Victorian era's elaborate decorative settings. Painted studio backgrounds are seen, sometimes with architectural details and furniture props for the sitter. Women are often shown at full length, some standing in profile to show a current hooped or bustled fashion (see figure 1-5). During the Civil War, officers posed in an affected military stance, many with the right hand placed inside the coat in a pose often seen in portraits of Napoleon. The subjects were photographed in the way they wanted to be seen, and their photographs reveal many of the fashionable affectations of the times (see figure 1-6).

Figure 1-4. The long exposure time required for daguerreotypes often resulted in stiff, rigid poses of the subjects who dressed in their Sunday best. *Daguerreotype courtesy of Thomas Featherstone.*

Figure 1-5. Painted studio backgrounds and architectural props created a Victorian setting in which women posed to show off their fashionable gowns. *Photograph courtesy of Thomas Featherstone.*

The styles of recognized, successful photographers were imitated by local practitioners who wanted to produce saleable photographs. Photographic styles swept across the country from east to west and filtered down from city to small town. Changes in portrait photography spread rapidly because this was the most lucrative part of the business. Full-length views gave way to close-ups, which made the subject more recognizable and thus pleased the sitter. Artful poses, with the subjects in natural positions, and enhanced with props of flowers or books, replaced the stilted poses that resulted when the subject sat or stood rigid and stared straight into the camera. Innovative camera placements presented new perspectives on familiar landscape and architectural scenes. A favorite scene, Niagara Falls, was photographed from countless viewpoints and camera angles to present a fresh approach to a scenic wonder that had been photographed repeatedly from the beginning of the daguerrean era. The subjects of scenic views, as well as new camera angles, were copied from well-known photographers—subjects such as the homes of the wealthy, busy thoroughfares, public buildings, and vistas in public parks. There was no market for photographs that recorded the life of the ordinary, lower classes. Even the photographs taken by amateurs reflected the more refined tastes, styles, and customs of the period. Amateurs learned technique from the study and imitation of the work of successful professional photographers.

Pictorial Photography

Toward the end of the nineteenth century, as technology advanced, photographers found ways to go beyond the simple action of light and chemicals to produce images that expressed their personal creativity. They manipulated their negatives and prints in the darkroom to imitate both the prevailing and the experimental ideas of contemporary painters; the result is known as pictorial photography. The soft focus that conveyed the Romanticism of the late nineteenth century was achieved to a very small degree in the camera, and to a large degree by long hours of handwork and alteration of the negative and print in the darkroom. Some of the resultant prints looked more like drawings, paintings, etchings, or lithographs than like photographs (see figure 1-7). These techniques were developed by photographers struggling to have photography accepted as art, and were adopted by professional photographers and skilled amateurs.

Straight Photography

A reaction to pictorialism in photography came in the 1920s and 1930s and resulted in what is called straight photography. Straight photographers concentrated on the real world, visible to their cameras, and carefully recorded it on film with as little alteration as possible in the photographic process. At the same time, technical advances in cameras, films, and the chemistry of photography occurred which made it possible for skilled photographers to achieve the highest level of photographic quality in the finished photograph without the need to manipulate or alter the negative or print.

Figure 1-6. Photographs of Civil War officers reveal stylized, affected military poses, many in a stance often seen in portraits of Napoleon. *Howard Collection, University Archives, Wayne State University.*

Figure 1-7. The work of pictorial photographers often looks more like a painting or drawing than like a photograph. "Rush Street ca 1930," bromide print by M. Bernstein, ICHi-18186. *Courtesy of the Chicago Historical Society.*

Characteristics of Photographs

"Photographs are not made, as a painting or drawing is, by the skill and attitude of the person wielding the brush or pencil following traditional schemes of expression. Rather, photographs are taken mechanically by a camera." Statements such as these are commonly used to support the conviction that photographs are authentic, objective representations of reality seen by the camera and by anyone present when the photograph was taken. "The camera doesn't lie" is a cliche repeatedly used to express this belief. In fact, the opposite is true. The clarity of the image, its coherence of composition, and its point of view are determined by the person behind the camera. A photographer makes choices and decisions that affect the message the image will convey to viewers.

John Szarkowski, curator of photography at the Museum of Modern Art in New York City, defines photography as a picture-making process based on selection. He discusses five issues of selection by the photographer that become inherent elements of a photographic image.[7] His discussion applies to all photographs in the photographic record.

The first issue a photographer considers is "the thing itself," or the subject the camera records in a photograph. The camera records an actual reality but the subject and the

_____

[7]John Szarkowski, *The Photographer's Eye* (Boston: New York Graphic Society, 1966).

picture of it are not the same thing, no matter how factually clear the photograph may be.

The second issue of selection is "the detail." A photographer can only record what he or she finds in nature, usually only fragmented pieces of a complete story or of the whole truth. The fragment or detail of the whole the photographer chooses to record becomes symbolic of the complete story or the whole truth. News photographs depend on one or a few images to represent the complete story; the pictures alone cannot make a clear story, but they can add life to it.

The third issue is "the frame." The central act of photography—the act of choosing and eliminating—forces an emphasis on the delineating edges or frame of the picture. The part of the whole subject or scene chosen to be inside the frame is spotlighted and gains an importance and meaning from being chosen and from the attention focused on it, while the remainder of the scene is eliminated from the picture by the frame.

The fourth issue is "time." All photographs are fragments of time and represent only the discrete portion of the time in which they were made. In the early days of photography, with its slow films and slow lenses, the segment of time recorded was relatively long and motions showed up in the photograph as blurs. As films became faster and more sensitive, and shutter speeds became faster also, the fragment of recorded time shortened and motion stopped in the picture. Each photograph portrays the scene or subject only in that moment of time in which it was made.

"Vantage point" is the fifth issue. The photographer, in choosing where and how the camera will record the scene, imposes a perspective or viewpoint that can emphasize, distort, or conceal the truth of the subject or scene. The bird's-eye view differs markedly from the worm's, and viewing the action from the front, back, or side can give three contradicting perspectives of the same event.

These issues are inherent elements of photography and offer the photographer—professional, serious amateur, and casual snapshooter—opportunities to affect the truthfulness and accuracy of the representation of the whole event in a photograph. For example, a photographer sent to photograph a sparsely attended political rally has the opportunity to take photographs that make completely opposite statements about the rally. If the photographer takes the exposure from the back of the hall, the photograph will record the small turnout. If the photographer chooses to stand at the side of the platform and include only the speaker and the first few rows of enthusiastic supporters, this photograph of the event will convey an entirely different and opposite message. The photographer chooses the position of the camera and the lens, which will determine the size of the subject in the image and the amount of coverage of the field of vision. The photographer selects the arrangement of the figures in relation to each other and to other objects, and within the frame of the overall picture. The object or subject takes on an importance by being photographed, by being singled out from all the choices to be recorded in a photograph. The instant chosen to click the shutter and record the scene is a unique, definite moment, like no other moment in the passage of time. All of these considerations by the photographer become crucial elements in a photograph and in its authentic representation of the reality of the scene.

Many photographs in archival collections may not seem to have been taken by a photographer who consciously and deliberately considered Szarkowski's five points. They may appear to be formless and accidental images. Nonetheless, in every case there was a reason for the making of the photograph, however casual the reason may have been. Even an unsophisticated amateur photographer chooses the subject and the pose, where to stand with the camera, and the moment to press the shutter button.

Photographs as Documentary Evidence

Photographs that provide evidence that something existed or that a particular event happened are called documentary photographs. The years of experimentation to discover a way to create a permanent picture were spent by men motivated by the desire to record reality. In the early years of photography, the camera was used mainly as a copier of nature, and it seemed miraculous that the camera could provide such a clear representation of what the human eye saw. The photographs were regarded as literal records or documents of nature as it existed. It was not long after photography gained acceptance as a visual reporter of the real world that photographers began introducing their own comments about that reality in the way they used their cameras and the images they created. Thus, photographs must be analyzed to test the truth and accuracy of their content, as must all historical records.

Photographers have always been eager to record history with their cameras. Just two years after the wet collodion process was introduced, Roger Fenton took his darkroom on a wagon to the Crimean War. From 1853 to 1856 the photographs he sent back to England were the first graphically real reports of war to government and people. Mathew Brady, perhaps the most famous of all early American photographers, also sensed the value of photographs as historical records. He took his staff of photographers from his successful Washington photographic studio onto the battlefields of the Civil War. Timothy O'Sullivan and Alexander Gardner worked for Brady early in their careers and went on to become famous in their own right as early documentary photographers. Their Civil War photographs were not, however, of actual battles in progress, since cameras and emulsions of the time did not allow for capturing action shots. Brady's photographers took their wagons into camps to photograph the soldiers and campaign preparations (see figure 1-8). As soon as the firing stopped, they were on the battlefield to record the grisly aftermath of battle. Their photographs of the Battle of Bull Run mark the beginning of American military documentary photography.

Photographs of the western survey expeditions of the late 1860s and early 1870s have become famous both as photographic art and as historical documents of the expeditions sent to record what lay beyond the waters of the Mississippi River. Americans wanted accurate information about the great wilderness. Adventuresome photographers, equipped with cameras, tripods, and portable darkrooms, climbed mountains in all kinds of weather and exposed huge glass plates sensitized with wet collodion (see figure 1-9). These breathtakingly beautiful documents from the cameras of Timothy O'Sullivan, William Henry Jackson, Carleton E. Watkins, and others influenced Congress to set aside regions as public lands for national forests and the first national park. In 1870 O'Sullivan also went with the U.S. Navy expedition to the Isthmus of Panama. His photographs formed part of the evidence in the report that construction

of the canal was possible and aided in the selection of the best route across the isthmus. Gardner and O'Sullivan also accompanied railroad survey parties through Kansas and the New Mexico Territory. Their images aided the railroad companies in determining the best routes for the tracks that opened the West to settlement and connected it to the business centers in the East. Local photographers were important members of their pioneer communities and helped to record the expanding and developing western frontier. Photographic documentation of frontier life is a rich resource that has been collected and preserved in many archives.

Social reform documentary photography began with Jacob Riis in New York City in the 1880s. Riis was a newspaper and magazine writer frustrated by the ineffectiveness of the printed word in his efforts to bring help and change to the poor in the tenements of New York City. He learned to use a camera and shocked New York with his documents of living conditions of the urban poor.[8]

---

[8]Jacob A. Riis, *How the Other Half Lives: Studies Among the Tenements of New York* (New York: Charles Scribner's Sons, 1890; republished, Dover Publications, 1971).

Figure 1-8. Mathew Brady's photographers captured campaign preparations with the slow emulsions and camera lens available at the time of the Civil War. Some of the men appear as blurs in the photograph because they moved during the exposure. "Massaponax Church, Va., May 21, 1864. 'Council of War': General Ulysses S. Grant (standing behind bench) examines map held by Gen. George G. Meade. Photo by T. H. O'Sullivan." *Courtesy of the Library of Congress.*

Figure 1-9. Adventuresome photographers with the western survey expeditions climbed mountains with their cameras and portable darkrooms to record the breathtaking views of the wilderness. "On the overhanging rocks, Glacier Point, 3,300 feet above valley, showing Yosemite Falls, photographing the wonderful Yosemite, California." *Photograph by Timothy O'Sullivan, courtesy of the Library of Congress.*

Lewis Hine is perhaps the most widely known of the American social reform photographers, and his fame continues to grow even today, years after his death. Several books of his work have been published, and exhibitions of his photographs have traveled across the United States in recent years.[9] He too found the camera more eloquent and effective than the written or spoken word. A sociologist, he took his camera to Ellis Island to record the immigrants arriving in the early years of this century. Hine documented their homes in the city slums and the sweatshops, mines, mills, and factories where they worked (see figure 1-10). His photographs recording the exploitation of children in all types of work helped lead to the passage of child labor laws.

Farm Security Administration Photographs

In 1935 an important event in photographic history began. When President Franklin D. Roosevelt created the Re-

[9]Lewis Hine published one book, *Men at Work* (New York: Macmillan, 1932; republished, Dover Publications, 1977). See also: Jonathan L. Doherty, ed., *Women at Work: 152 Photographs by Lewis W. Hine* (New York: George Eastman House in association with Dover Publications, 1981). *America and Lewis Hine* (New York: Aperture, Inc., 1977). Judith Mara Gutman, *Lewis W. Hine and the American Social Conscience* (New York: Walker and Company, 1967).

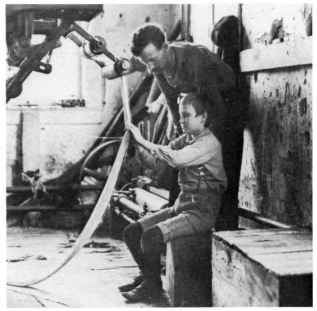

Figure 1-10. Lewis Hine's photographs of the exploitation of children in all types of work helped lead to the passage of child labor laws. "Hosiery mill, 1909," by Lewis W. Hine. *Courtesy of the Archives of Labor and Urban Affairs, Wayne State University.*

settlement Administration to provide economic assistance to poverty-stricken farmers, the Historical Section was created to photographically document the agency's activities. In 1937 the Historical Section became part of the Farm Security Administration (FSA), and for eight years its staff created the contemporary visual history which is known as the FSA File of Photographs.[10] The work of the twelve photographers under the direction of Roy Stryker "turned the direction of photography."[11] Following the tenets set down by straight photographers, they developed a style that attempted to make an accurate record and a moving comment in the language of pictures. They aimed not to expose or exploit the unfortunate people they photographed.

The type of photography that evolved out of this project affected the style of photography that appeared in the two popular picture magazines, *Life* and *Look*, for the next twenty-five years. It set new standards for the art of photography with the fresh application of old and the development of new techniques and the use of new equipment. FSA photographers were the first in the United States to use the small, 35-mm Leica camera on professional assignments; and with this camera they were able to stop action and photograph events as they took place. FSA photographs look natural and unposed, yet the photographers used accepted portrait photography techniques, such as having the subjects look directly toward the camera, to photograph ordinary people in their own surroundings, far from photographic studios. FSA photographers used flash bulbs to light the interiors of homes that had never been photographed before, such as simple log cabins and modest farmhouses in remote rural areas. All of these techniques were new to American photography at that time and have become standard techniques of photographers today.

Dorothea Lange's "Migrant Mother" photograph is one that has come to symbolize the work of the FSA Historical Section. Lange happened on the desperate widow and mother in a peapickers' camp in Nipomo, California, in March 1936. The pea crop had frozen and there was no work. The woman had sold the tires from her car to buy food and could not move on. In ten minutes' time Lange took the series of five photographs from which came the single most reproduced photograph of the FSA file.[12] The series of five

images does give additional information about the plight of the 32-year-old stranded woman, but their main function may be to authenticate the veracity of the one image, which carries its message almost without caption (see figures 1-11, 1-12, 1-13, 1-14, and 1-15). The photograph represents the 1930s meaning of a documentary photograph: a subjective interpretation of a social circumstance, a "human document."[13]

Photojournalism

Photojournalism, the branch of photography that has more influence on public thinking and opinion than any other today, evolved from this great period of documentary photography in the 1930s. It was fostered first by the picture magazines such as *Life* and *Look,* then by newspapers that made lavish use of the photo story and news photos. After World War II, interpretive documentary photography faded from popular use, to be replaced by the factual visual reporting of photojournalism.

Newspaper photographs were taken in vast quantities to supply the daily newspapers' demand for pictures. Frequently the photographs were shot hastily in a series of exposures in rapid succession, and thus the photographer had little control over the composition of the image through framing, detail, time, or vantage point. Often it was not until the film was developed in the darkroom that the photographer could be certain that at least one exposure from the group adequately represented the event and could be reproduced in the employer's publication. Today, modern high-speed cameras with automatic film winds are responsible for millions of such news photographs created each year. Newspaper photographs vary widely in their content; some depict exciting news events while others are posed, static, and highly repetitive. Nevertheless, newspaper photo files can be a rich chronicled source of local photographs that are not available elsewhere.

Amateur Photographs

Amateur photographers have contributed to the photographic record from the earliest times. In the early years of photography, amateur photographers were among the wealthier class, for pursuing photography as a hobby required time and a capital investment in equipment, in addition to an understanding of the chemistry of the process. In the 1880s a series of new developments made picture taking easier. Gelatin dry plates could be purchased already sensitized by the manufacturer, eliminating the messy, time-consuming, and exacting processes of preparing wet plates immediately before exposure in the camera and developing them immediately after exposure. Hand-held cameras were much more convenient and mobile than those dependent on a tripod for steadying. Futhermore, the faster exposure times of glass plate negatives and later roll film eliminated the

[10]There are 80,000 prints and 200,000 unprinted negatives in the Farm Security Administration Photograph File in the Prints and Photographs Division of the Library of Congress, Washington, D.C.

[11]Ansel Adams quoted by Susan K. Reed in an interview, "Ansel Adams Takes on the President," *Saturday Review* (November 1981): 32–34, 39.

[12]Dorothea Lange, "The Assignment I'll Never Forget," *Popular Photography* 46 (February 1960): 42, 126. See also: Karin Becker Ohrn, *Dorothea Lange and the Documentary Tradition* (Baton Rouge: Louisiana State University Press, 1981). Roy Emerson Stryker and Nancy Wood, *In This Proud Land* (New York: Galahad Books, 1973). Therese Thau Heyman, *Celebrating a Collection: The Work of Dorothea Lange* (Oakland, Calif.: Oakland Museum, 1978). Milton Meltzer, *Dorothea Lange: A Photographer's Life* (New York: Farrar, Straus, Giroux, 1978).

[13]William Stott, *Documentary Expression and Thirties America* (New York: Oxford University Press, 1973), 5–12.

Figure 1-11

Figure 1-13

Figure 1-12

Figures 1-11, 1-12, 1-13, 1-14, and 1-15. Dorothea Lange's series of five photographs document the plight of the destitute mother and her children in a peapickers' camp in California. The 5th photograph (p.20) became the best known photograph in the Farm Security Administration Files and the visual symbol of the California migrant workers of the Depression. ''Migrant Mother, Nipomo, California 1936.'' *Photographs by Dorothea Lange, courtesy of the Library of Congress.*

Figure 1-14

Figure 1-15

need for a camera on a tripod. The emergence of commercial processing laboratories eliminated amateur photographers' need for a darkroom.

In 1888, for an investment of $25 in George Eastman's Kodak camera, photography became as simple as the Kodak advertising slogan: "You press the button, we do the rest." The ease of using this camera gave a strong impetus to snapshot photography—a term used to describe photographs casually made with a hand-held camera. For the first time a wide range of people had the means to make their own pictures. No longer were personal photographic records infrequent, stiffly posed professional photographs taken only on special occasions. They became frequent, casually snapped images that recorded people engaged in everyday activities as well as at special events.

Many amateur photographers formed camera clubs to acquire and perfect technical skills, learn the art of photography, and share experiences. Camera clubs have contributed significant photographic records to archival repositories. For example, each year since 1949 the Chicago Area Camera Clubs Association has donated to the Chicago Historical Society the results of an ongoing project to photographically document the growth and changes in Chicago neighborhoods (see figure 1-16).[14]

Amateur photographers created great numbers of personal and family collections of photographs, many of which are now housed in archival collections. George Talbot discussed family photographs and albums in the exhibit catalog, *At Home*:

> "Most of the photographs were made by or for people in the ordinary course of their lives. They were intended to be family keepsakes, not objective documents. They showed what people were proud of, thought interesting, and what they wanted to show to others. . .Taken as a whole, these amateur picture collections are an extraordinary record of almost everything that was considered acceptable by the middle class or at least those aspects of life the middle class felt free to make public."[15]

Details of home environments are revealed in amateur photographs taken with portable cameras (see figure 1-17). The standard, stylized background of the photographic studio gave way to an accurate rendering of the family surroundings. By their selection and arrangement of photographs, family albums suggest the personality of the owner as well as the social and cultural customs of a time and place.

Local Professional Photographers

Local history collections in historical societies, public libraries, and archives are enriched both by family photograph collections and by the works of local professional photographers. The changes that industry and technology brought to towns at the end of the nineteenth century were exciting and provided subjects for saleable photographs. The laying of water mains, gas lines, sewers, and streetcar

---

[14]Glen E. Holt, *"Chicago Through a Camera Lens: An Essay on Photography as History," Chicago History* 1 (Spring 1971): 158–69.

[15]George Talbot, *At Home: Domestic Life in the Post Centennial Era, 1876–1920.* (Madison, Wis.: State Historical Society of Wisconsin, 1976), iv,vi.

Figure 1-16. "The Chicagoland in Pictures" documentary project of the Chicago Area Camera Clubs Association records the growth and changes in Chicago neighborhoods each year and donates the photographs to the Chicago Historical Society. "Carnicerias Jimenez, North Avenue and Keeler. Photo by John McCarthy, May 29, 1983." ICHi-18170. *Courtesy of the Chicago Historical Society.*

Figure 1-17. Family photographs show the prevailing styles of interior decoration, especially those items that are considered symbols of success in the world, such as fancy stoves and elaborately patterned wallpaper. Notice the photograph of Niagara Falls hanging over the parlor table. "Christmas 1910, J.P. Jacobson, photographer." *Photograph courtesy of University of Wisconsin Area Research Center Archives, River Falls, Wisconsin.*

Figure 1-18. Local photographers documented the changes industry and technology brought to cities and towns toward the end of the nineteenth century. *Bureau of Public Roads #30-N-15423 photograph, courtesy of National Archives and Records Service.*

tracks; the paving of streets (see figure 1-18); the installation of electricity lines and street lights; and the construction of large, important buildings were recorded by the town's professional photographers. In many cases the photographs were taken on assignment for a government agency or a commercial client; also, many photographers with business acumen recognized the potential for sales to townspeople, civic organizations, and local businesses interested in a town's growth and technical progress. Often it was a personal interest in a facet of town life that led to the creation of a valuable photographic record of community history. Workmen began to be idealized and romanticized in many of these photographs. There was a saying in the lumbercamps from Michigan, across Wisconsin and Minnesota, to the Northwest, "You're not a lumberjack until you've had your picture taken with your axe, saw and a big tree" (see figure 1-19). Many photographs were taken to advertise commercial establishments and the services they offered. The photograph of the butcher with all his wares displayed over the front of his store is typical of these images (see figure 1-20). It is one like thousands taken to document commercial life in a developing frontier town.

From its beginnings as the invention of scientists, photography has been practiced by thousands, professionals and amateurs alike, who shared no common tradition or training. Most photographers have been self-taught and have learned by imitation or by serving a short apprenticeship with another photographer. Some have regarded photography as a science that needs to be continuously improved and developed by scientific experimentation; others have used it as a recording tool for scientific endeavors of all kinds. Still others have been artists continually searching for ways to use photography as a medium of creative expression. Some photographers have regarded photography as a medium of communication and documentation, and others have seen it as a business directed by the needs of the client. Millions of photographers—professional and amateur alike—have used photography for their own entertainment and pleasure. Some photographers have achieved a mastery of the photographic process and have expressed themselves with superior artistic and technical skills, making a significant contribution to photography. By scholarly consensus of art and photographic historians, they are designated master photographers. Much of the legacy from these diverse creators of the photographic record survives in archival repositories across the country.

Photographs in the Art World

The developing interest in historical photographs was paralleled by a growing recognition of photography in the art world. In 1937 Beaumont Newhall mounted the first major exhibit on the history of photography in an American art museum.[16] As a result of its success, in 1941 Newhall became the first curator of the Museum of Modern Art's Department of Photography. After World War II, Newhall organized the George Eastman House collection of photography in Rochester, New York, and he served as its first curator. George Eastman House, renamed the International Museum of Photography in 1972, exerted a major influence on the collection of art and historical images and on scholarly research. "The Family of Man," an exhibition mounted in 1955 by Edward Steichen for the Museum of Modern Art in New York City, traveled throughout the world in the late 1950s and continues to be one of the most famous photographic exhibitions. The catalog has sold millions of copies. These two exhibitions were major factors in establishing photography as an art form and in encouraging other prominent art and historical museums to collect and exhibit photographs.

The 1970s saw not only an unprecedented market for photography as art, but also the emergence of scholarly

---

[16]The exhibit was such a success, both critically and with the viewing public, that the catalog to the exhibit was published as a hardcover book, *Photography 1839–1937*. In 1938 Newhall, to fill the need for a history of photography from the art perspective, expanded it as *A Short Critical History of Photography*. In 1949 it was rewritten as *The History of Photography*, and it was revised in 1964 and 1982. Another acclaimed history was written in 1938 from the technical and cultural viewpoint: Robert Taft's *Photography and the American Scene: A Social History 1839–1889*.

Figure 1-19. Photographers began to romanticize the ordinary working man in their pictures, and poses such as this one became commonplace across the country. *Photograph courtesy of the Archives of Labor and Urban Affairs, Wayne State University.*

Figure 1-20. Many photographs taken to advertise commercial establishments and the services they offered are now a historical record of the development of frontier towns into urban centers. *Photograph courtesy of the Wiskmann Collection.*

research in photography. The number of articles, monographs, books, and exhibitions on all phases of photography, including technical, historical, artistic, and critical aspects, increased dramatically. In 1973 the Smithsonian Institution installed a permanent exhibition on the history of photography in the History and Technology Museum. In 1974 the Whitney Museum of American Art in New York City mounted the exhibition, "Photography in America," a survey of the history of American photography. Books devoted to the retrospective works of nearly all the well-known photographers, from Mathew Brady and the daguerrean era to Richard Avedon and contemporary high-fashion photography, were published as photography continued to grow in popularity.[17] Scholarly works, art publications, and popular publications created an even greater awareness of photographs and a favorable public response to auctions, gallery shows, and museum exhibitions.[18]

Publicity given to record-setting prices paid for single photographic images by famous photographers brought widespread attention to the collecting of photographs. Photographs attained the status of art investments. In 1970 the Parke Bernet (later Sotheby–Parke Bernet) auction house in New York City presented an auction at which photographs sold for unexpectedly high prices. The collection offered contained historical photographs, photographic apparatus such as cameras, rare books about photography, and books with original photographs tipped into the pages of the text. The works by masters as well as little known and anonymous photographers were the same kind of photographic materials often found in archival collections. This auction set the standard prices for many types of photographs; and these prices, in many instances, have continued to grow. The auction houses have influenced sales and prices even in remote antique shops. As a result, archival institutions that purchase photographic materials in the art and antique market have had to pay the higher and sometimes inflated prices.

The art market divides photography into photographica and fine art. Photographica includes cased photographs, such as daguerreotypes, ambrotypes, and tintypes; card photographs, such as stereographs, cartes de visite, and cabinet cards; and antique cameras and photographic equip-

ment. All of these photographic materials, largely from the nineteenth century, are widely available at antique shops, flea markets, and trade fairs. Fine-art photography encompasses images made from the beginning of photography to the present and includes select examples of the forms from the photographica group, especially if they are from a well-known photographer or are rare images of an important individual, scene, or event. Fine-art photographs usually are large paper prints—rare historical images, prints of master photographers, and work of newly acclaimed contemporary photographers. Fine work from previously unknown nineteenth-century photographers is also becoming available as a result of the growing public awareness of the historical and monetary value of such photographs.[19]

Some collectors and dealers assume the high prices quoted for fine examples of historical images or master photographers' prints apply to all images from the same time period, even those of unknown origin and poor technical quality. This has had a serious impact on archival collecting programs. Many people who previously would have donated photographs to institutions now wish to sell them; and collections that actually would have little monetary value in the market, but are important to a repository's collection, must be purchased at the inflated price if the institution is to acquire them.

Archivists and curators whose collections contain examples of photographica and fine-art photography should keep informed of current market prices, as reflected in prices realized by Sotheby–Parke Bernet, Christie's, and Swann in New York. These auction houses set the standard for photography galleries throughout the country. Their catalogs are helpful in determining the monetary value of a repository's collection. Such an appraisal might indicate a need for increased insurance coverage and special security measures, such as vault storage and very limited access, for the more valuable items in the archives.

Research Uses of the Photographic Record

Biographical and institutional studies have long been interests of historical research. In the 1950s, research trends changed to include topics such as work and workers, labor organizations, women's studies, ethnicity, and local history; these subjects began to gain attention from researchers in American culture, anthropology, and archaeology, as well as history. The new fields of research were accompanied by a dramatic increase in the use of photographs and other illustrations to supplement written texts. Re-

---

[17]For example, see Dorothy Meserve Kunhardt and Philip B. Kunhardt, Jr., *Mathew Brady and His World: Pictures in the Meserve Collection* (New York: Time-Life, 1977); Richard Avedon, *Portraits* (New York: Farrar, Straus, and Giroux, 1976).

[18]An example of the scholarly works published is *Mirror Image: The Influence of the Daguerreotype on American Society* (1971) by Richard Rudisill. The scholarly journal, *History of Photography*, which is international in scope, began publication in 1977. Art publications such as *Art News, Art in America*, and *Portfolio* regularly print articles on photographs. The popular publications, such as *American Photographer*, which first appeared in 1978, and *Camera Arts*, begun in 1980 (and merged with *American Photographer* in 1983), brought an awareness and appreciation of photography as an art form to a wide audience.

[19]Peter H. Falk, *The Photographic Art Market* (New York: Falk-Leeds, International, 1981). Other guides to the photographic market are: Richard H. Blodgett, *Photographs: A Collector's Guide* (New York: Ballantine Books, 1970). Landt and Lisl Dennis, *Collecting Photographs: A Guide to the New Art Boom* (New York: E. P. Dutton, 1977); Margaret Haller, *Collecting Old Photographs* (New York: Arco Publishing Co., 1978); and Lee D. Witkin and Barbara London, *The Photograph Collector's Guide* (Boston: New York Graphic Society, 1979).

spected historical journals used photographs for the first time to illustrate articles. Many state historical journals changed their size, format, and paper stock to accommodate photographic reproductions. One of the most successful of all historical journals of this period was *American Heritage*. Begun in 1947 as the official organ of the American Association for State and Local History, the magazine was acquired by a private publishing firm in 1954. It became one of the most popular history journals of all time and had a great influence on historical publications in general. Encouraged by the success of *American Heritage,* publishers began marketing pictorial histories in book form. Time-Life published whole series with historical themes. These also became financial successes and the heavy demand for historical photographs began. Initially, the large collection in the Prints and Photographs Division of the Library of Congress was the major source of images. As the need for previously unpublished images expanded, publishers searched through hundreds of archives, libraries, and historical societies across North America. Archival institutions, historical agencies, and libraries were deluged with requests for illustrations for the new publications.

Photo editors and free-lance photo researchers, working for publishers of textbooks and other publications, began to use the popular pictorial history books as illustrated guides to national photographic collections. Researchers often requested reproduction prints for their books from the selections seen on the pages of the pictorial histories. The practice has resulted in the repeated use of some images to illustrate a topic or event.

The successful uses of historical photographs in popular publications and the acceptance and exhibition of photographs as an art form by respected museums contributed to a general heightened awareness of photography. This newly focused interest in photography in all its facets directed increased attention on historical photograph collections. Repositories and their staffs, as well as researchers, began to appreciate the important contributions collections of photographs can make to historical research.

In the past, historical photographs have been used mainly as illustrations to make both scholarly and popular publications more visually attractive and enticing to their readers, and this use continues to predominate today. Writers often left the choice of illustrations to the editor or a photo researcher. The placement of photographs in the publication was determined by layout design and production costs rather than by relationship to the information contained in nearby text. Researchers and scholars from many disciplines were unfamiliar with the use of photographs as primary source materials and were reluctant to include them in their research. This reluctance is slowly fading as more scholars find photographs a valuable source of information and evidence that is not available in traditional written research materials.

Social historians, whose approach to the study of the American past is through the study of ordinary people, find much of the information they seek in the photographic record. The rich resources of family and local history collections in particular contain information and evidence in visual form that is not available in other records. Social historians use photographs as primary resources for the study of workers, racial and ethnic groups, women, children, the elderly, families, urban and rural communities, social behavior and value systems.

Sociologists, anthropologists, ethnographers, and folklorists use photographs as analytical tools for studying society's institutions and the patterns of societal values, attitudes, and behavior. Wedding photographs, funeral pictures, photographs of other traditional family celebrations, and those from government and social agencies are sources for this type of research.

A procedure for the use of photographs in research for any of the social science disciplines has been suggested by Howard Becker, a sociologist. He recommends that a number of photographs on the same topic, subject, or event be studied, examined, and compared as a safeguard to support the reliability of any conclusions that are drawn from a photograph. Each photograph should be submitted to a test of its truthfulness: has the camera, with the help of the photographer, lied? The test questions he suggests are the following: 1) What is the "truth" the image asserts? 2) What part of a "greater truth" is the "truth" the image asserts? (One photograph cannot show "the whole truth.") 3) Is this "truth" representative or characteristic of the subject matter shown in the photograph, or is it posed, faked, or somehow manipulated? 4) What is known about the photographer and his artistic style that may have biased the "truth" of the photograph? and 5) Has the archivist contributed to the censorshop of the "truth" of the photograph by the process of selection or elimination of other photographs of the same topic, subject, or event?[20] Other evidence supplied by other photographs, written documentation, oral interviews and site visits where possible, as well as the knowledge of the technical and aesthetic aspects of the time period in which the photograph was made, must also be weighed. The researcher should guard against interpreting nineteenth-century photographs by twentieth-century moral, cultural, and technical criteria.

Anthropologists and archaeologists have used photography as a recording tool in their research methodology. They continually use historical photographs from their anthropological archives for comparative evaluations and research. Also, anthropologists have developed the photo elicitation technique, an information-gathering research

[20]Howard S. Becker, "Do Photographs Tell the Truth?", *Afterimage* 5 (February 1978): 9–13, and "Photography and Sociology," *Afterimage* 3 (April–May 1975): 22–32.

method of showing a photograph to a number of people and encouraging them to talk about the photograph. This technique has been adopted as part of the procedure in many of the copy clinic outreach projects undertaken by archives and historical agencies to collect and preserve local history photographs.

Urban historians, urban planners, and historic preservationists often seek photographs of domestic and public architecture among collections of local professional photographers and architectural and real estate firms. Many homes and buildings scheduled for historic preservation have deteriorated or have been altered so that the original design is no longer evident, and only old photographs can aid in restoring them to their original appearance.

Students of fine-art photography, art historians, and other scholars use collections of historical photographs to study the development of aesthetic taste and to learn to recognize the distinctive photographic style of various photographers. They also use study collections containing examples of historic photographic processes to learn to recognize the individual characteristics of the many processes. Students and scholars of material culture use historical collections for research on photographs as artifacts of American culture.

Documentary filmmakers use archival collections of still photographs in the preliminary stages of filmmaking as they research the subject of the film and the availability of existing visual images. They may use still photographs in the production of their films not only to supplement motion-picture footage, but even to take the place of film footage when specific scenes cannot be located in a film archives. They also use still photographs as an artistic change of pace or in a montage. Local and national television news producers use historical photographs to illustrate anniversaries of historical events, especially when motion-picture footage is not available on short notice for a news telecast.

A major new use for photographs since the 1950s has been in museum exhibitions. Interpretive exhibits have become the norm and replace the open storage style of display. Enlargements of photographs are used to show the context in which artifacts were created or used, or as a supplement when certain artifacts are not available or cannot be placed on exhibition.

Many institutional, organizational, and corporate donors draw upon their collections of historical photographs placed in archival repositories to provide materials for their publications, particularly for those produced to mark important milestones in their history. Exhibitions that feature historical photographs are also created for these anniversaries; other exhibitions at conventions and conferences, when properly mounted, create a favorable public image for both the donor and the archival repository that houses the collection. Archival repositories use photographic collections for their own publications and outreach projects, and as resources for exhibitions mounted at the repository or at off-site locations for special occasions, conferences, and professional meetings.

The photographic record that accumulated and has been actively collected since the beginning of photography is preserved in archives, libraries, historical agencies, and museums. This vast record includes the first permanent image by Niepce[21] and examples of the creations of the many practitioners of the art, science, and business of photography—a visual history of life since the pioneers began recording it in photography's many forms. Repositories that house this visual history have assumed the responsibility of preserving and making the record available for study, research, and viewing.

---

[21]Niepce's first photograph was found in 1952 by Helmut Gernsheim, and is in the Gernsheim Collection at the University of Texas at Austin.

2 History of Photographic Processes

Gerald J. Munoff

Uses of Technical Knowledge

The study of the development of the technical processes of photography is critical to many, if not all, archival uses of photographs. The archivist, librarian, curator, scholar, researcher, writer, and publisher can all benefit by acquiring at least a rudimentary knowledge of this aspect of photography. For the photographic archivist, such knowledge must be an integral part of a detailed and comprehensive understanding of the complex and far-reaching medium of photography. A technical knowledge of photography can allow the archivist to develop important skills necessary for dealing with many aspects of photographic collections. In some areas, such as conservation and storage, this knowledge will have specific consequences for action. In other areas, such as identification and interpretation, a knowledge of processes, case mats and mounts, photographers, etc., are simply clues, usually not definitive, that can aid in the identification and interpretation of a photograph. Consequently, technical knowledge must be used in conjunction with other information. The following four broad areas describe the archival activities that can benefit most from a knowledge of the technical history of photography.

Conservation

Because photographs are chemically and physically more complex than most archival materials, a basic understanding of how they were made and how they age is essential to their proper care. Different processes require different storage materials and environmental conditions. Also, for copying and duplicating it is important to identify unstable processes, such as diacetate negatives, cellulose nitrate negatives, and poorly processed prints. Compromises often must be made when deciding on storage materials, environmental conditions, and handling of originals, but these decisions should be made with an awareness of the possible consequences. Chemical research on photographs is in its infancy, but important information is beginning to appear, and a technical knowledge of photography is essential to understand and apply this information.[1]

---

[1] Klaus B. Hendriks and Brian Lesser have recently published research on disaster recovery for photographs that have immediate practical applications. See: "Disaster Preparedness and Recovery: Photographic Materials," *American Archivist* 46 (Winter 1983): 52–68. James Reilly has recommended practical storage considerations for nineteenth-century prints in a forthcoming book (to be published by Eastman Kodak) entitled: *Photographic Prints of the Nineteenth Century: Care and Identification.* Alice Swan's recommendations for care of prints are based on her research. See: "Conservation of Photographic Print Collections," *Library Trends* 30 (Fall 1981): 267–96.

Identification of Images

There are two basic activities in dealing with photographs as primary resource materials: identifying the date and subject of the photographs and then interpreting what the image means. The identification is often viewed as primarily the responsibility of the archivist, while the interpretation is viewed as the responsibility of the researcher. The divison of activities is becoming less distinct, however, and the photo archivist is often called upon to interpret photographs. As can be seen from the chronology (see figure 2-1), identification of a photographic process can give an approximate date of the image. Identifying the process may only date the image within a decade, but this may be more specific than can otherwise be determined. At the very least, identifying the process establishes the earliest date at which the image could have been taken.

In dating the image, knowledge of technical aspects is often the most important, if not the only, clue. Photographic technology did not develop, however, in a linear manner with one process forming the basis for a new process which immediately made the older process obsolete. As the chronology shows, at most times a number of processes were in use because of their ability to render various aesthetic effects and because a range of variously priced processes appealed to clients of a wider economic spectrum. Nevertheless, an ability to identify processes and understand their characteristics and a knowledge of mounts or cases, toning, and hand-coloring, together with an interpretation of the internal evidence observed in the image, can often lead to a dating and identification of an otherwise unlabeled image. The internal evidence can be the date on a license plate of a car, for example, or the presence of gaslights instead of electric streetlights, or the style of the subjects' clothing.

Interpretation

After as much identifying information as possible has been established for a group of photographs, their meaning must be interpreted. The photographic archivist must determine why they were taken, if the images are representative of the time and place, if they are accurate or truthful, and how the images were used. As with dating images, knowledge of the technical process aids in interpretation. For example, a knowledgeable observer will realize that the lack of action photographs of the Civil War does not indicate that photographers were not present during battles, but rather, that the long exposures required precluded taking photographs in which the subject moved.

Another key technical aspect of interpretation involves the ability to distinguish copies of photographs from originals. Copies of photographs are often altered by cropping or, at the very least, loss of detail, if not more overt manipulation. Also, copies of historical photographs often are in a different medium than the original. Consequently, the failure to recognize that a photograph is a copy in a different

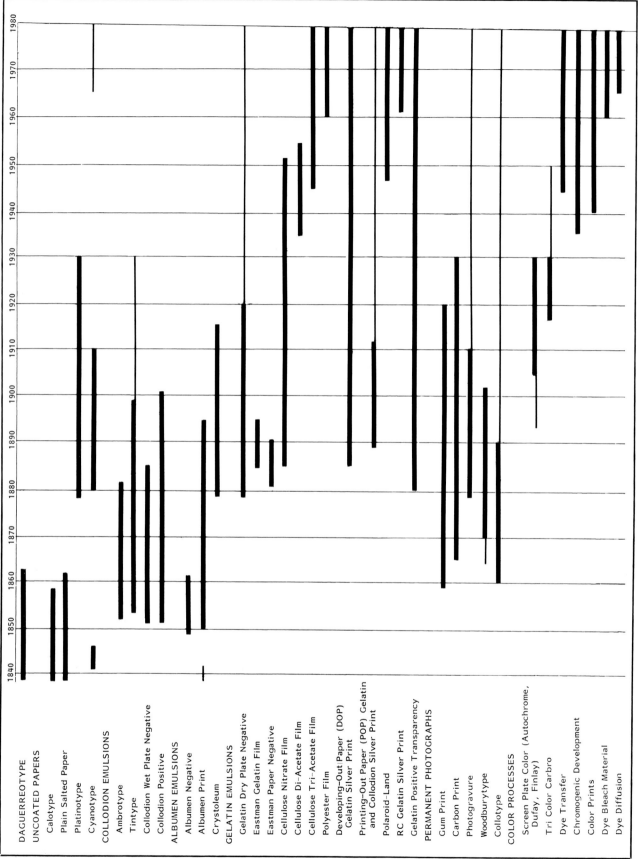

Figure 2-1. Chronology of use of photographic processes. The dates represent approximate dates of use in the United States rather than invention or discovery. Dates are approximate and will vary by geographical area and photographer. The thickness of line indicates relative use. Processes listed are those most commonly found in repositories, with the exception of calotypes, crystoleums, and some of the color processes.

Figure 2-2. Copy photograph. The image on the left is a tintype copy of the daguerreotype on the right. Using the dates of the tintype process for the image could result in an error of more than ten years. *Courtesy of Special Collections, University of Kentucky Libraries.*

medium may lead to inaccurate dating of the image (see figure 2-2).

Appraisal

While many factors affect the appraisal of photo collections and individual images, technical knowledge plays an especially important role. There are usually three general opportunities for appraisal: 1) When determining if a collection should be accepted by the repository; 2) When assigning priorities to the various collections for processing (based on a number of factors, including uniqueness of materials, subject content, relationship to other collections, potential research use, and preservation concerns); and 3) While determining which groups of materials in a new or existing collection should be processed and to what degree (see Chapter 4, Arrangement and Description). Technical knowledge will help to determine if a collection contains early or rare photographs and whether their quality is good or poor. It is important to consider whether the image or the information contained in it is unique.

The appraisal of images for their monetary value has become more important as prices of photographs have increased. Being able to determine monetary value relates not only to appraising materials donated to a repository but also to buying and selling images. The monetary value of a collection or item may also determine the type of physical care that is given from conservation and security perspectives, as well as the type of insurance coverage needed.

Basic Photographic Principles

A few basic terms and concepts are applicable to all photographic images. A knowledge of these is important to understanding individual processes.

Polarity

Photographic images are either negative or positive (see figure 2-3). This is referred to as polarity. In a negative image, light areas of the object photographed appear dark and dark areas appear light. In photographic terms the tonal value or polarity has been reversed. For example, in a negative image of a newspaper, the type appears white and the paper black. In a positive, the tonal value or polarity is true to life. Thus, in a positive image of a newspaper the type appears black and the paper appears white. Both negatives and positives can be on either paper, glass, or film.

Base and Emulsion

Most photographs, both negatives and positives, have a base and a light-sensitive emulsion (see figure 2-4). The exceptions are daguerreotypes and the plain paper processes. The base provides support for the light-sensitive emulsion. Bases can be made up of any material but usually are on metal, glass, film, or paper. More unusual processes use ceramic, leather, or cloth. Emulsions are made up of many different substances and the light-sensitive materials they contain are composed of different chemicals. Most emulsions are either albumen, collodion, or gelatin, and the most

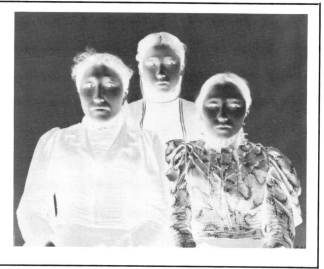

Figure 2-3. Polarity. All photographic images are either positive or negative images. The image on the left is positive, the image on the right is negative. *Photograph courtesy of the James T. Whitely Collection, Alaska and Polar Regions Department, University of Alaska-Fairbanks.*

common light-sensitive materials are silver salts. It is important to be able to distinguish which side of a photographic object is the emulsion side. When viewed with reflected light, the emulsion side of photographic film, which contains the image, appears less reflective and duller than the base side, which is generally either glass or plastic (see figure 2-5). The base material does not determine the polarity (negative or positive) of the image.

On positive photographic prints the emulsion side contains the image while the base side is blank paper. Emulsions on paper prints are different from those on film or glass in that the emulsion side of the paper is usually shinier than the base side. One ongoing element in the history of photography has been the development of different combinations of base and emulsion materials to produce desired effects.

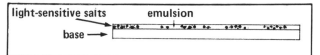

Figure 2-4. Emulsion and base. An emulsion coats the base material and contains the light sensitive substance. *Drawing by Pamela Spitzmueller.*

Processing

In studying technical processes it is helpful to have a basic understanding of the chemical processing of photographic images.

Image Formation

The formation of photographic images (negative or positive) begins when a light-sensitive emulsion (usually coated on paper, glass, or film) is exposed to light under controlled circumstances. The exposure can be from reflected light, such as that produced with a camera, or transmitted light, such as that introduced when making a contact print or enlargement.

A contact print is made by placing a negative in direct contact with the sensitized paper (hence the name contact print) and exposing it to light. This produces a print that is the same size as the negative. Early photographic prints were exposed to sunlight; gaslights were used later, and finally electric light was used. Enlargements were not commonly made until the end of the nineteenth century, when electric lights and more sensitive printing papers made them practical. An enlarger projects a negative image through a lens system over a short distance to the print emulsion. The

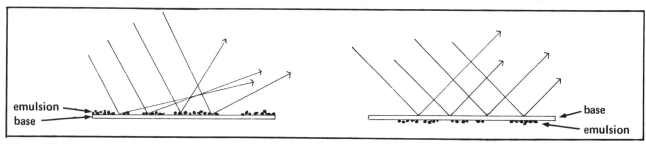

Figure 2-5. Base and emulsion. The drawing to the left represents a negative with the emulsion side up. The relief and surface texture of the emulsion diffuses reflected light and appears less shiny than the glass or plastic base as shown in the drawing to the right. *Drawing by Pamela Spitzmueller.*

projection enlarges the image and can be controlled by the photographer.

The image (negative or positive) on the light-sensitive material can be made visible by "printing-out" or by "developing-out." Only positive prints will be discussed here since most negatives are made by developing-out.

Photographic papers are either printing-out papers (POP) or developing-out papers (DOP). The earlier papers were POPs; after the late 1890s most papers were DOPs. Printing-out papers are placed in contact with a negative and exposed to light through the negative. The exposure continues until the image appears on the paper, sometimes for a day or more. Developing-out papers are exposed for a much shorter time, either in contact with the negative or by enlargement. The calculation of the exposure time, usually varying from a few seconds to a few minutes, is based on the sensitivity of the paper used, the quality of the negative, and the strength of the light. After the calculated exposure is given, there is no image on the paper. Such paper is said to possess a latent image, that is, the image has been formed on the light-sensitive emulsion but is invisible. The paper must then be chemically developed to produce the image. Various developers are used, the choice depending on the particular paper and the desired effects.

The next step is "fixing" the image, that is, making the image stable by desensitizing the emulsion in a fixing bath. This removes the unexposed silver so that it will not continue to darken upon exposure to light. The chemical commonly used is sodium thiosulphate (often called "hypo" by photographers). Proper fixing and subsequent washing to remove the fixer is critical to image stability. Chemical washing aids are often used to insure a thorough washing. Residual hypo is one of the major problems of photographic image stability. Early development of photography was hindered by the inability to fix images made by the actions of light on various materials. Both Louis-Jacques-Mandé Daguerre and William Henry Fox Talbot took advantage of Sir John Herschel's suggestion in 1839 to use hypo to fix the image.

Many nineteenth-century prints were then toned. Albumen prints were always gold toned. Printing-out papers were red before gold toning, which gave them a purple or plum color. Platinum toning gave POPs a brown color, and a neutral black could be obtained by toning in gold and platinum successively. POPs less frequently were toned in sulfur to produce a green tone. This treatment, however, caused fading and staining. DOPs can be toned with many different chemicals to produce a variety of colors.

Description of Processes

This chapter describes photography in terms of photochemical processes, i.e., the nature of the light-sensitive medium and its technical processing to produce a direct positive, a negative, or the subsequent positive print. This approach contrasts with the more common methods of describing support materials (metal, glass, film, paper, etc.) and the emulsion on each, or listing the processes in chronological order.

Most of the photochemical processes discussed are illustrated in this manual. However, copies of these photographs reproduced in halftone on paper lose much of the richness, detail, and mystery of the originals. It is simply for the sake of reference and preliminary studies that the illustrations are included. To gain a full understanding of technical processes, one must study originals. Original photographs can be found in most archival repositories around the country and one should seek them out in order to see firsthand the unique characteristics, subtleties, and beauties of each individual process.

Dates for technical processes given in the chronology only approximate their actual use. Often new processes were not taken up by photographers immediately or were not used until some years after their introduction, which in turn was often some time after the theoretical development of the procedure. While the beginning dates of a process are tentative the ending dates of a process are even more so. Both dates varied widely by location and also by the specific practitioner. While some photographers were eager to try new processes, others were content with the existing process and were not eager to make a change until a new process had fully proven itself. Other photographers were content to continue to use the process they were most familiar with even when a new process had proven itself. If a stock of materials for a particular process were on hand, these would generally be used up before the photographer switched processes. Consequently, when establishing the date of a photograph, one must use discretion. It becomes the responsibility of individual photographic archivists to establish more definitely a chronology of photographic processes for a particular region and for the major photographers represented in a repository. This can be done through the use of many resources, city directories and newspapers in particular. Both of these carry advertisements in which photographers listed the processes they were using. This was often done because processes changed quickly and the photographer wanted to convey that the studio was either up to date or was still offering a particular process. However, it must be kept in mind that photographers were in business first of all to make a living. It is possible that in their eagerness to attract clients and to have clients return they occasionally exaggerated the types of processes they had at their disposal, as well as the quality of the end results. Consequently, the advertisements should be confirmed by extant prints in collections throughout the region.

The description of the development of technical processes will reveal several trends. Photography has moved from materials handmade by the photographer and requiring a knowledge of chemistry, optics, and considerable manual dexterity, to fully manufactured products requiring no preparation but only exposing, developing, and printing by the photographer. In this transition from handmade to manufactured materials there has been a general trend of emulsions becoming faster and more convenient to use. For example, the wet collodion negative required extensive preparation by the photographer to sensitize the plate, followed by immediate exposure and development after exposure. Later, gelatin emulsion negatives were bought prepared and could be exposed and developed at the convenience of the photographer. The gelatin emulsion was usually more sensitive and required shorter exposures, but the tonal range was not as long as that of the collodion negative and did not produce as sharp and clear an image.

Modern photographers are interested in historical processes for a number of reasons. Historical print processes, such as albumen or salt prints, are often used for authenticity in printing negatives contemporary with these print processes. In some cases only these processes will faithfully reproduce the long tonal scales and details of original negatives. Some contemporary photographers are interested in using historical processes to create modern images. Sometimes this is done for the novelty of the process or to achieve characteristics not found in modern materials. Many photographers are interested in reintroducing the handmade quality of early processes. The use of modern negatives and handcrafted print processes such as cyanotypes, plain salt prints, albumen prints, and hand-coloring allow this handwork. Consequently, even positive identification of a process can only serve as a clue to dating and identification of photographs, since, for example, it is possible for an albumen print to have been mde in 1975 instead of 1875.

Daguerreotypes

Daguerreotypes are named for the Frenchman Daguerre, who introduced the process in 1839. A number of people experimented with light-sensitive materials prior to Daguerre. The daguerreotype, however, is generally considered to be the first fully successful and practicable photographic process. It was commonly in use from 1839 until the late 1850s, with some daguerreotypes being made into the 1860s and beyond (see figure 2-6).

The term daguerreotype is sometimes used incorrectly to mean any early cased photograph. However, the term correctly refers to the chemical process involved and the resultant photograph and not to the manner in which it was presented or encased. Two other major processes that also were encased will be described later.

Daguerreotypes were made by the following process: a copper plate was coated with silver and then cleaned and finely polished. The plate was placed in a small box, where it was exposed to iodine vapors for five to thirty minutes. The result was a film on the surface of the plate composed of silver iodide, a light-sensitive substance. This sensitized plate was then placed in a camera and exposed to light for

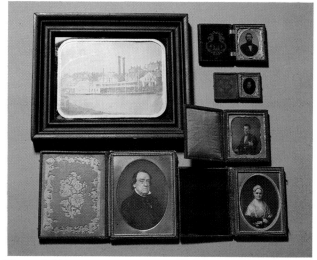

Figure 2-6. Daguerreotypes were made in a variety of sizes ranging from whole plate (8½″ × 6½″) to sixteenth plate (1⅜″ × 1⅝″) and were placed in frames or cases. *Courtesy of Chicago Historical Society.*

five to seventy minutes. After 1840, improved lenses and more sensitive plates allowed exposure times to be greatly reduced to approximately five to forty seconds, thus making daguerreotypes more practical for all uses, but especially for portraiture. After exposure, the plate was removed from the camera and placed in another box, which held the plate at a 45° angle over a pan of mercury, which was heated to a temperature of 167° F. A small hole in the box allowed the plate to be inspected during development. When the mercury vapors had sufficiently brought out the image the plate was removed, washed in distilled water, saturated with common salt or with hyposulphide of soda, and then dried over a flame. By 1841, toning in a bath of gold chloride was added for protection of the emulsion as well as to improve the appearance of the image.

Because the silver plate acted as a mirror, daguerreotypes were difficult to view. It was necessary to hold them at an angle to the light in order to see the positive image clearly. The image was laterally reversed, as in a mirror image, because it was a direct positive. Consequently, lettering on a sign would be reversed or a wedding ring would appear on what seemed to be the right hand instead of the left. When taking outdoor views, a daguerreotypist might use a prism or mirror in front of the lens, so that the image would not be reversed, but as this increased the exposure time it was not always done. Because this technique was rarely used with portraiture, most daguerreotype portraits are laterally reversed. Each daguerreotype is unique in that it is a direct positive image and there is no negative. To reproduce the image the plate must be rephotographed.

Daguerreotypes were made in a variety of standard sizes, from a whole plate (8 1/2″ × 6 1/2″) to a sixteenth plate (1 3/8″ by 1 5/8″). Quarter plates (3 1/4″ × 4 1/4″) and

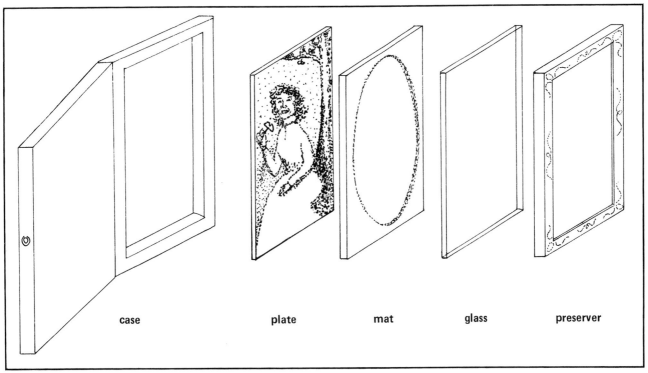

case   plate   mat   glass   preserver

Figure 2-7. Case daguerreotypes contained various layers. The mat kept the glass from touching the delicate surface of the plate, while the preserver added decoration and allowed the unit to be easily inserted into the case. A preserver was not used on early daguerreotypes. *Drawing by Pamela Spitzmueller.*

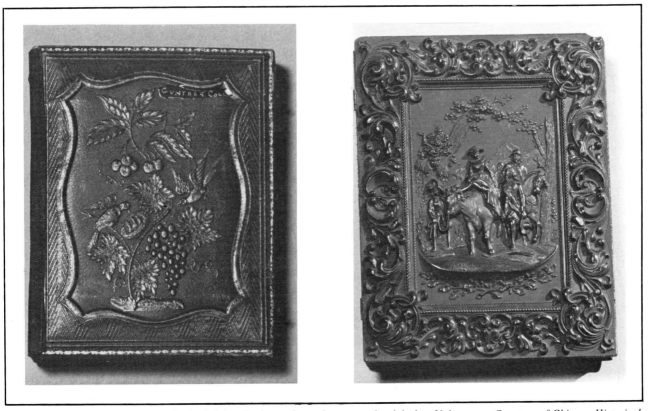

Figure 2-8. Daguerreotype cases. On the left is a leather and wood case; on the right is a Union case. *Courtesy of Chicago Historical Society.*

sixth plates (2 3/4″ × 3 1/4″) were the most common. After they were dry the images were commonly colored by hand, usually with just a touch of red on the cheeks (although often gold was applied to jewelry and other colors to garments). The coloring was done with varying degrees of skill and success. The plates were then put under glass and in appropriately sized cases (see figure 2-7). Because similar cases were used for daguerreotypes, ambrotypes, and sometimes tintypes, the latter two processes are sometimes incorrectly referred to as daguerreotypes.

The cases themselves are of interest aside from the images they hold (see figure 2-8). They were made in a variety of designs from various materials, the most common being wood covered with tooled leather or embossed paper that simulated leather. Union cases, the first items manufactured of thermal plastic, date from 1854. These cases, of particular interest to collectors, were made in approximately 800 different designs, some produced in large quantities and others in small numbers.[2] The methods of manufacture of cases can be clues to dating the images they contain. Until the early 1850s, for example, daguerreotypes were assembled without a preserver. The design of the mats can also be an aid in dating, with the simplest designs usually the earliest. Caution must be exercised, however: cases, mats, and preservers were sometime switched, and failure to notice this could lead to inaccurate dating.

[2]Cases are dealt with extensively by Floyd and Marion Rinhart in *American Miniature Case Art* (New York: Barnes, 1969), and to a lesser degree in William Welling, *Collectors' Guide to Nineteenth-Century Photographs* (New York: Collier, 1976).

Uncoated Paper Processes

Plain Salted Prints

Uncoated paper prints do not make use of an emulsion to suspend light-sensitive material. Rather, the light-sensitive material itself is soaked into the paper (see figure 2-9). The earliest form of this process is the calotype process,

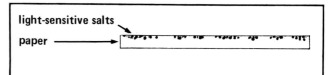

Figure 2-9. Uncoated paper prints do not have an emulsion, the light sensitive material is soaked into the paper. *Drawing by Pamela Spitzmueller.*

developed by Talbot in approximately 1839. The calotype process makes use of a paper negative to produce a plain (uncoated) salted paper print (see figure 2-10). Later, other types of negatives, such as wet collodion glass negatives, were used to make plain salted paper prints (see figure 2-11). While daguerreotypes were a direct positive process, the calotype process was the first of the negative/positive processes, which dominate photography today. Unlike the daguerreotype process, which was purchased by the French government and awarded free to the world, the calotype process was patented by Talbot. Consequently, the calotype process was not used as widely by professionals in the United States. However, amateurs in this country sometimes ignored the patent and used the calotype process with-

Figure 2-10. Callotype. A paper negative and plain salt print from that negative circa 1850, by John Shaw Smith. *Courtesy of International Museum of Photography at George Eastman House.*

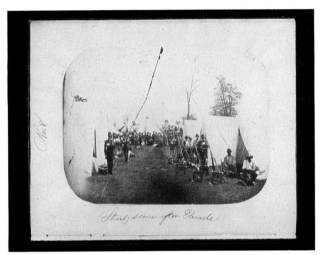

Figure 2-11. Plain salt print. This salt print of the Kentucky State Guard was made from a cracked glass negative circa 1860 by Garret and Nickerson. *Courtesy of Special Collections, University of Kentucky Libraries.*

out paying fees since it was cheaper and easier to execute than the daguerreotype. Nevertheless, calotype negatives do not seem to be widely represented in archival collections.

The calotype process involved making paper negatives using silver iodine as the light-sensitive substance. After exposure the latent image was developed-out in gallic acid, although the earliest images (1836-1840) were printed-out. After being fixed and dried, the negative was often waxed or oiled to increase its transparency.

The paper prints, however, were printed-out. They were made by applying a solution of sodium chloride (common table salt) to a fine grade of paper by brushing or soaking. The paper was dried and then floated on a bath of silver nitrate, thus forming light-sensitive silver chloride in the paper. The sensitized paper was then placed in contact with the paper negative and exposed to daylight. The exposure was continued until the image on the paper appeared as desired. The exposure was then stopped and the print was fixed, washed, and dried.

The calotype and plain salted paper processes and the daguerreotype were introduced and in use at approximately the same time and were viewed as being in direct competition with each other in Europe. Each had its advantages and disadvantages. The daguerreotype was much more difficult to view because of its mirror-like quality, and could not be reproduced without being rephotographed. The calotype was much easier to view, not having a metal reflective surface, and could be reproduced by making multiple prints from negatives. Daguerreotypes, however, had a full rich tonal range with extremely sharp detail. With the calotype, the paper fibers of the negative diffused the light sufficiently to give a softness to the print that, while being

pleasing, did not reproduce sharp detail. While the salt print was rich, the tonal range was not as full as that of the daguerreotype. Although the daguerreotype was the most popular at the time, the negative/positive process employed by the calotype has dominated the development of photography and reigns almost exclusively today.

Platinum Print or Platinotype

The platinum print or platinotype is an uncoated paper print in which the light-sensitive materials are soaked into a plain paper (see figure 2-12). The process was first introduced in 1873 by the Englishman William Willis but was not in wide use until 1880. Its use continued into the 1930s. Platinum prints have a silvery gray color and are soft in

Figure 2-12. Platinum print. A plain paper print that exhibits rich details and a long tonal range. *Courtesy of Photographic Archives, University of Louisville.*

texture and detail much as are plain salted prints, due to the visible grain of the paper. This process was accomplished by applying a mixture of a ferric oxalate solution and potassium chloroplatinite to a plain piece of paper. When dried the paper was exposed to light (often the sun) under a negative until all the details of the image were faint but distinct. The exposure was then ended and the paper was placed in developer until the full tonal range emerged.

The print was then fixed, washed, and dried. The chemical process created images of metallic platinum, which is extremely stable and gives a full, long range of tones. Platinum prints were preferred by many creative photographers around the turn of the nineteenth century.

Cyanotype

Cyanotypes or blueprints, another plain paper process, were introduced in 1842 by Sir John Herschel (see figure 2-13). They did not become popular, however, until the 1880s, when their low cost and easy processing appealed to amateur photographers. Their ease of processing also allowed professional photographers to use them to proof their negatives in order to decide which they would select for finished prints. The use of cyanotypes as final prints, however, was restricted because many people objected to the blue tones, particularly for portraits.

Figure 2-13. Cyanotype. The distinctive blue color identifies this plain paper process. *Courtesy of Photographic Archives, University of Louisville.*

The process was accomplished by coating well-sized paper with a light-sensitive solution. There were many different formulas for this solution, but the original formula called for potassium ferricyanide and ammonium ferric citrate. After the paper was dry, it was exposed to light under a negative, and then simply washed in water. The ferric salt on the sensitized paper changed to a ferrous salt when exposed to light. These ferrous salts then reacted with the ferricyanide and became blue in color, while the ferric salts protected from the light remained unchanged. These were subsequently dissolved away during washing, allowing the white paper to show. Van Dyke prints, a variation of the blueprint, were made by immersing a cyanotype in an ammonia solution and then in a solution of alum, tannin, and water. The resultant prints are brown in color.

Collodion Emulsions

The collodion emulsion process was developed by Frederick Scott Archer, an Englishman, in 1848 and was published in 1851. It was in extensive use until approximately 1880 and continued to a lesser degree for some time after

that. The collodion emulsion was a fine grain emulsion with clear, creamy highlights and gray shadows. The emulsion had a low sensitivity to light and required long exposures, although not as long as daguerreotypes or calotypes. Collodion, a mixture of gun cotton (the result of combining purified cotton with nitric and sulfuric acid), ether, and alcohol, could be mixed with potassium iodide or bromide and poured evenly over the surface of the base material. It was then soaked in silver nitrate solution, placed in a holder, exposed in a camera, and developed, all while still wet: hence the name "wet plate" collodion process. Collodion emulsions were used primarily to produce ambrotypes, tintypes, and wet plate negatives.

Ambrotypes

Ambrotypes are a particular application of the wet collodion process developed by Archer (see figure 2-14). When Archer published his process without restrictions, James A. Cutting of Boston was granted three United States patents in 1854 relating to the wet plate process for the production of ambrotypes. To produce an ambrotype, a well cleaned and polished plate of glass was sensitized as previously explained. The plate was underexposed in the camera and, after development, was sometimes bleached. This produced a fainter negative image than normal, with a white silver image rather than a black silver iodine image. To make the image appear positive, the plate was backed by a black material, either cloth, paper, metal, or paint. The black backing showed through mostly where the negative image was thinnest, thus changing the light areas in the negative into dark areas. Dark areas in the negative image allowed the least amount of black to show through, thus appearing light (see figure 2-15).

Cutting's main patent was for the method of assembling the layers of glass and black backing to produce an ambrotype. Because Archer published the wet collodion process without restrictions, Cutting could not patent the process itself and ambrotypes were soon being assembled in many different ways in order to circumvent Cutting's patent. Some were made using only one plate of glass, some were on colored glass (ruby or dark green) to substitute for black backing, and some consisted of two unsealed pieces of glass, one holding the image and the other painted black. Consequently, archivists must be careful when dealing with the artifact (see Chapter 5, Preservation of Photographic Materials).

Ambrotypes were similar to daguerreotypes in many ways; in fact, at one time they were called daguerreotypes on glass. Like daguerreotypes, ambrotypes were also direct positives—nonreproducible, unique items. Ambrotypes were also colored by hand and put in cases. They were, however, much cheaper than daguerreotypes. They were most popular in the United States in the mid 1850s but were commonly available from 1852 until 1881. Unlike daguerreotypes, however, ambrotypes usually were not laterally reversed even though they were direct positives. In order to protect the emulsion of the ambrotype, as well as to reverse the image, the negative was usually turned over so that the base, i.e., the glass, instead of the emulsion was facing the viewer, thus presenting the image in the correct way.

The ambrotype is easily distinguished from the daguerreotype because of the latter's reflective mirror quality. While the cover glass of the ambrotype might reflect some light, it will not exhibit the silver metallic reflectance of the daguerreotype.

Tintypes

The tintype was developed by Hamilton L. Smith of Kenyon College, Ohio, and patented by him in 1856 (see figure 2-16). Peter and William Neff later purchased the patent rights for the manufacture of the plates. The tintype, like the ambrotype, was a particular application of Archer's wet collodion process. It too was a direct positive image that was necessarily laterally reversed. Instead of being on glass, however, tintypes were on thin sheet iron that had been lacquered black or chocolate brown. Since they were on metal plates, tintypes, unlike ambrotypes or glass plates, could not be corrected by turning them over.

Tintypes, sometimes called melainotypes or ferrotypes, were more durable and less expensive than daguerreotypes or ambrotypes, and, consequently, they were frequently mailed to friends and relatives. They were sometimes put into cases, as were ambrotypes and daguerreotypes, but more often they were placed in paper mats or albums (see figures 2-17 and 2-18) or were left loose. The image was often duller than ambrotypes and was grayish black or brownish rather than a crisp black and white. They were often colored by hand, as were daguerreotypes and ambrotypes.

Although tintypes were also made in Europe, they enjoyed great popularity only in the United States, starting just before the beginning of the Civil War and continuing into the twentieth century. Because tintypes were relatively inexpensive and more durable than other photographs, they were attractive to Civil War soldiers. Many soldiers, eager for their families to see them in uniform, posed for the photographers set up at the military camps and sent the tintypes home. This practice, combined with the popular notion that the tintypes were less expensive and thus less precious than other photographs, may explain the dented, scratched, and rusted tintypes found in many collections.

Collodion Wet Plate Negatives

These were negative images on glass produced by the wet collodion process (see figure 2-19). They were introduced in the United States in approximately 1855 and were extensively used by 1860 and into the 1880s. Wet collodion

Figure 2-14. Ambrotypes. Like daguerreotypes, ambrotypes came in a variety of sizes and were usually in cases. *Courtesy of Chicago Historical Society.*

Figure 2-15. Ambrotype. The left side is backed with white and the right side with black to show the negative/positive aspect of this process. Courtesy of private collection.

Figure 2-16. Tintype. This wet collodion process is often found in a case similar to ambrotypes and daguerreotypes. *Courtesy of Photographic Archives, University of Louisville.*

Figure 2-19. Collodion wet plate negatives have a gray and cream tonal range and are lower in contrast than modern negatives. *Courtesy of Photographic Archives, University of Louisville.*

Figure 2-17. Tintypes of various sizes can be found in albums designed for that use. *Courtesy of Chicago Historical Society.*

Figure 2-20. Collodion wet plate negatives will often have an uneven emulsion coating with one corner exhibiting the thumb print of the photographer who coated the plate. *Courtesy of Photographic Archives, University of Louisville.*

Figure 2-18. Tintypes may be found loose, particularly larger sizes as with this whole plate (8½" × 6½"). Note the reversed lettering caused by the direct positive process. *Courtesy of Special Collections, University of Kentucky Libraries.*

Figure 2-21. Wet plate collodion positives were produced as lantern slides for projection (top left: Palmer House, Chicago; top right: Chicago Fire, 1871, Lake Street east from LaSalle; lower left: Chicago Fire, 1881), or as stereos for view with transmitted light (lower left: panoramic view of Sicily, Italy). *Courtesy of Chicago Historical Society.*

negatives are distinguishable by the often rough edges of the hand-cut glass plate and by flow lines near the edges and in the corners, where the photographer attempted to evenly coat the plate but often left thumbprints or plate holder marks (see figure 2-20). Seen by reflected light, the dark areas are a grayish black and the highlights are a creamy white, rather than stark black and white as in modern negatives.

Until the introduction of the collodion wet plate negative, the direct positive processes (daguerreotypes, ambrotypes, and tintypes) had been used in part because of the unsatisfactory nature of paper negatives. The wet collodion negatives replaced the paper with glass, however, and thus removed the major objection (i.e., paper grain and fuzziness) to the negative/positive process. When the collodion negative came into use the major mode of photography shifted from direct positives to the negative/positive process using wet collodion negatives and albumen prints (to be discussed later). As noted earlier, the name wet plate came from the fact that the plates had to be coated, sensitized, exposed, and developed, all while the plate remained wet. While these procedures were less of a restriction in the production of studio portraiture, for other uses the wet plate process presented serious obstacles. In order to photograph outside the studio, as was often done with wet collodion negatives, the photographers needed to have chemicals, glass plates, and a darkroom tent nearby. Working in a darkened tent the photographer coated the plate and loaded it into the camera. The photographer then left the tent to expose the plate in the camera, took it back into the tent, and then developed the plate, all before the plate dried out, within five to fifteen minutes. Under conditions of high temperature and low humidity, this would be an even shorter time. One of the major problems encountered by photographers in the Southwestern territories is noted in the contemporary literature: their chemicals would boil inside the darkroom tent because of the summer heat. At the time enlargements were not practical because of technical limitations, so the glass negatives were made in the size of the desired prints (20″ × 24″ not being an uncommon size), resulting in heavy, awkward, and easily breakable negatives.

Collodion Positive Transparencies

The collodion process was also used from 1851 until the early 1900s to make positive transparencies on glass for both lantern slides and stereo transparencies (see figure 2-21). Lantern slides were created either by printing negatives exposed in a camera onto another negative (thus producing a positive for projection) or by exposing a sensitized glass negative directly in the camera and developing it in such a way as to produce a positive. The fine grain and excellent detail rendered by the wet collodion process were ideal for this application. The wet collodion process was also used to produce glass stereographs, which, unlike card stereographs, were viewed by transmitted light instead of reflected light. The glass collodion stereos give a much more realistic stereoscopic effect then did card photographs.

Collodion was also used for print papers from about 1889 to 1910. These prints were produced by the printing-out method and, although employing collodion, were essentially different from the developing-out wet collodion process.

Albumen Emulsions

The albumen emulsion was used to produce negatives, prints, and crystoleums from 1848 to 1895, although the albumen process was first suggested in the photographic literature in 1839.[3] Albumen negatives were first developed by Abel Niépce de Saint-Victor in 1847 in France, while albumen prints were first introduced by Louis Blanquart-Evrard in 1850 in France. Albumen negatives were not widely used because of long exposure times required (five to fifteen minutes). The process was impractical for portraiture but was used to a degree for architecture or landscapes. The very fine detail achieved, however, made the process ideal for copy work on lantern slides, and it continued in this use until it was replaced by collodion in the late 1850s. Albumen prints, however, became the dominant printing process of the nineteenth century.

Albumen Prints

Albumen prints from wet collodion negatives comprise approximately 80 percent of the extant prints in nineteenth-century historical collections in the United States[4] (see figure 2-22). To create the emulsion, albumen (the white of

---

[3]*Journal of the Franklin Institute*, 24 (1839): 71.
[4]Reilly, James, *The Albumen and Salted Paper Book: The History and Practice of Photographic Printing* (Rochester: Light Impressions, 1980).

Figure 2-22. Albumen print. This view of High Bridge in Kentucky by Lexington photographer James Mullen exhibits characteristic yellowing of highlights. *Courtesy of Special Collections, University of Kentucky Libraries.*

egg) was beaten and mixed with sodium or ammonium chloride. This was coated on the base paper. After it had dried the paper could be stored for months or years before being sensitized, but once sensitized, it had to be used immediately. The albumenized paper was sensitized by floating it in a solution of silver nitrate. The sensitized paper was a printing-out paper (POP) and was exposed until the image appeared. The print was then washed, toned, fixed, and given a final wash. The albumen gave a more glossy coating to the paper than the plain salted print gave and albumen paper was described in the contemporary literature as glossy paper. However, to modern viewers, who are accustomed to 8″ × 10″ glossy gelatin silver prints, most albumen prints appear to have a slight sheen rather than a high gloss. Not until the late 1880s when attempting to compete with newly introduced gelatin paper, were albumen prints burnished to achieve a true gloss. Consequently, the surface of albumen prints varies between a slight sheen and a moderate gloss. With the albumen process the photographer could coat the paper or buy it coated and sensitize it as needed. Later, sensitized albumen paper could also be bought. To print on albumen paper, it was placed in contact with the negative, exposed in a printing frame in the sun, and left until the image came out to the desired darkness. It was then rinsed in water, toned in gold chloride, and fixed in hypo. Albumen prints usually exhibit a yellowing of highlights and middle tones. The yellowing occurred both at the time of their making, because of attempts to shortcut the processing by mixing the gold chloride with the hypo, and also over time as a result of the natural aging of the egg albumen and storage in high humidity. So widespread is this deterioration that yellowing is often considered an intrinsic identifying characteristic of albumen prints. However, unless one has seen a non-yellowed albumen print, it is difficult to realize the extent of this deterioration. Another identifying characteristic of albumen prints is the cupping, or cockling and minute cracking, of the albumen emulsion. Under magnification this is readily observable, although it is more obvious in the low- and medium-luster

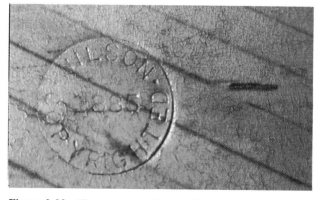

Figure 2-23. Albumen print. This detail shows the tiny cracks in the albumen emulsion easily visible under magnification. *Courtesy of Photographic Archives, University of Louisville.*

albumen prints than in the high-gloss albumen prints (see figure 2-23).

Albumen prints were made on very thin paper and trimmed to the edge to minimize the expense of gold toner. Because the thin paper was susceptible to tearing or curling, albumen prints are most often found mounted on cards, either of standard commercial size or of a size to accommodate the individual photographer's formats (see figure 2-24).

Figure 2-24. Albumen prints were often mounted on 2½″ × 4¼″ cards which were called cartes-de-visite. *Courtesy of Special Collections, University of Kentucky Libraries.*

With mounted as well as cased images it is important that archivists distinguish between a format and a technical process. In this instance, the albumen process is the photographic process. Mounts, such as cartes de viste, cabinet cards, and stereographs, are simply the format used to present the image, regardless of the technological process employed. This is important to remember because the format (i.e., the size of the card) may not always contain an albumen print. Salt prints, silver gelatin prints, cyanotypes, platinum prints, and collodion prints can be found on one of the standard sized cards (see page 41, Card Photographs). It was noted earlier that cased ambrotypes and tintypes are sometimes incorrectly identified as daguerreotypes, in part because encasement, the form of presentation usually associated with daguerreotypes, is used to identify the process. Misidentifying a tintype as a daguerreotype could cause an inaccurate dating of the image as well as improper care and handling. Therefore, it is essential that a distinction be made between process and format.

Crystoleums

Crystoleums, also called chromo-photographs, are one of several lesser known variations of the more dominant albumen process (see figure 2-25). Crystoleums will sometimes be found in collections but are not easily identified. They are included here to show how a major process could be altered, and to illustrate one of the many variations of the major processes. Neither the developer nor the date of introduction of crystoleums has been established, although they were described as early as 1883 and were still being

Figure 2-25. Crystoleums. A variant albumen print process that resembles a painting on glass (left) by coloring details and background on the back (right). *Courtesy of Special Collections, University of Kentucky Libraries.*

used in 1912.[5] A crystoleum, intended to look like a framed painting on glass with very delicate colors, was usually made on curved glass in a variety of sizes. At first glance it appears to be a painting on glass, but closer inspection reveals that the coloring of the image is behind photographic detail. The crystoleum was accomplished by taking an albumen print and pasting it with starch paste or gelatin face down to the inside of a concave glass. When dry, the print was made transparent either by rubbing away most of the paper backing and then applying wax, or by saturating the paper with a combination of canada balsam, chloroform, and wax. All the fine details in the print were colored by hand and then either a second piece of glass was put on the back and the broader areas crudely colored or the broad coloring was done directly on the back of the print over the detailed coloring. The pieces were then bound together and framed. Crystoleums are delicate fine images that integrate the photographic process and painting to a greater degree than crayon or pastel colored photographic prints.

---

[5]Jones, Bernard Edward, ed. *Encyclopedia of Photography* (1911; reprint ed., New York: Arno Press, 1974).

Formats

Card Photographs

Card photographs, especially cartes de visite, were the most popular form of presentation of nineteenth-century photography (see figure 2-26). Cartes de visite take their name from French calling cards, which they were supposedly meant to replace. Measuring 4 1/4″ × 2 1/2″, they were the same size as calling cards but were seldom used as such. The invention of the carte de visite is the subject of speculation, but it is certain André Adolphe Disdéri patented the process in Paris in 1854. It did not become popular, however, until 1859, when Napoleon III, leading his troops out of Paris, stopped in front of Disderi's studio to have his portrait taken. From that time on, except for a period in the United States when the tintype was most popular, card photographs were the principal style of portraiture throughout the world.

Cartes de visite were usually produced with albumen prints from wet collodion negatives, but most paper print processes, including plain salted prints through gelatin silver prints, were used. A special camera with four, eight, or more lenses and a movable plate holder was used to make as many images as possible of a single pose or different poses

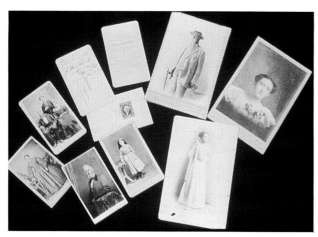

Figure 2-26. Card photographs. Prints of many different types of processes were mounted on various standard sized cards including cartes-de-visite (left), and cabinet cards (right). *Courtesy of Photographic Archives, University of Lousiville.*

Figure 2-27. Card photographs often carried printed information concerning the photographer or studio that is useful for dating and identifying images. *Courtesy of Chicago Historical Society.*

Figure 2-28. Stereo cards measured approximately 4½″ × 7″ and used prints by various processes, which were sometimes hand colored. *Courtesy of Chicago Historical Society.*

on a single plate. A contact print was then made and the individual photographs were cut apart and mounted onto cards. This procedure allowed the mass production of photographs of popular public figures. Studios produced cartes de visite by the thousands each day. When interest in these small portraits began to wane, the studios introduced photographs and cards in larger sizes: Cabinet, 4 1/2″ × 6 1/4″; Victoria, 3 1/4″ × 5″; Promenade, 4″ × 7″; Boudoir, 5 1/4″ × 8 1/2″; Imperial, 6 7/8″ × 9 7/8″; Panel, 8 1/4″ × 4″. The popularity of card photographs continued until after the turn of the century. After approximately 1895 gelatin and collodion printing-out papers superseded albumen on the cards.

The cards were often decorated and contained important information regarding the photographer (see figure 2-27). At the time, this information (the photographer's or studio's name, address, awards, prominent clients, and speciality) was a form of advertisement; today, however, it is an important source of information on photographers. People often wrote captions and identifying information for the photograph on the card.

Stereographs

Stereographs (see figure 2-28), like card photographs, are a format and not a technical process. Many different photographic processes were used to produce stereographs, including daguerreotypes, ambrotypes, wet plate glass positives, and mounted salt prints, albumen prints, and gelatin prints. Regardless of the process used, stereographs were formed of two images placed side by side. These were most commonly produced with cameras that had two lenses side by side, 2 1/2″ apart, so that the two exposures were made simultaneously. The lenses were spaced to approximate the view a person would have, with each eye receiving a slightly different image. When properly viewed, stereographs give a remarkable sense of three dimensions. Card stereographs were viewed on a stereoscope, the most popular being a hand-held model developed by Oliver Wendell Holmes in 1861. Other types of processes (daguerreotypes, ambrotypes, glass) were inspected through various viewers designed to give the three-dimensional effect.

Daguerreotypes and ambrotypes were used to create stereographs up to the early 1850s. Glass stereographs were in use from 1852 to 1860. Paper prints from wet collodion negatives were the most convenient means of producing card stereographs and contributed to the popularity of stereographs in the United States from approximately 1850. Cartes de visite and other card photographs briefly overshadowed stereographs but from about 1867 until after the turn of the century they again enjoyed popularity.

Photo Albums

The photo album was first introduced in 1860.[6] It had recessed pockets to hold tintypes and card photographs of

---

[6]Welling, *Collectors' Guide to Nineteenth-Century Photographs.*

Figure 2-29. Albums. Card photographs of various sizes will often be found in early albums. *Courtesy of Chicago Historical Society.*

various sizes (see figure 2-29). By 1870, E. & H. T. Anthony offered over 500 styles of family albums. Albums were usually made of leather with metal clasps, but some were made of cloth or wood. The albums contained portraits of family and friends as well as those of celebrities of the day. Many albums also contained views that were purchased on trips, a practice that continued until the 1890s when the picture postcard appeared. Family albums of the nineteenth and early twentieth century give a context for many photographs that would be of less interest on their own. The albums often show various family members at several ages and if a family member was an amateur photographer, details of home life might be shown as well. The families' likes and dislikes are indicated by the choice of celebrities included in their albums. Careful consideration should be given before dismantling albums and thereby destroying not only the order in which they were kept but also their integrity as a collection.

Gelatin Emulsions

Gelatin emulsions were introduced in 1871 by an Englishman, Richard Leach Maddox. They have been in use in the United States since 1879 and are the principal emulsion in use today. Gelatin emulsions were used to form negative and positive images on glass, film, and paper, and form the basis for many photo-mechanical printing processes. The gelatin emulsion was a dry process that was completely manufactured. Consequently, the photographer could buy paper or film already sensitized and ready to use. The gelatin emulsion was much more sensitive to light and, consequently, a faster emulsion than the wet collodion. This factor, together with the problems of the wet collodion process involving extensive hand work and the necessity of performing all the steps of the process while the collodion was wet, made the gelatin emulsion a revolutionary development in photography. Although professional photographers were slow to change to the gelatin emulsion, amateur photographers were enthusiastic about the process and readily

saw its potential. The availability of gelatin emulsions contributed to a tremendous increase in the number of amateur photographers. In his book *Photography and the American Scene: A Social History, 1839 to 1889*, Robert Taft observed that "to be an amateur in wet plate days required a fondness for the art verging on fanaticism." And so it did. However, gelatin emulsions changed all of that.

Gelatin emulsions could be purchased fully manufactured and required no preparation by the photographer; they only required processing, which could be done at any time after exposure (see figures 2-30 and 2-31). The emulsion was made with a slightly acidic solution of gelatin and either bromide or chloride, combined with silver nitrate to produce silver bromide or silver chloride, respectively. This was coated on the base material, which could be either glass, film, or paper.

Figure 2-30. Gelatin dry plate negatives were purchased completely prepared ready to expose. *Courtesy of private collection.*

Figure 2-31. Gelatin paper of various types and in many different sizes could also be purchased ready to use. *Courtesy of private collection.*

In the wet collodion process, the collodion emulsion was applied to the base material and then the light-sensitive material was formed in the collodion. In the gelatin process, the light-sensitive silver halides were dispersed throughout the gelatin emulsion and then spread evenly on the support material.

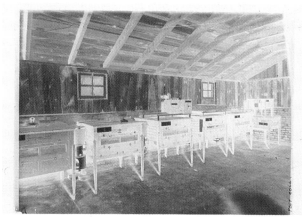

Figure 2-32. Gelatin dry plate glass negatives exhibit stark black and white tones and more contrast than collodion wet plate negatives. *Courtesy of Photographic Archives, University of Louisville.*

Dry Plate Negative

The gelatin dry plate plate negative was first offered for sale in the United States by John Carbutt in Philadelphia in 1879, with George Eastman following soon after. It was used predominately until 1920, although it continues to be used in certain scientific applications. The plates were produced on thinner glass with edges more even than those of wet collodion negatives, and with a smooth, even coating of emulsion (see figure 2-32). A comparison of the glass of a gelatin dry plate negative and a wet collodion plate reveals the difference between a manufactured and hand-crafted object. A side-by-side comparison also reveals that the emulsion of the gelatin dry plate negative has rich black shadows and white highlights, in contrast to the cream and gray colors of the wet collodion. The gelatin negative also appears to have more contrast in reflected light. Because they were manufactured items, gelatin plates came only in standards sizes, such as $4'' \times 5''$, $5'' \times 7''$, $8'' \times 10''$, and $11'' \times 14''$. Wet collodion negatives were often available in these sizes as well, but because they were handmade, they could be made in any size.

Eastman Paper and Gelatin Negatives

Although the gelatin emulsion freed the photographer from much darkroom work, allowing a greater mobility and freedom in selection of subject matter and location, the weight and fragility of the glass plate still continued to be a problem. In an attempt to eliminate the heavy glass negative, George Eastman developed the Eastman paper negative in 1883. This process was in use for only a few years and was available in sizes of $4'' \times 5''$ or smaller. It was difficult to keep larger sizes flat in the camera's focal plane, and flatness was necessary for sharp images. Paper coated with a gelatin emulsion was used in the camera in place of the glass photographic plate. After exposure and development, the paper was made translucent by use of oils. Prints were then made directly from these paper negatives onto

sensitized gelatin paper. While the paper support solved the problem of the weight of the glass negatives, Eastman's paper negative had the same problem experienced by Talbot, i.e., the grain of the paper negative interfered with the detail and sharpnes of the resultant print. While the Eastman paper negative is not often found in repositories, it is an intermediate process important to understanding the transition from glass plate negatives to roll film.

In 1886 the Eastman gelatin film, also known as Eastman paper stripping negatives, was introduced (see figure 2-33). The process was accomplished by coating paper with a layer of soluble gelatin and then with a gelatin emulsion. Long rolls of 100 exposures were loaded onto roll holders and placed in a camera. After the images were exposed, developed, and fixed, the roll of paper negatives was pressed face down on a coated glass plate. Hot water was applied to the paper back. This melted the soluble gelatin layer, allowing the paper to be removed and leaving the negative emulsion on the glass plate. A thin sheet of fresh gelatin was moistened and pressed on the back of the roll of negatives and allowed to dry. The roll of negatives, now supported by clear gelatin instead of paper, was then removed from the glass plate as one unit. The negatives were then printed.

Figure 2-33. Paper stripping negatives from a Kodak No. 2 camera are composed entirely of gelatin. *Courtesy of Photographic Archives, University of Louisville.*

With these methods Eastman was able to solve not only the problem of the weight and fragility of glass negatives, but also the problem of having to use an individual plate for each exposure. By using negatives in a roll, a photographer could make numerous exposures simply by advancing the film rather than changing plates. This process, in combination with the dry gelatin emulsion and Kodak's complete developing and printing service, encouraged amateur photography to bloom, aided by the promotional efforts of Eastman Kodak. The Eastman gelatin film was used in the early Kodak cameras offered for sale with the slogan: "You push the button, we do the rest." These cameras were purchased already loaded with film. The purchaser exposed each frame, advanced the film between frames, and sent the entire camera to Rochester, where Eastman Kodak unloaded the film and developed and printed the pictures. Kodak then reloaded the camera with fresh film and sent the pictures and the loaded camera back to the customer. The Eastman gelatin film negatives had circular image areas, and the resultant prints were round and mounted on square mats. Depending on the camera, the images were either 2 1/2″ in diameter for a Kodak No. 1 (1888) or 3 1/2″ in diameter for a Kodak No. 2 (1889). The edges of the negatives are uneven and frilly, and the negative may be brittle. While the negative may look like a plastic film, it is completely gelatin and hence very fragile.

Cellulose Nitrate Film

Although he had solved two major problems, Eastman continued to develop negative materials, and in 1887 he introduced cellulose nitrate film (see figure 2-34). The film was comprised of a nitrocellulose base (also known as celluloid), a layer of nitrocellulose dissolved in wood alcohol and solvents, and the dry gelatin emulsion. It was first used for roll films and, beginning in 1913, for sheet films. It

continued in use until approximately 1950. Although the cellulose nitrate film was stronger than the gelatin film, presented fewer problems of breaking, and would lie flatter in the roll holder for a sharp picture, time has shown that it has a number of problems. Nitrate film is highly flammable and because of inherent instability it deteriorates easily, resulting in a loss of image. (For information on the hazards of nitrate film, see Chapter 5, Preservation of Photographic Materials.)

Figure 2-35. Diacetate safety film. The shrinking base wrinkles the emulsion and thus obscures the image. *Courtesy of Photographic Archives, University of Louisville.*

Safety Film

In 1937 Eastman Kodak began the use of safety film for X rays, and, except for a few graphic arts films, safety film replaced all other types of film by 1951. The first safety film, in use from 1937 to 1956, was cellulose diacetate film (see figure 2-34). By changing the base material of the gelatin negative from cellulose nitrate to cellulose acetate, manufacturers removed the fire hazard. After further experimentation, Kodak began to produce portrait and commercial sheet film on a cellulose diacetate base. However, diacetate film underwent complex chemical reactions that

Figure 2-34. Nitrate and safety sheet film are difficult to distinguish visually if neither has deteriorated. Nitrate (top) and safety (bottom). *Courtesy of Photographic Archives, University of Louisville.*

resulted in the base material shrinking by as much as 9 percent, while the gelatin emulsion did not shrink. Consequently, deteriorated cellulose diacetate negatives can develop large wrinkles and ripples in the gelatin emulsion that result in a loss of image. Also, tiny bubbles often form in the emulsion and yellow staining can occur overall or in local areas (see figure 2-35).

In 1947, in an attempt to deal with this problem, Kodak introduced another type of safety film, cellulose triacetate, which is still used today. In 1960, polyester was introduced as yet another type of safety film. This together with triacetate are the two materials currently used for films.

Figure 2-36. Developing-out paper. Cool black and white tones are identifying characteristics of this paper. *Courtesy of Special Collections, University of Kentucky Libraries.*

Figure 2-37. Printing-out paper. Warm tones that may be in a variety of colors may be an indication of a printing-out paper. *Courtesy of Photographic Archives, University of Louisville.*

Gelatin Silver Prints

As well as being used for negatives, gelatin emulsions were also used for printing papers (see figures 2-36 and 2-37). Gelatin papers were produced in two basic types. One was developing-out paper (DOP). This required that the paper be exposed for a short time and then, with no image visible on the paper (latent image), be placed in chemical developers until an image appeared (hence the name developing-out paper). The other type of gelatin paper was printing-out paper (POP). This was exposed to light for a period of time until the image appeared on the paper, with no developing required. Prints were then gold toned, fixed, and washed. Developing-out paper was a cooler-toned paper with deep rich grays and dark blue-blacks. Printing-out paper had warmer tones with brownish and purplish colors. During the period from the mid-1880s to just after the turn of the century, gelatin printing-out papers, gelatin developing-out papers, and collodion printing-out papers were all competing to supplant albumen prints in the marketplace. Since about 1910, gelatin silver bromide developing-out paper has dominated the market, mainly because of the speed of the paper and the range of colors and surface textures available.

Since the turn of the century few changes have been made in photographic prints. Those few, however, have been significant. In 1947 Edwin H. Land introduced the Polaroid-Land process (see figure 2-38). This involved the use of Polaroid film in a special camera to produce a finished print in seconds. Negatives could also be produced with some Polaroid films. The Polaroid-Land film combined the film negative (triacetate or polyester), the silver gelatin positive print, and the developing chemicals in one unit. After exposing the film in a Polaroid camera, the photographer pulled the film out of a slot on the camera. In exiting the camera the film passed through two rollers that broke pods of chemicals contained in the film and spread them evenly over the film. After waiting the required length of time for the particular film being used (usually between fifty and ninety seconds), the photographer peeled the negative and chemicals apart from the print. With some films the negative could not be used further and was discarded. In other types (665 and 55P/N) the negative could be chemically treated and subsequently used to make additional prints on conventional photographic materials. Polaroid prints and negatives are thinner than conventional photographic materials. Prints tend to curl easily and are often found mounted on self-adhesive boards provided with the film. Most prints are 3 1/4″ × 4 1/4″ or 4″ × 5″ and may be labeled Polaroid on the back.

In the early 1970s another significant change in gelatin paper prints occurred with the introduction of resin-coated (RC) paper by Eastman Kodak (see figure 2-39). The paper base was coated on both sides with synthetic resins, and

Figure 2-38. Polaroid. This 4″ × 5″ print is a copy print of a historical photograph. *Courtesy of Special Collections, University of Kentucky Libraries.*

Figure 2-39. RC paper may be used for prints of modern or historical negatives. Here it was used to print from a dry plate glass negative. *Courtesy of Special Collections, University of Kentucky Libraries.*

the emulsion was placed on top of the plastic. The plastic coating kept the paper from becoming wet and absorbing chemicals, thus significantly reducing the time required for fixing, washing, and drying. However, there have been problems with the stability of RC papers and at present they should not be used for archival copies (see Chapter 5, Preservation of Photographic Materials).

Permanent Photographs and Photomechanical Processes

Many of the processes of early photography produced unstable prints. This was of considerable concern to photographers at the time as it continues to be today for curators and archivists. Because of these problems, means of making more permanent photographs were sought. Some of the processes devised were the result of hand work, and others were produced mechanically on a press. Mechanically produced prints were in part an attempt to further integrate pictures and text for the illustration of published materials. One of the earliest experiments of Nicéphore Niépce was to produce images on plates that could be printed with ink on paper. As daguerreotypes and other photographic processes were developed and put into practice they too were investigated as means to illustrate books. At various times daguerreotype plates were etched with acids in order to make suitable printing plates, although this process was never completely developed and was never fully successful. One of Talbot's early uses of the calotype was to produce the book called *The Pencil of Nature*.[7] He later continued to be active in producing calotype prints for book illustrations.

Salt prints and albumen prints were both used heavily to illustrate books, but problems persisted not only with their lack of permanence but also with their manner of production and integration with book production. Because photographic prints were made separately and then tipped by hand into blank spaces or pages in books, these books were expensive. The unit cost of production of photographs did not decrease as the number of items produced in a run increased, as is generally the case with printed text. These problems helped lead to the development of permanent photographs that could be produced more cheaply and quickly than original prints. Work on these processes eventually resulted in the complete integration of photography and printing.

Many of these processes were also used to produce prints aside from book illustrations. In addition to their permanence, some processes offered the ability to produce multiple copies easily. Others offered desirable aesthetic qualities or the opportunity to employ handwork on the surfaces. Some photographers used these processes as their major means of producing images and today these are sold and exhibited with photographs.

Permanent photographs did not employ light-sensitive metallic salts (silver or platinum) and were not processed with photographic chemicals. Consequently, they were very stable (and thus termed ''permanent''). Perhaps the most obvious identifying characteristic of these prints is that they do not exhibit signs of image deterioration.

Since permanent photographs did not employ silver as the light-sensitive material, a number of other light-sensitive materials were used, the most common being bichromated gelatin. Potassium bichromate was added to gelatin (normally soluble in water), causing it to be tanned or hardened when exposed to light. Thus a sheet of bichromated gelatin exposed under a negative, as a photographic printing paper might be, would not turn shades of gray and black as the paper would, but would harden in proportion to the amount of light the negative had allowed to fall on it. When washed with hot water, the bichromated gelatin sheet washed away where not exposed to light and did not wash away

where hardened by the light. Various degrees of hardness were caused by the amount of light and, consequently, varying amounts of gelatin were washed away.

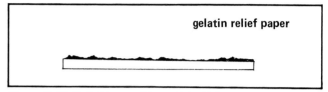

Figure 2-40. Relief image. Many of the bichromated gelatin permanent photographs exhibit a slight relief image. *Drawing by Pamela Spitzmueller.*

The result was a relief image (see figure 2-40). That is, the dark areas in the negative produced a thin area of gelatin while the light parts produced a thick area. If the gelatin had been colored or if coloring was added after exposure and washing, the tone would vary depending upon the thickness of the gelatin.

This slight relief is one of the ways of identifying permanent photographs produced by a bichromated gelatin process. Other permanent photographs produced with ink on paper must be examined for indications of the use of a plate and a pattern for applying the ink. Also, when ink is used there is no continuous gradation of tones as in a true photographic print. The ink is only one color (black, for example) and must be applied to the paper in varying densities of a pattern to establish tonality. If black ink is applied in a dense pattern, the appearance is of black. If black ink is applied in a less dense pattern the appearance is of gray.

The most common modern printing process for photographs is called halftone. This is used for newspapers, magazines, books, and most other printing. This process uses varying densities and sizes of black dots to produce the appearance of gradation of tones of gray. This characteristic is readily identifiable when viewed under magnification (see figure 2-41). Halftone reproductions are not considered one of the permanent photograph processes.

Identification of permanent photographs is aided by examination of a magnified area of the print. Viewing prints through a loupe will reveal one of four things: the regular dot pattern of a halftone reproduction with no relief; a lack of relief and true continuous tones ranging from white through grays to black with no pattern to the coloration, indicating a photographic emulsion print; a slight relief image and continuous tone with no pattern, indicating one of the bichromated gelatin processes; or no relief and an irregular pattern of one color of ink, indicating one of the printed images.

Gum Bichromate

Although not used extensively for book production, the gum print was a permanent photograph that was used extensively by fine art photographers from 1858 until the 1920s (see figure 2-42). Prints were made on uncoated paper spread

---

[7]Talbot, William Henry Fox, *The Pencil of Nature* (London: Longman, Brown, Greens, and Longurans, 1844–46).

Figure 2-41. This detail shows the observable dot pattern of a halftone reproduction. *Courtesy of private collection.*

Figure 2-42. Gum prints were used extensively by fine art photographers of the early twentieth century. *Courtesy of Photographic Archives, University of Louisville.*

with a solution of gum arabic to which had been added a pigment and potassium bichromate. After drying, the paper was exposed under a negative and then developed in water, which washed away the gum that had not been exposed to light and left the gum that had been hardened and made insoluble through exposure to light, similar to the bichromated gelatin process. The prints were low in contrast and had a very short tonal range. They appeared to be very silvery overall and did not have brilliant highlights or rich shadows. They often exhibited some slight three-dimensional relief on the surface of the paper and, when used by fine art photographers, often showed handwork on the surface in imitation of brush strokes. The process was not capable of rendering fine detail and consequently was used to emphasize subtle tones and lights and darks.

Figure 2-43. Carbon print. Rich details and a long tonal range often characterize this bichromated gelatin process. *Courtesy of Photographic Archives, University of Louisville.*

Carbon Print

The carbon process was patented by Sir Joseph Wilson Swan in 1864 (see figure 2-43). This process used bichromated gelatin which, as explained earlier, became soluble where not exposed to light and insoluble when exposed to light, thus allowing parts of the gelatin to be washed away. Carbon prints were usually executed on a smooth-surface paper, and they have an exceedingly long tonal range with rich shadows and bright highlights. Although the name of the prints derives from the fact that carbon black was most often used for the coloration, any other pigment could be used and carbon prints could be in a range of colors. The most common color, however, is a very rich, deep black. This color, in combination with a slight relief when viewed under magnification, is the chief identifying characteristic.

Photogravure

The photogravure was patented in 1879 in Vienna by Karl Klíč and was used extensively for book illustration from 1880 until well into the twentieth century. The photogravure process was an intaglio printing process similar to engraving. A metal printing plate was sensitized with bichromated gelatin and was then exposed and washed. The plate was then etched in acid and cleaned before being inked and printed in an engraving press. The process produced extremely detailed and long tonal range prints that are very fine and sharp. Under magnification the photogravure does not exhibit a dot or regular grid pattern such as can be seen in a halftone, but instead shows a random and irregular pattern. Since this was an ink on paper process, any color was possible. The photogravure process was used extensively for book illustration, one notable example being *The North American Indian* by Edward Curtis[8] (see figure 2-44). However, many photographers used it as a print medium aside from book illustration. Paul Strand (1890-1976), an important fine art photographer, published many of his portfolios in photogravure.

[8]Edward S. Curtis, *The North American Indian* (Cambridge, Ma.: The University Press, 1907). 20 volumes of text, 20 volumes of portfolio. Photogravures on tissue, tipped-in.

Figure 2-44. Photogravure. A plate from the *North American Indian* by Edward Curtis. Courtesy of Special Collections, University of Kentucky Libraries.

Woodburytype

The woodburytype was patented in England by Walter Bentley Woodbury in 1866 (see figure 2-45). It was a true continuous-tone process, often indistinguishable from actual photographs and considered by many to be the most beautiful of the photo mechanical processes. Like most of the other permanent photographic processes it relies on bichromated gelatin. A hardened gelatin relief print similar to a carbon print was impressed into a sheet of lead at high pressure, imparting the relief to the lead. This sheet was then covered with warm pigmented gelatin and used as a printing plate in a hand press. The resultant print had varying tonal gradations due to the varying depths of the pigmented gelatin. The process was used mainly for book illustration but also to produce loose prints. In addition to the slight relief of the print, an identifying characteristic is that each woodburytype was trimmed to the edge of the image. During printing the excess gelatin was squeezed out on the edges of the paper and had to be trimmed off. *Paris Theater* was an outstanding publication that used woodburytype portraits of famous actors, actresses, writers, and composers, taken by most of the leading nineteenth-century French photographers.[9]

Collotype Process

The collotype (no relation to the calotype process of Talbot) also made use of the bichromated gelatin process. In this process, however, the gelatin was used to produce a printing plate that was inked and printed on paper. It was developed primarily in the 1880s and 1890s and continues to be used even today, mainly for fine art reproduction. In the hands of a master printer the collotype process is capable of producing an exceedingly accurate reproduction and beautiful prints. The collotype was used to produce the important work by Eadweard Muybridge called *Animal Locomotion*[10] (see figure 2-46).

Color Processes

From the very beginning of investigations into photographic materials, early researchers were interested in capturing color in their images. When the search for a direct color-sensitive photographic medium was not successful, photographers turned to hand-coloring images in order to produce the desired results. Nevertheless, hand-coloring fell far short of the rich natural colors desired in photographs, and the search continued. Many processes were successful in producing some images in color. However, most of these early attempts were not commercially viable because the

[9]*Paris Theatre: Journal hebdomadaire*. Paris: Paz, 1873–78. Année 1–5, no. 1–251 (1873–78).

[10]Eadweard Muybridge, *Animal Locomotion: An Electro-Photographic Investigation of Consecutive Phases of Animal Movement*. (Philadelphia. 1887.) Published under the auspices of the University of Pennsylvania. Plates printed by the Photogravure Company of New York.

Figure 2-45. Woodburytypes are said to most resemble an emulsion photograph but often exhibit relief on the surface of the print. *Courtesy of Photographic Archives, University of Louisville.*

methods were not easily and consistently reproducible. Most repositories will have only modern color materials dating from 1935, but that factor makes earlier images even more valuable from historical, artifactual, and monetary perspectives.

Screen Plate Color

Joly Plate

The earliest commercially available color photographic materials were various types of screen plate color processes. John Joly introduced the Joly plate, a line screen process, in 1896. This process involved exposing a black-and-white negative through a sheet of glass ruled with alternate lines of red, green, and violet, 200 lines to the inch. The colors blocked varying amounts of light and caused the black-and-white emulsion to record varying shades of gray. The photographic plate was then developed as a positive image and bound together with the color line screen behind the black-and-white emulsion. The various shades of gray allowed the lines of colors to show through in varying amounts, thus giving the appearance of natural color. These Joly plates were dark and difficult to view and, consequently, were not widely used. Also, if the plate and screen were the least bit out of alignment, the color effect was ruined.

Autochrome

Far more successful was the Autochrome process, patented in 1904 by the Lumière brothers, but not commercially available until 1907 (see figure 2-47). Starch grains, microscopic in size and colored orange, green, and violet, were sprinkled on the glass plate so that the colors were

Figure 2-46. Collotype. A plate from *Animal Locomotion* by Edweard Muybridge. *Courtesy of Photographic Archives, University of Louisville.*

Figure 2-47. Autochrome. The first practical, commercially available color photographic process. *Courtesy of Photographic Archives, University of Louisville.*

evenly distributed. Approximately 2,500 starch grains filled an area of one square millimeter. The space between the grains was colored black, thus making the autochrome a four-color process. A silver gelatin emulsion was coated over the starch grains. The plate was exposed through the glass side with the colored starch grains acting as a filter, as the lines did in the Joly plate. The plate was then developed as a positive. The result was a glass transparency with color similar to a pointillistic painting. The colors are soft and subtle and can produce very beautiful effects. Autochromes were produced until 1932 in all standard glass plate sizes. They are often found in holders that allow backlighting for viewing.

Tri Color Carbro

The tri color carbro was a fairly stable process that made use of three superimposed color gelatin images (see figure 2-48). Three separate black-and-white negatives were each exposed through a different colored filter—red, blue, and green. A separate gelatin bromide print was made from each negative and each print was dyed a separate color— cyan, magenta, and yellow. The gelatin emulsions were stripped from their paper bases and superimposed on one sheet. The resultant print has deep, bright, rich colors. Carbro prints were used mainly in magazine and display advertising during the late 1920s and 1930s. There is currently a commercial revival of this process due to its permanence.

Dye Transfer Prints

Also known as the imbibition process, the dye transfer process makes use of three color separation negatives (see figure 2-49). These negatives are used to make three pos-

itive gelatin reliefs on film in a manner similar to bichromated gelatin prints. The three gelatin relief positives are dyed cyan, magenta, and yellow, and after drying are transferred to a special paper. The process was introduced by Kodak in 1946 and is still in use, having enjoyed a revival in the 1970s among contemporary creative photographers.

Figure 2-48. Tri color carbro. A high stability color print process. *Courtesy of Photographic Archives, University of Louisville.*

Figure 2-49. Dye transfer. A fairly stable color process that has enjoyed a revival among contemporary creative photographers. *Courtesy of Photographic Archives, University of Louisville.*

Chromogenic Development Materials

The direct recording of more natural colors was achieved with chromogenic development materials (see figures 2-50 and 2-51). These are called tripack materials because all three color-sensitive materials are incorporated in layers into one piece of film. These produced more natural colors than earlier processes because during processing the silver images are changed into color dye images by the use of color formers or dye couplers. With some chromogenic development materials the dye couplers are contained in the developing chemicals, while in others they are contained in the tripack itself.

The first of these materials was Eastman Kodak's Kodachrome film, which was introduced as 16-mm motion-picture film in 1935 and as 35-mm still film in 1936. Kodachrome was developed as a direct positive transparency or slide. These early slides could only be viewed by transmitted light or by projection. In 1941 Kodak introduced Kodachrome prints, a direct positive paper that produced prints from the slides. These prints were often stamped with the date at the time of processing. Kodachrome's dye couplers were in the processing chemicals rather than in the tripack. Consequently, the process was complicated and exacting and could only be done at a professional processing lab, not by the photographer.

In 1936, Agfacolor, a transparency film with the dye couplers in the tripack emulsion, was introduced. Because the color couplers were in the tripack emulsion instead of in the developing chemicals, the development was less critical and could be done by the photographer. Kodak's Ektachrome film, introduced in 1940, also contained the color couplers in the tripack emulsion and could be developed by the photographer. In current color film terminology, a trade name ending in ''-color'' denotes a negative film, while one ending in ''-chrome'' indicates a positive transparency. (Agfacolor was an exception.)

In 1942, Kodak introduced Kodacolor, the first American color negative process. Kodacolor used different types of color couplers, which allowed better color balance when a print was made. These couplers, however, were in the chemicals, not in the tripack emulsion, and the film could only be developed in a professional laboratory. With a color negative not only are the tones reversed, as in a black-and-white negative, but the dye image is in the complimentary colors of the original object. When the negative is printed the process is repeated in the paper so that the print appears as the correct colors. Black-and-white prints can also be made from Kodacolor and similar color negatives by using special papers.

Color Prints

As mentioned, the first color print materials were Kodachrome prints. Photographic materials normally yield the opposite tone or color value when printed. Hence, if a positive image on a color slide were printed, the resultant print

Figure 2-50. Chromogenic development materials. Kodachrome (upper right and lower left) and Ektachrome (upper left and lower right) transparencies exhibit varying degrees of stability. *Courtesy of Photographic Archives, University of Louisville.*

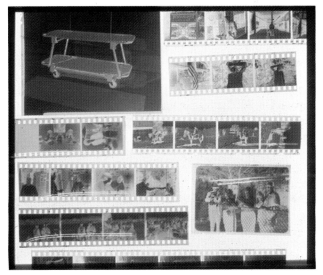

Figure 2-51. Chromogenic development materials. Kodacolor negative film is obtainable in a variety of sizes. *Courtesy of Photographic Archives, University of Louisville.*

Figure 2-52. The most common modern color prints are on RC paper and have varying degrees of stability. *Photograph by Gerald J. Munoff.*

would have the complimentary colors of the original: blues would be orange, etc. Consequently, it is necessary for the print to reverse this during processing to yield the same colors as in the slide. Prints made from negatives are called positive prints since they yield a positive image from a negative, while prints made from slides are called reversal prints. A variety of color print materials have been available since 1941 (see figure 2-52). Unless they are labelled, as were the early Kodachrome and Kodacolor prints, it is not easy to differentiate between them. Ektacolor prints also may be labelled if they were processed at a laboratory, but they were not if processed by the photographer.

Color prints are often called, generically, Type C prints if printed from a negative and Type R prints if printed from a transparency. These terms technically refer, however, to particular types of Kodak print papers processed with certain Kodak chemicals that were in use primarily from 1955 to 1959. Nevertheless, the terms "Type C" prints and "Type R" prints are widely used to refer to many types of color prints. For purposes of display and conservation, information on the exact type of paper and chemicals used should be obtained from the photographer if possible, since different types of color prints have widely varying degrees of stability. The majority of modern color prints are on RC paper and, in addition to the instability of the color dyes, suffer from problems similar to black-and-white RC papers.

Dye Diffusion Transfer Processes

Instant color prints are technically known as the dye diffusion transfer process. In 1965, Polaroid Corporation introduced Polacolor peel-apart negatives and prints. This material incorporated the three-color layer emulsion for the negative, the developing chemicals, and the color printing paper. The film was exposed and processed similarly to Polaroid black-and-white materials. However, the color negative could not be further used and was discarded.

In 1972, Polaroid introduced SX-70 film and cameras

(different groups of Polaroid films required particular types of Polaroid cameras; see figure 2-53). In this film the negative, developing chemicals, and print paper were in a sealed package that remained intact. Originally available only in an image size of approximately 3 1/8″ × 3 1/8″, it is now available in other sizes up to 8″ × 10″. Eastman Kodak introduced the Instant Print Film PR 10 in 1976.

Each of the instant color prints is unique. They do not produce a negative that can be used for making additional color prints, but must be rephotographed in order to produce slides, negatives, or prints. The fact that they are unique should be a factor in their appraisal, arrangement, description, and preservation. In addition, these color prints, like all direct color materials, present serious problems of stability that must be addressed by the archivist.

The evolution of photography from the unique daguerreotype to the unique instant color print has produced truly marvelous results. While photographic processes produce personal mementos, they also play a central role in mass communications, culture, and society through the accumulation and transmission of knowledge.

Figure 2-53. Dye diffusion transfer. Polaroid SX-70 prints are commonly 3 1/8″ × 3 1/8″, but can be larger. *Photograph by Gerald J. Munoff.*

3 Appraisal and Collecting Policies

Margery S. Long

As quantities of photographs are added each year to the photographic collections already housed in archives and historical agencies, it is increasingly evident that the archival process of appraisal needs to be applied to photographs as well as records and manuscripts. The ever-growing size of the photographic record requires evaluation and selection to attain collections that have a focus to their historically valuable research materials.

In the years when archives were struggling to establish their collecting programs, little thought was given to formulating criteria for evaluating the relatively small numbers of photographs they received. Following World War II there were many changes in the administration of archives and the archival profession. Existing federal, state, and local archival programs were expanded in scope and staff. Hundreds of new archival programs were established. Local and regional historical societies, local public libraries, business firms, professional organizations, social agencies, and churches inaugurated new programs to preserve records. Colleges and universities throughout the United States and Canada established archives to preserve their own records and to collect historical records on a variety of subjects and themes.

Archival practices involving the acquisition of photographs have varied widely depending upon the type of archival institution, its collecting scope or theme, and its size, facilities, and staff. There were a few institutions that developed separate photograph or picture collections—like the Prints and Photographs Division of the Library of Congress and the Still Pictures Branch of the Audiovisual Archives Division of the National Archives and Records Service. In most archives, photographs were collected as a part of or supplement to archival or manuscript collections. As late as 1950, many repositories considered photographs to be of secondary importance. Historians and other scholarly researchers seldom considered using photographs to illustrate their manuscripts, let alone using them as source materials. Archivists and historians, less familar with visual images than with the written word, did not know how to deal with photographs as historical documents. Their uncertainty about the historical value of photographs and the place photographs should have in archival and manuscript collections kept archivists from disposing of the photographs acquired by the repositories. Since they were used so infrequently, decisions about arrangement, description, and access were postponed; and the passive accumulation continued.

The general interest in photography as historical docu-

mentation, as technology, and as art, which increased dramatically in the 1970s, resulted in an ever increasing demand for historical images from archival collections. It was not long before it became evident that the old methods that allowed photographs to accumulate in collections of records and manuscripts with few descriptive aids to permit efficient retrieval were outdated and highly impractical. Lack of consistent order in the arrangement of photographs and lack of proper description in finding aids made retrieval of the photographs extremely difficult and time-consuming. Many existing collections of photographs needed appraisal to determine the relevance of their subject content to the repository's collecting program. Clearly it was time to apply the function of appraisal to the administration of photographic collections.

Appraisal

The function of appraisal applies to photographs as fundamentally as it does to other archival materials.[1] The Society of American Archivists' *Basic Glossary for Archivists, Manuscript Curators, and Records Managers* defines appraisal as "the process of determining the value and thus the disposition of records based upon their current administrative, legal and fiscal use; their evidential and informational or research value; their arrangement; and their relationship to other records."[2] Records deemed to have archival significance have a continuing usefulness after the original purpose for which the records were created has been served. Any material—a manuscript, map, sound recording, or photograph—can be appraised by these criteria.

The appraisal of photographs is a critical aspect of the archivist's work. As in the case of written records, only a small percentage of photographs have enduring qualities that justify their preservation. It is the responsibility of the archivist to make this evaluation and judgment, always tempered with the knowledge that those photographs designated as not worthy of preservation in an archives may be destroyed and lost forever. The appraisal function thus becomes one of the most important and demanding responsibilities of the archivist.

Appraisal judgments about photographs should be supported by a firm background in the subject field of the archival repository. The archivist must know the important events and persons involved in the history of the subject, and be alert to recognize them in photographs. An archivist who is appraising photographs should be able to recognize the various photographic processes and the time periods in

[1]References for discussions of archival appraisal are: Maynard J. Brichford, *Archives & Manuscripts: Appraisal & Accessioning* (Chicago: Society of American Archivists, 1977); and T. R. Schellenberg, *Modern Archives: Principles and Techniques* (Chicago: University of Chicago, 1956).
[2]Frank B. Evans, Donald F. Harrison, and Edwin A. Thompson, *A Basic Glossary for Archivists, Manuscript Curators, and Records Managers*. Reprinted from the *American Archivist* 37 (July 1974): 415–33.

which they were most commonly made. An appraiser also needs to be aware of the modern photographic techniques that can be used in copying stained, chemically deteriorated photographs, and thus be able to preserve valuable historical information before it is completely lost. A basic reference collection of periodicals and books such as the one suggested in the bibliography (see Appendix B) is a useful resource when making appraisal decisions.

Unfortunately, photographs, like written records, have no inherent features or labels that indicate they have permanent, enduring value. As a matter of fact, what is considered to be of archival quality and worthy of permanent preservation by one archives, may be considered to be worthless by another.

Appraisal Guidelines

The repository collection policy is the basic factor in the formulation of appraisal guidelines; and the collection policy, in turn, is derived from the mission statement and goals of the parent institution of the archives. The collection policy of the archives should specifically define the archives' purpose and the focus and sphere of its collections.

For example, the mission statement of a college or university may state that it is dedicated to the education of the citizens of a particular state, region, or religious denomination and that it will contribute to and support scholarly research. The archives collection policy may then define its focus for the acquisition of primary resource materials as the history of the institution and a field of knowledge or discipline for which the university is particularly known or in which it excels. The archives of a religious college or university may be chosen to be the repository of the archival records of the religious order or denomination as well as its own institutional records. A local, state, or regional historical society may declare that its mission is to collect and preserve the social and cultural history of a prescribed geographic area, and educate its citizens in that history. The archives of the historical society may use the same parameters, confining itself to written, visual, and oral records of historical value. The particular geographic area it represents may also suggest a subject specialty, such as agriculture, lumbering, railroads, shipping, automobiles, or pioneer life. The objective of a business or industry, naturally, is to develop its product or service and sell it to consumers for a profit. The policy of the archives of such an enterprise may state that its purpose is to collect and preserve evidentiary records of the history, function, and operation of that business or industry. The archives also may develop a special subject collection related to the product of the corporation, such as the history of paper in a paper manufacturing company, and thus serve the scholarly community as well as its own research staff.

Developing a Photographic Collection Policy

The photographic collections should complement and be relevant to the subject focus of the archival and manuscript collections. Since most photographic holdings come into a repository as part of the collections of written materials acquired under the guidelines of the archives collection policy, they are most likely relevant to the archival and manuscript holdings. When seeking out and acquiring separate collections or individual photographs, however, special care should be exercised to adhere to the collection policy and apply the appraisal guidelines. A focused and well balanced photograph collection requires careful planning and long-range goals. This plan should be expressed in the collection policy statement, in clearly defined terms that will guide the staff in appraising photographic materials. The collection policy statement should provide a concise statement of the institution's goals and objectives for prospective donors. The policy statement should contain the full name of the institution, a brief history of the repository, and a description of the current character of the collection. The definition of the subject field should include the parameters of the geographic area from which the materials will be sought. An explanation also should be given of why the material is wanted and, briefly, how it is prepared for use.

Appraisal Factors

Once established, the collection policy becomes the frame of reference for the factors of the appraisal of photographs. These factors are: evidential value, informational value, research value, age, form, volume, copyright, relationship to other archival materials, and intrinsic value.

Evidential Value

Photographs that contain visual evidence of the structure, organization, function, and activities of an institution, organization, or business are usually created originally for or by them. However, these evidential photographs may have research value beyond the uses anticipated by the originator. For example, archives that serve as the official agency for an organization or institution—such as one serving a college or university—may give priority to photographs of officers, distinguished faculty and alumni, campus buildings and scenes, inaugurations, graduations and other educational ceremonies, student life and customs, and important campus events. Photographs such as these should be evaluated for the evidence they provide on the structure, organization, development, and function of the college or university. In addition, they may meet broader research needs, such as studies of student life and political activism.

Research Value

The majority of photographs considered for acquisition, and those already contained in archival collections, are valued for the information contained in the images that is useful to research in topics or subjects unrelated to the original purpose for taking the photograph. The most obvious example is photographs of people. Originally portrait studies or candid poses of individuals were valued by family and friends because of their associational value, but now researchers study them because of interest in costumes, social mores, cultural customs, and conventions of posing. Backgrounds in the photographs yield information about interior decorations, exterior architecture, work settings, leisure activities, and public and family ceremonies. One rather typical photograph made by an itinerant photographer reveals a great amount of visual information about a pioneer homestead family pictured in front of their frontier home in Nebraska. "Reading" the photograph (see figure 3-1), the viewer may deduce the effects of pioneer life on the parents, who appear to be older than the number and ages of their children would indicate. All, with the exception of the young woman on the right in the photograph, are wearing plain and simple clothing, not the "Sunday best" usually worn in portraits. The farm animals and equipment assembled for the photograph are a sign of the material success of the farmer and the scale of the farming operation. The house in the background is a sod house, typical and unique to the Nebraska prairie. Its design is strictly functional and there are no architectural features or decorative plantings to soften its stark utilitarianism. A few saplings have been planted near the house for future shade and protection. Some furnishings are visible and the windows have curtains. The windmill is evidence of the water supply for the farm and

the household. This information and more can be gleaned from one photograph. The researcher's task then is to authenticate the deductions and verify the photograph's representativeness with written accounts, other photographs, manuscripts, and documents.

The information contained in photographs may be unique—it may not be found in any other source of primary material, or it may not exist in as complete or usable form. In reviewing all other sources of information about a subject or event, such as newspapers, books, documents, manuscripts, and accounts of interviews with participants made at the time of the event, the photograph may contribute substantial accuracy to the visual conception of the event. One of the most important events in labor union history illustrates this point. The event, called the Battle of the Overpass, is a confrontation that took place at the Ford Motor Company in Dearborn, Michigan, in May 1937, between members of the United Auto Workers union and the company security personnel. The photographic documentation of this event numbers around fifty images, some of which were shot hastily during the rapidly developing confrontation. The camera used by news photographers in the 1930s was a bulky, heavy Speed Graphic, which used sheet film in holders. It was not capable of producing a quick sequence of exposures in the way a small 35-mm camera does today. Photographers had to scramble for vantage points (there were many photographers on hand for the confrontation they suspected would happen); and they had to aim their heavy cameras and change film holders rapidly to

Figure 3-1. The photograph of a Nebraska family assembled before their sod home for a portrait by an itinerant photographer reveals much information about pioneer life to a photo researcher adept at "reading" photographs. "Custer County Nebraska c. 1890." *Photograph by Solomon Butcher, courtesy of the Library of Congress.*

Figure 3-2. All of the exposures a newspaper photographer makes of a rapidly unfolding event are not of publication quality, but may contribute to the complete and accurate visualization of the event. During the Battle of the Overpass photographers inadvertently got into some of the pictures, making them unusable for publication but valuable for research. *Photograph courtesy of the Archives of Labor and Urban Affairs, Wayne State University.*

catch all of the action. Some of the shots are blurred, and some show other photographers who obscured the camera's view of the battle (see figure 3-2). However, all are important to a complete and accurate visualization of the event; they were used as evidence in the National Labor Relations Board hearing on the battle. Three of the photographs have become symbolic representations of the battle.

The information and evidence contained in a photograph must be credible. There should be no question of the reliability or authenticity of its visual evidence, though most photographs need to be substantiated by other photographs of the same scene or event and by other documentary records or manuscripts that corroborate and verify the evidence. There should be no indication or suggestion of deliberate staging of the event, nor doctoring or manipulating of the negative or print to change its meaning or influence its interpretation. There should be no pasting together of two images, or superimposing one upon the other, without due notice that this has been done. A close examination of the photograph of the angry spectator interrupting Martin Luther King, Jr. (see figure 3-3) reveals it is a composite of two separate negatives. There is evidence

of the overlap at the point where the image of the podium nearly obliterates the man's coat collar. In reality, the man would be in front of the podium. While doctored photographs can pose intriguing research questions, archivists must insure that they are not misrepresented in photographic collections.

Completeness of the visual documentation of a collection of photographs is necessary to support research into the history or development of a subject or topic. The chronological span of the photographic materials' should be of sufficient breadth and scope to permit the drawing of valid, supported conclusions within the proper context. A collection of single, isolated curiosities, even within one subject field, might satisfy the needs of a picture file used only for illustration of specific events and persons, but usually does not comprise a research collection. Appraisal decisions must take into account both the extant photographic resources on a given topic and the kinds of research use they are likely to engender.

Photographs valued for their informational content are researched by two groups of users with different needs. The largest group consists of researchers looking for the one arresting photograph that represents an event or subject, to be used in a publication, an exhibition, or perhaps on a television news broadcast. These researchers require photographs that have sharp, clear detail and tonal qualities that will reproduce well.

The second group of users is scholars from many disciplines who use photographs as primary resource materials and therefore need a photographic record that is as thorough as possible. A series of successive photographs made of the same subject or event at one shooting supplies a more complete representation and documentation of a subject, event, or person from different perspectives and different moments in time than do one or two images. A sequential series of photographs or similar images representing the same subject or event does not contain duplicate images, because each photograph represents a different viewpoint, moment of time, and detail.

Uniqueness as a factor in appraisal of photographs for research value may be judged based on the physical form or the intellectual content of the photographs. The photographic image or images may be a unique physical form, such as an original print of a photograph of which there is no other known print. A photograph, or group of photographs, may also be designated unique if it contains information in visual form that is not available in any other archival materials, i.e., records or manuscripts.

The quality of the image is a major factor in evaluating the research value of photographs. The image must be in proper focus to have sharpness in detail, it must have proper exposure for a contrast of tones, and the subject must be composed in an arrangement that creates a meaningful image. Without these qualities the image may not be clear enough to impart information and may have very little, if any, visual appeal. The exception, of course, would be photographs created by pictorialist photographers, who deliberately created fuzzy, soft-focus images as an expression of their photographic technique. An image that is badly stained and out of focus may appear to be useless to the

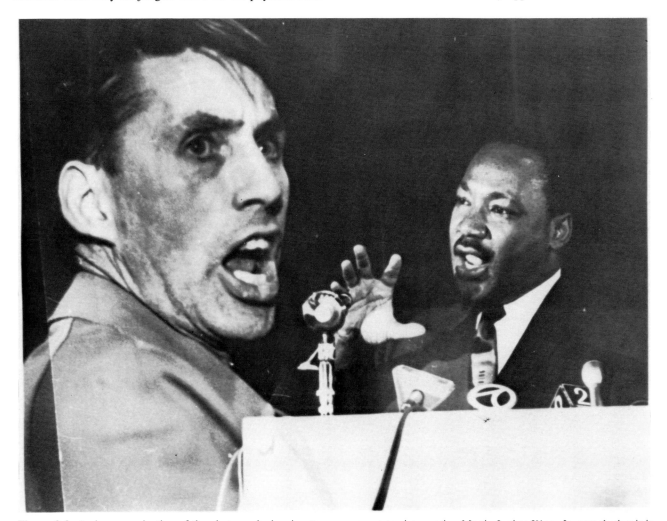

Figure 3-3. A close examination of the photograph showing the angry spectator interrupting Martin Luther King, Jr. reveals that it is a composite of two separate negatives, not a single photograph accurately representing what happened during the speech. The proportions of the men's heads are not in correct perspective, and the podium partly conceals the spectator's coat collar, which in reality would appear in front of the podium. A dramatic picture has been manufactured by the photographer from two separate pictures. *Photograph courtesy of the Archives of Labor and Urban Affairs, Wayne State University.*

Figure 3-4. A stained, out-of-focus photograph that appeared to have little visual appeal or research value proved upon closer examination and study to be the only known, extant photograph of an important event. It is a photograph of the performance of the Paterson Silk Strike Pageant, written by John Reed for the Industrial Workers of the World strikers in 1913. *Photograph courtesy of the Archives of Labor and Urban Affairs, Wayne State University.*

collection as a photograph capable of being reproduced for illustration in publications. It may be useful, however, for the information contained in the image, in spite of its physical blemishes. In one instance, for example, an unidentified, stained, out-of-focus 2½″ × 3½″ print had been overlooked for years in the Industrial Workers of the World Collection at Wayne State University (see figure 3-4). Careful examination by a knowledgeable researcher and corroboration in the manuscript collection made possible the identification of the only known extant print of the performance of the Paterson Silk Strike Pageant in Madison Square Garden, June 1913. Later the photograph was used in research for set designs for a stage production and a motion picture based on the history of the Industrial Workers of the World.

Age and Form

Photographs from the nineteenth century have intrinsic value beyond their subject content; it derives from their age,

from the fact that they have survived to the present. The cased photographs—daguerreotypes, ambrotypes, and tintypes—were unique images at the time they were created. Many of the early paper prints, such as salt paper, albumen, and platinum, have become unique prints because they are the only survivors—and the wet plate glass negatives they were printed from have not survived in most cases. These early forms of photography are valued as artifacts, and as such, may have both monetary as well as research value. If an archival repository does not want to retain nineteenth-century images because their subject matter does not fit its collection policy, they should be offered to another institution. Such materials have become increasingly scarce and should never be destroyed.

Volume

In archival appraisal, the larger the quantity of materials, the more selective the appraiser must be. However, in judging photographs for historical value, the archivist must consider the often fragmentary nature of single photographs as recorders of an event or subject, and place an appropriate value on a series of successive images that may be of great research use in documenting an event or interpreting a subject or topic. Although users who consider photographs as primary source materials prefer the total available record for their research, clearly useless images should be weeded from the collections. Photographs in which the subjects or persons are nearly obscured by lack of focus, light-struck patches or chemical stains, and those that are redundant waste storage space and staff and researchers' time. The appraiser should eliminate them from a research collection after ensuring by careful investigation that they are totally inferior and the image cannot be improved by copying.

Massive collections of photographs may be appraised for the most significant images and for those most pertinent to the overall photograph collection. The group selected as the most significant and useful from the mass of photographs (for example, of a large newspaper collection) may then be given proper containers, arranged, described in finding aids, and placed in accessible archival storage. The remainder of the large collection may be stored as ''unprocessed materials'' with only minimum inventory control, although they may be made available for research use. Actual research use may then be the criterion for transferring photographs to the processed collection. Such an approach allows photographs appraised to be of marginal research value at the time of acquisition to be reappraised for research potential at a later date.

Copyright

Copyright is an important consideration in the acquisition of photographs for research use in a repository. If the copyright cannot be acquired with the photographs, their value may be seriously restricted, since most users assume they can request copy prints of the photographs. Copyright status does not, however, affect their value for pure research. Archives themselves want the right to reproduce photographs in their collections for publications and exhibitions. Without ownership of copyright on photographs, an institution may find that expensive and time-consuming correspondence and record keeping are involved with each use of the photographs. Consult Chapter 6 for a more complete discussion of copyright.

Relationship to Other Archival Materials

Appraisal considerations include judging the relationship photographs have to the archival record and manuscript collections. The subject content of the photographs collected by a repository will have a complementary and supplementary relationship to the other images in the photograph collections and to the archival and manuscript materials, if a well-stated collecting policy is used as the guide to what to collect. All of the appraisal factors discussed above should be applied within the framework of the collection policy and its defined subject focus and sphere.

Intrinsic Value

Records determined to have intrinsic value should be preserved in their original physical form.[3] Original photographs such as daguerreotypes, ambrotypes, and tintypes have qualities and characteristics that are not preserved in copies. While it is true that the subject content can be preserved in copy photographs, the evidence of the physical nature of the particular photographic process cannot be preserved in a modern copy print.

These appraisal factors are meant to be used as guidelines; they are not universal standards. It is not possible to achieve complete consistency in appraising photographs. Each repository places emphasis on different factors in the evaluation of photographs individually and as a group. A priority for one repository would not be a major consideration for another. Each body of photographs considered in appraisal will suggest greater weight for some factors than for others. Appraisal decisions require common sense as well as a basis of knowledge of the subject represented and of photography.

Appraisal decisions are difficult to make, but archivists should keep in mind that retaining large quantities of marginal materials diminishes the overall value of the holdings and take space and resources away from especially significant collections. Limited space, funds, and staff should be used judiciously for the preservation of the most important, significant, and relevant photographs.

Archivists should appraise photographs initially at the time they are considered for acceptance into the archival or manuscript repository. This is customarily a cursory examination, since conditions in the field are usually not conducive to careful appraisal of the entire contents of a collection. The donor's storage site may be physically uncomfortable—a dark, hot attic; a dark, damp basement; or a cluttered, unheated building—and usually there is not enough time to make a thorough investigation. If the collection looks at all promising, it is wiser to ship it to the repository and appraise it there before accessioning it. On the archives' premises, a more careful evaluation can be made, using the repository's appraisal guidelines to determine if the photographs have potential for historical research and are worthy of permanent retention.

Collecting Scope and Policies

There are several major factors to be considered in developing a policy for collecting photographs. The first and most important is the overall collecting or acquisition policy

---

[3]*Intrinsic Value in Archival Material.* Staff Information Paper 21 (Washington, D.C.: National Archives and Records Service, 1982).

of the archival institution. What is the scope of the existing archival holdings? What are the plans for the future? What is the coverage of the existing photographic collection in the archives? What are its strengths and weaknesses and where are the gaps? It is obvious that a collection policy specifically for photographs should be developed and that the staff member in charge of donor contacts and collecting should be apprised of the needs of the photographic holdings. It is highly desirable to develop a want list describing in general the types of photographs needed, including specific items—scenes of a particular street, building, event, group, etc.

Another factor to be considered in developing a photographic collection policy is the facilities and staff required to develop and administer the collection. It should be obvious that maintaining a photographic collection involves special expenses. These costs include supplies and equipment, conservation materials, and copying costs, as well as special environmentally controlled storage facilities. Also, there may be special fees for legal counsel and other consultants, and for the publication of guides or other appropriate finding aids. These monetary considerations, as well as the broader ethical questions of collecting without proper archival facilities for the care and preservation of the photographs obtained, must be carefully weighed.

The prospective research use of photographs in the archives is a third factor to consider in developing a collecting policy. How and by which groups of researchers will the photographs be used? Will there be a steady demand for photographs by local television stations, film companies, newspapers, publishers, and other similar users? Does the institution have an exhibit program that will require an extensive use of photographs, or are there museums, schools, or other organizations in the area that need such materials for displays? Are the collections of the archives in demand nationwide or only on a local basis?

Statistics on the uses of photographs may be gathered from researcher forms and from order forms for reproductions of photographs. These forms will indicate present research interests and the photographs most frequently ordered. Analysis of the researcher forms and finding aids may indicate gaps in the subject coverage of the photographic collections as they relate to present research topics and those that are gaining strength, and may give indications of new directions in historical research. The awareness and foresight that may be gained from a survey of research uses of the existing photographic collections will aid the archivist or curator in planning new dimensions or new directions for the collection policy.

The collecting policies of other archival institutions in the same geographic or subject area should also be assessed. If major photographic archival collections already exist in the subject field of the developing archives, consideration should be given to the implications of duplication of effort. If possible, a cooperative agreement should be worked out between institutions delineating major collecting spheres. On the other hand, archives often find themselves in a position of accepting photographic (and other archival) collections because no other institution is active in the area. If such materials are not solicited or accepted, they may be destroyed.

The archivist should know the location of significant collections on specific topics. Publications that will be helpful in locating them are: *The NHPRC Directory of Archives and Manuscript Repositories, The National Union Catalog of Manuscript Collections, Picture Sources 4*, and *Index to American Photographic Collections*,[4] and the journals listed in the bibliography. An archivist working with photographs should become familiar with the materials published in the subject field represented by the archives' photograph collections and should be especially cognizant of the photographs used to illustrate the publications and to which repository they are credited.

Archivists should keep informed of the current auction and antique prices of photographs, whether or not the repository regularly purchases individual items or entire collections of photographic materials. An awareness of current market values is necessary in the buying and selling of photographs. Monetary values also play an important part in the determination of the appropriate conservation, storage, and security measures for valuable photographs, including vault storage, limited access procedures, and additional insurance.

An archives or historical agency may need the services of an appraiser if a donor requests a monetary appraisal for income tax purposes, when it plans to sell or exchange a collection, and when it renews insurance policies or makes an insurance claim. Any damage assessment for losses suffered in an accident, vandalism, fire or water damage, or theft requires an accurate monetary appraisal. Such an appraisal is also necessary when making loan agreements for exhibitions and similar purposes.

Establishing the monetary value of photographic collections is best left to outside, trained appraisers when there could be any question of conflict of interest. A conflict of interest arises when an archivist is asked to appraise the value of a collection the owner plans to donate or sell to

---

[4]National Historical Publications and Records Commission, *Directory of Archives and Manuscript Repositories* (Washington, D.C.: National Archives and Records Service, 1978); *The National Union Catalog of Manuscript Collections* (Washington, D.C.: Library of Congress, 1962—); Ernest H. Robl, ed., *Picture Sources 4* (New York: Special Libraries Association, 1983); James McQuaid, ed., *Index to American Photographic Collections* (Boston: G.K. Hall Library Catalogs, 1983).

the repository. In addition to the issue of appropriate procedure and objectivity in appraising a collection in which the archivist has an interest, the Internal Revenue Service may question the validity of the valuation in such a situation. However, as a professional courtesy, archivists often perform appraisals for other historical or archival institutions.[5] An appraiser should be competent to judge the monetary value of historical photographs, should have broad knowledge of the history of photography and its many technical processes, and should be informed about the current market prices in the geographic area of the repository as well as the New York City auction market. In addition, the appraiser must be competent to place a value on the historical content of the images. This may require special research and documentation. Often the archivist can be of help in supplying the background information the appraiser needs to make this judgment.

The development of a collecting policy requires careful study and planning based upon the particular needs and programs of an archival institution. Furthermore, such a collecting policy requires constant review and analysis. The acquisition policy of a new archival institution can be and usually is quite different than that of a more established one. There is a natural tendency to accept all photographs in the beginning stages of an archives' development. Later, as a collection expands and as the staff becomes more familiar with potential photographic resources and potential research use, the scope of the photographic collection can be more narrowly defined.

Sources of Photographs

Once the scope of the collection is defined, the photographic archivist must locate relevant holdings. As in the case of locating and obtaining archival and manuscript collections, this work requires imagination, hard work, perseverance, and, in some instances, luck. Nevertheless, certain sources of photographs should be considered in a carefully developed collecting program.

Most donors of archival material, whether organizations, governmental agencies, or families—especially since the late nineteenth century—have photographs in their collections. Often, such photographic material is transferred to the archives along with written records, publications, etc. In many instances, however, donors neither consider photographs to be historical records nor realize that an archives is interested in such materials. Moreover, many are hesitant to part with photographs unless they are informed of their historical and research value. More concerted attention must therefore be given by the archives representative to specifically soliciting photographs. It is often possible, for ex-

ample, to work out an arrangement whereby the archives makes a copy of certain photographs for return to a donor. Or, if this approach is not possible, an archives may make reproductions of the desired photographs and return the originals to the donor.

There are many local sources of photographs in almost every subject sphere. Commercial photographers produced a wealth of local historical materials, usually over a long span of years. In Michigan the Manistee County Historical Society, for example, obtained the files of a local photographer who had a studio in this once thriving lumber mill town on Lake Michigan from 1880 to 1910. These photographs give a magnificent picture of life in the area over several decades. Scenes from the lumber camps, deep in the white pine forests, depict various and fascinating aspects of the life of the lumbermen and their work of cutting logs and getting them to the saw mills. The homes of lumber barons and the churches, theatres, and schools they built, along with the homes of the workers, are captured in these photographs. So too are the ships that docked in Manistee Harbor to pick up finished lumber, salt, and other cargo, as well as local parades, circuses, fires, and other events. This photograph collection has become the core of the Manistee County Historical Society and its museum.

Commercial photographers in larger cities are also a valuable source of photographs. In addition to portraits and special events, they often specialize in a particular area or work for special clients. One famous commercial photographer of Washington, D.C., provided services for most of the major international unions headquartered in the capital city. From his collection, which was recently given to an archives, one can obtain photographs of most of the labor leaders of the past half century.

Other commercial photographers pursued their special personal interests with the camera. A commercial photographer of Sault Sainte Marie, Michigan, was interested in Great Lakes shipping and over a fifty-year period took photographs of hundreds of ships that passed through the locks connecting Lakes Superior and Huron. Although the collections of many commercial photographers have been discarded or destroyed, such collections are still a potential source that should be explored.

Newspaper photo files are voluminous, diverse collections that form a unique and continuous record of a locality. Unfortunately, they present serious problems of access, processing, and conservation. Also, there may be legal complications in the use of newspaper photo collections. Copyright may not belong to the newspaper. Wire service photographs are sold to newspapers with specific time-use restrictions, and these wire service prints may be in the newspaper's files. Also, individual photographers may have personally copyrighted their own photographs and sold only specific uses to the newspaper. Newspaper photographs were

---

[5]Dexter D. MacBride, "Appraisals: of objects in historical collections," Technical Leaflet 97, *History News* (July 1977). Nashville: American Association for State and Local History.

produced in a variety of processes over the years, and most are in a chemically unstable condition because of hasty development in the darkroom to meet press deadlines. Chemical instability presents serious conservation problems to an archivist wishing to preserve any of the images and requires isolated storage so that the residual processing chemicals will not contaminate the other photographs in the repository.

A newspaper collection's historical value will depend on the thoroughness of the newspaper's photographic coverage of community life and events and the retention and weeding policies of its photo library (or morgue as it is sometimes called). Some newspaper cumulative files range back to glass plate negatives and the introduction of the halftone process that is used to reproduce photographs in print; others are only from the recent past. Some contain every photographic negative and print received by the library from staff photographers and the wire services. Others may have periodic weeding schedules and rid the files of wire photo service prints that are not locally important, have restrictions on use, and are available in the archives of the originating wire service. Some newspaper libraries weed out the extraneous shots of each photo assignment. Shots not chosen for immediate publication and which have not been used at any time since origination are weeded on the basis that they have no future news or historical value to the newspaper. As a result, the collection of news photos offered to an archives from an operating newspaper may be only discards; in addition, their original filing organization may have been destroyed or lost by the weeding process. In contrast, many newspapers have ceased publication, thereby placing huge historically valuable photograph collections in jeopardy.

Photographic clubs and organizations are another source of historical photographs. Although the quality of the work of members of such clubs varies greatly, depending upon the experience and expertise of the individual photographer, valuable collections can come from camera clubs. In recent years, many camera clubs have been involved in projects to systematically take pictures of historic buildings, streets, and neighborhoods before they are altered or destroyed. Many archives encourage such projects and provide leadership, meeting space, and financial support for such endeavors. The archives, in turn, becomes the depository for the photographs it selects for the collection.

Private collectors, whose interests cover myriad topics, should also be cultivated. Some collectors have developed their photograph holdings around a particular event or era, such as the Civil War, and others have an interest in automobiles, railroads, ships, or sports figures. Some collectors concentrate upon the history of photography and collect daguerreotypes, ambrotypes, tintypes, card photographs, stereographs, etc. Although some of these private collectors would never consider parting with their collections because of their emotional attachment or financial investment, many

have been willing to place them in an archives under certain conditions, or to lend them for special exhibitions. Some archives have made arrangements with such donors, whereby the collection retains the name of the donor or is highlighted in an exhibit or publication. In order to acquire valuable research collections that also have commercial potential, it may be necessary to require that a fee be paid to the donor each time a photograph from the collection is copied. Another approach that has met with success is for a collector to will his or her material to an archives.

Book and antique dealers should also be contacted as a source of historical photographs. Because of their contacts in the community and their involvement in the appraisal of estates and other property, they are in an unusual position to locate photographs and related archival materials. For obvious reasons, such dealers usually will require payment for their finds, but it can be a worthwhile investment for an archives. It is wise for the archivist to maintain contact with such dealers to apprise them of the types of photographs wanted. Another related source is the local paper and junk dealer, who occasionally acquires valuable photographs, books, and manuscripts. Some of the major private collectors and archives in the United States have enriched their holdings from such sources.

Archival institutions whose responsibility is to a single parent institution, such as a unit of government, church, service organization, business firm, or college or university, may have an unusual advantage in developing a photographic archives. Not only can an archivist solicit photographs from each department within the organization that maintains them, but he can recommend a policy or guideline that provides for the actual taking of photographs of certain topics. For example, a business firm might, as a matter of policy, obtain and preserve portraits of all officers in an unbroken sequence from the founders to the current office holders; take photographs of all properties and buildings, all products manufactured, and employees and staff in typical work situations; and acquire originals of all publicity photographs released by the company. Scenes of special events, staff picnics, strikes, and retiree programs might also be specified as worthy of systematic photographic documentation.

Amateur photographs in personal collections are prime sources of a photographic chronicle of ordinary people performing the tasks of their everyday lives, expressing their pride in their labors, their joys, their celebrations, and, sometimes, the sadness of family life. Nearly every family owns scrapbooks and albums containing old and new photographs of life on farms, in villages, and in towns, cities, and suburbs. Estate sales are a good source of family photograph collections; some sales bring forth examples of images and processes from the early daguerrean era up to the present-day snapshots.

Copy clinics have become a popular, very successful way to uncover new sources of local photographs that document social history. A copy clinic is a concentrated effort to draw photographic contributions from the general public. The repository sponsoring the copy clinic project advertises throughout its geographic area the specific time and place of the clinic to encourage citizens to bring their old photographs to the site, where the originals will be copied and returned immediately to the owners if that is their wish. Of course, the original photographs are usually preferred by the repository, but owners are not pressured to part with them. A taped or written interview of predetermined questions is conducted with the owner to elicit and document all pertinent information about the photographs. The oral history evoked from memory by viewing old photographs usually requires verification in other archival and historical sources. It is important to have forms for the transfer of reproduction rights on hand for signature at the time the photographs are copied and assumed into the archives' collection. Legal issues of copyright ownership should be resolved at this time, for without the transfer of copyright, the photographs cannot legally be reproduced or exhibited by the repository that acquired them in a copy clinic. Many small historical societies have used the copy clinic successfully and have added historically important local photographs to their collections. The Georgia Department of Archives and History conducted a statewide project, "Vanishing Georgia," to gather and ensure the preservation of photographs documenting Georgia's history from private collections around the state. The project used a mobile darkroom to carry the copy clinic to carefully planned locations throughout Georgia.

In collecting photographs, the negative as well as the prints should be sought from the sources or donors. The negative is the original form of the image created in the camera. An original negative in good condition will produce a print today that is of a quality nearly equal to the print originally made from it. The tonal rendition and detail of the image will be transmitted most precisely by the original negative. Some degree of clarity, sharpness, and detail of the original photograph is lost in making a copy negative.

When it collects photographs, a repository incurs the ethical and financial responsibility to arrange and describe the items and make them accessible for use and to physically preserve them for the historical record. Some photographs will require a greater commitment of staff time and financial expenditure than others. Repositories should be aware of the obligations and the alternatives before the photographs are accepted.

For example, negative collections have special problems of conservation and require a substantial investment to convert to copy negatives or to make file prints when none exist. Glass plate negatives and nitrate negatives have individual requirements, which are discussed thoroughly in Chapter 5, Preservation of Photographic Materials. Also, by accepting color photographs the repository assumes a responsibility to attempt to preserve fugitive images. For years, many archives made the decision not to accept color photographs into their collections, in an attempt to avoid all the problems of preserving color images. However, color has been the prevalent medium in both personal and commercial photography for over twenty-five years. If archives do not make an effort to collect and preserve color photographs, a period of history will be devoid of visual documentation.

Lead Files

Given the variety of sources available to the photographic archivist, it is obvious that a planned, systematic approach to collecting is essential. In any active collecting program, the archivist will develop scores of leads to photographic holdings. These leads to potential photograph collections will come from a variety of sources—from donors, friends of the archives, book dealers, newspaper articles and obituaries, and from careful research by the archives staff. In some cases prospective donors will express an interest in giving their collections "someday," possibly at retirement, but not at present. A systematic way to collect and record data about potential photographic acquisitions is thus required. The fallibility of the human memory is in itself justification for such a control; the need for continuity in the event of changing archival staff is equally important.

The format of a lead file can vary according to established procedures of an archives. It can be maintained in a card file, log book, or file folder (see figure 3-5). Indexes to the data can be arranged by geographical location, name of the prospective donor, type of photograph collection, and date of next contact. The file itself should give information on the sources of the lead and biographical information on the donor (see figure 3-6), such as positions held, major interests and associations, family history, date of retirement, and address. Data compiled on organizations should include founding date and brief information on history, officers, goals, and activities. If possible, the lead file also should contain an inventory and description of the photographs. These files should be reviewed periodically and updated. Color coding or special tabs can be used to remind the archivist when further action should be taken.

Collection File

When the photographs have been received from the donor, the archives' lead file becomes the collection file. It should contain all of the correspondence, telephone messages, research notes, field trip reports, lists of items removed or discarded, and other records relating to the collection. The deed of gift, transfer of copyright, statement of access rules and restrictions, purchase invoice, inventory of the photographs, and other relevant documents should also be placed in the collection file. The accession number assigned to the collection should be affixed to each pho-

CONTACT SHEET

Name of Contact_____   Date Entered_____

Address-Home_____   Telephone-Home_____

_____

Address-Office_____   Telephone-Office_____

_____

Source of information_____

Brief biographical sketch (include affiliations, reasons for interest, special notes)

_____

_____

_____

_____

_____

_____

_____

_____

Date	Visit Summary (Include any follow-up Date!)

Figure 3-5. Information on potential donors can be recorded on a contact sheet.

ARCHIVES OF LABOR AND URBAN AFFAIRS
BIOGRAPHICAL QUESTIONNAIRE

Name_____   Telephone_____

Current Mailing Address_____

Permanent Address (if different than above) _____

Name of Parents_____

Place of Birth_____   Date of Birth_____

Married_____   Widowed_____   Date of Marriage_____   Name of Spouse_____

Children (names and addresses) _____

_____

_____

(In answering the following questions, please include dates if possible. If you need more space
for any item, use the other side of this sheet.)

Education and other training_____

_____

Occupations followed (list only your main occupations, not temporary activities)_____

_____

Memberships (in unions and/or other organizations) _____

_____

Office held in these organizations (if any)_____

Government positions held, elected or appointed (if any)_____

Awards or honors_____

Publications (any articles, pamplets or books written)_____

___ _____

Other information of interest about yourself and your career_____

_____

_____

_____

_____

Figure 3-6. A biographical questionnaire that meets the needs of the repository should be developed. *Reproduced with permission of the Archives of Labor and Urban Affairs, Wayne State University.*

ACCESSIONING WORK SHEET
ARCHIVES OF LABOR AND URBAN AFFAIRS

Copy 1 2 3
  of   1 2 3

Date received_____

Collection title_____

Accession #_____   _____New accession

Sent by: _____
          (name)

          _____
          (address)

          _____
          (city, state, zip code)

# of boxes received_____

# of boxes shelved_____ (storage boxes)

Other_____

Comments:

Location_____

Accession checklist:

_____Acknowledged   _____Rolodex

_____Information requested   _____Index card

_____Log   _____Case file

_____Accession sheet   _____Master list

Figure 3-7. Accessioning work sheet. Reproduced with permission of the Archives of Labor and Urban Affairs, Wayne State University.

ACCESSION SHEET

Name of collection_____   Accession #_____

Given by_____   Date received_____

Address_____

Conditions of deposit_____

Preliminary summary of items received (printed and manuscript, audiovisual materials, photographs, memorabilia)	Location	Inventory Completed
_____	_____	_____
_____	_____	_____
_____	_____	_____
_____	_____	_____
_____	_____	_____
_____	_____	_____
_____	_____	_____
_____	_____	_____
_____	_____	_____
_____	_____	_____
_____	_____	_____
_____	_____	_____
_____	_____	_____
_____	_____	_____
_____	_____	_____
_____	_____	_____
_____	_____	_____
_____	_____	_____
_____	_____	_____
_____	_____	_____

Additional items, duplicates and discarded material may be listed on reverse side.

Figure 3-8. Sample accession sheet.

tograph to provide a link to its provenance.

The collection file contains documentation that both establishes the legal right of the archives to a collection and provides intellectual control over it. As such, it is a vital record, and special precautions should be established for its security. The file should be maintained in fireproof and locked cabinets and should be accessible only to designated staff members. If possible, microfilm or other copies of the documents in the file should be stored off-site.

Accession records provide the repository with physical and intellectual control over the collections of photographs, no matter where they are filed or stored in the archives facility. Information that should be available in accession records for each collection of photographs includes: the accession number or symbol, the date of acquisition, the source of the collection, terms of use, copyright ownership, name of the creating photographer or photographers if known, the place and date of creation if known, the approximate or actual quantity of photographs in the collection, and inclusive dates of the collection (see figures 3-7 and 3-8). It is important to keep a record of the number and size of the boxes or containers the materials were originally shipped in and the date they were received by the repository. The number and description of the containers the collection was subsequently placed in, and the storage location of these containers, should also be recorded. If the collection is received in continuing deposits from such sources as departments of government, colleges or universities, organizations, or businesses, this information should be recorded for each supplement. Collections from individual donors who are presenting portions of their collection of photographs at various intervals should be documented in this manner also. Consult Chapter 6, Legal Issues, for thorough discussion and explanation of legal documents and contracts in the acquisition of collections.

4 Arrangement and Description

Gerald J. Munoff

Arranging and describing photography collections are complex tasks that are best viewed as problem solving activities involving gathering and analyzing information, setting objectives, and planning and implementing solutions. This problem solving is assisted by a few basic archival principles, by experience and accumulated knowledge, and by sensitivity to and knowledge of the photographs themselves. Definitive answers are few, but the flexibility and adaptability of archival principles challenge the photographic archivist to develop a system that harmoniously combines the many variables into a customized method of arrangement and description best suited to the repository and its collections. The arrangement and description of the collections can have a strong affect on how the collections are used and how much they are used.

In this chapter both the planning and the implementation of archival systems for the arrangement and description of photographic collections will be examined. The physical arrangement of collections should not be undertaken without proper planning to insure good access to individual collections and to create consistency throughout the repository. Consistency gives researchers a reasonable expectation of the way they will find photographs arranged and described and demands less time of the archivist in maintaining the collections and adding new collections.

The system selected for the arrangement and description of photographs depends upon a variety of factors. The scope of a repository's holdings is a major consideration. A repository concentrating on a particular subject area such as a specific area of science or social welfare, or a particular institution, such as a business or a religious order, may contain fewer and perhaps more narrowly focused collections of photographs than will a general historical collection in a university or historical society. Future plans for the acquisition of photographic collections should also be considered in developing procedures for establishing intellectual control over existing materials. The provenance of the collections—the manner in which the photographs came into existence and their original order—is given special attention by the archivist. The potential research value of the photographs and how and by whom they are likely to be used are also factors to be considered. Often, in order to accommodate all of these factors, more than one system of arrangement and description will be used.

For some photographic archives, it may be possible to provide item-level descriptions and access for each photograph within the various collections with extensive indexes and cross references. The practical limitations of staff, time, and money, however, usually require systems where the minimum amount of processing time will afford researchers a reasonable amount of access. Comprehensive systems can be developed that allow work to progress from the collection level to item level as required while permitting good access at each interim level. Defining the goals and developing these systems is one of the most important responsibilities of the photographic archivist.

Archival Approach

The archival approach to photographs makes judicious use of two concepts: provenance (respect des fonds) and the registry principle (sanctity of original order). The concept of provenance applies to collections and requires that materials created or assembled by a person, family, organization, or other single source should be kept together and not be intermingled with other sources. The registry principle applies to organization below the collection level and states that materials should be retained in their original organizational pattern or structure and in their original filing arrangement in order to preserve all relationships. In practice these two concepts are followed to varying degrees depending on the type of repository and the materials involved. Nevertheless, they are the basis of most archival systems of arrangement and description and warrant careful study from both a theoretical and practical perspective.[1] Although it is often impossible for the archivist to follow these concepts completely because the photographs have been intermingled or rearranged before the repository receives them, the concepts should form the basis of any system of arrangement and description.

The record group/collection concept is basic to both provenance and original order. Although individual photographs are important, a group of photographs and the interrelationships between individual items within this group take on additional significance. Groups of photographs encourage comparisons, document changes made over a period of time, allow interpretation of both the photographer's or collector's intentions or points of view, and permit reasonable judgments of the meaning of the photographs.

Archival approaches to arrangement and description, consequently, deal first with the larger body of materials: record group or collections. The sheer volume of materials in many collections necessitates the processing of groups rather than single, discrete items. Similarly, collections of photographs, especially contemporary collections of con-

---

[1] As stated in the introduction, the authors assume a basic archival knowledge on the part of the reader. Basic information on archival arrangement and description can be found in: S. Miller, J.A. Feith, and R. Fruin, *Manual for the Arrangement and Description of Archives*, trans. Arthur H. Leavitt (New York: Wilson, 1968); David B. Gracy II, *Archives & Manuscripts: Arrangement & Description* (Chicago: Society of American Archivists, 1977); T.R. Schellenberg, *The Management of Archives* (New York: Columbia University Press, 1965).

siderable volume, will be more useful to researchers if they contain analytical descriptions of groups of materials at the collection, series, or folder levels. Nevertheless, each collection must be dealt with on the basis of its merits and processing systems must allow flexibility in dealing with photographs at whatever level is appropriate: collection, series, folder, or item.

Planning Considerations

Thorough planning is essential to the development of systems for arranging and describing photographic collections. Archivists have only general principles to follow and no widely accepted rules for arrangement and description. There are many diverse systems for handling textual materials, and there is probably even less agreement on dealing with photographs. Implementing a suitable system for a specific repository or revising an existing one places a great responsibility on the photographic archivist. At the same time, however, this is a challenge that allows freedom to devise efficient and effective systems tailored to the specific characteristics and needs of the collections and the repository.

Specifics of implementation must follow general planning. If specifics are decided without first forming an overall system, then complexities, disunity, and confusion may follow. A common example is that of assigning subject headings to photographs without first having established an authority control. While the master list of subject headings must be appropriate for the collections at hand, a comprehensive list that works in hierarchical order for the series, subseries, folder, and item levels should be selected or developed before sorting is begun. If subject headings are devised as the collections are arranged many false starts and revisions will result. This will also cause inconsistencies between collections. Various systems of selecting or devising subject headings will be discussed in detail later.

Institutional Profile

The first step in planning is to develop an institutional profile that indicates how and for whom the repository is attempting to accomplish its mission and goals. First, a repository must define its purpose. This will vary for each repository, and the mission statement of a repository or its parent institution may provide a point of departure. However, a general mission statement may need further interpretation and refinement to make it meaningful for the photographic collections and to give unifying objectives toward which the system is working. The range of holdings currently in the repository and those likely to be accessioned should be examined. Whether these coincide or new directions are sought, a collecting policy should be developed as a guide for acquisitions (see Chapter 3, Appraisal and Collecting Policies).

While mission and goal statements can often be used to determine the purpose and collecting scope of a repository, the types of patrons served are harder to determine. Many archivists assume they know their patron profile without examination. Often it is necessary to gather data from patrons to determine their interests, uses of materials, and research methodologies. This is not to say that systems in a repository necessarily must be planned to accommodate the majority of researchers. The mission statement or policy may specify that the purpose is to serve a specialized audience that makes up only a small portion of the total number of users. However, it is important to balance the needs of actual researchers against the targeted researchers in order to know how to allot resources and staff time and to plan archival systems. Obviously, an institution's status as either public or private is an important factor. Examining these points can result in an important overall understanding of what a repository is attempting to do, and how and for whom it is attempting to do it. These points are fundamental for developing any information system.

Provenance

After determining the institutional profile the archivist must consider several concepts regarding the materials. Chief among these is the concept of provenance. Using provenance as an overall organizing concept allows access to materials through a knowledge of the activities of the person or organization creating the file and through the structure of the organizing principle of the file.[2]

Most manuscript and archival materials, and especially photographs, are sought for purposes more numerous and often very different from the original reasons for creating them. Consequently, the immediacy of the need for direct access to small groups or items by content (subject, name, or geographical location) can conflict with the original organization of the materials. This conflict is often addressed by two means: by making compromises on the extent to which provenance is applied; and by content indexing, regardless of the overall organization scheme.

Photographs are brought into archival repositories singly, in groups, and as parts of larger collections containing other types of materials, usually manuscripts. With individual photographs the question of maintaining groups of materials together is not a concern. The individual photographs may be grouped together to form artificial collections or may be added to a general file. Artificial collections may be formed around any one of a number of organizing elements including: content elements of the image (event, person, place, time, subject), or aspects of the photograph itself (technical process, photographer, format). The collection is considered artificial because the items are gathered by the archivist from a variety of sources. General files give organization

[2]Richard H. Lytle, "Intellectual Access to Archives: I. Provenance and Content Indexing Methods of Subject Retrieval," *American Archivist* 43 (January 1980): 64.

to photographs that are brought into the repository individually or with other materials with which they have no substantive relationship. Usually these files are arranged by subject although other arrangements can be appropriate, especially for specialized collections.

Collections of photographs should be left intact and not mixed with other photographs to form artificial collections or dispersed into a general file. A related group of photographs often has greater informational value as a group than as individual photographs. Individual photographs that are part of a collection offer more information when they can be studied in relation to the other photographs in the collection. There is a synergism in collections in that the information gained from the whole collection is more than the sum of the information gained from the individual objects. The relationship of the individual photographs to each other, their different perspective, the different segment of time, and the changes documented over time are all elements that cannot be analyzed from individual photographs. The enhanced informational possibilities of photographs as a group can give entirely new perspectives.

Photographs that are important to be kept together are: (1) the work of a particular photographer or photographers; (2) those that were created or systematically and deliberately collected by one individual or institution; (3) groups that were produced or collected about one subject or topic; (4) collections comprised of a particular format or process (for instance, a collection of daguerreotypes or an album); (5) photographs that are sequential in number or time or that document a particular event, place, or person; or (6) any collection that has any other sort of internal order, particularly if there are related written materials. Nevertheless, there are times when photographs that do not constitute a valid collection come into a repository, and it is necessary to have a system to arrange these photographs. In these cases the photographs may be dispersed and handled, as are single photographs, by forming artificial collections or by placing individual photographs in a general file. The dispersal of a group of photographs into artificial collections or a general file must be carefully documented. The photographs should retain the accession number of the original group that entered the repository. A list should be made indicating the specific location of each photograph placed in a collection or in a general collection. This list will be invaluable if it becomes necessary to reassemble the collection. For example, after a collection is dispersed, information may become available indicating a unifying element that makes it desirable to reassemble the collection. Without proper record keeping reassembly would be very difficult.

Photographs that are part of larger manuscript collections have more complex provenance issues. Any relationship between the photographs and written materials must be maintained or documented in some form. This will provide the greatest informational possibilities for researchers using either the written materials or the photographs.

Because of the different natures of written documents and photographs, and the means by which each is generated and used, the two types of materials often will be separated before arrival at the repository. However, if photographs are found interfiled with written materials, such as correspondence, a construction report, a scientist's laboratory notes, or an anthropologist's field notes, the relationship must be carefully analyzed before a decision is made to separate the materials. Although maintaining written materials and photographs physically together can present problems of description and conservation, these problems can be overcome if it is determined that the best way of maintaining the link is to leave them together. Too often archivists have removed photographs from such files and placed them in a separate series or in a general photograph file without first examining the relationship or documenting the original order.

Where there is an intimate relationship between the written materials and the photographs (for example, a lengthy written description of a construction project that refers directly to the photographs for specific details), it may be best to leave the photographs in the file. Conservation requirements can be met by sleeving the photographs in a transparent material or using copy prints. If the photographs and written materials do not directly refer to each other, such as is often the case with many family collections, the photographs can be removed to create a separate series within the collection. Very often personal collections will arrive at the repository with this type of organization. However, some repositories, particularly institutional archives, strictly adhere to the principal of provenance and the registry principle and always maintain all materials together and in the order in which they were received.

Before developing an overall plan for arrangement and description, it must be decided if there will be a uniform policy regarding the organization of all collections or if a decision will be made for each separate collection or record group based on the content of both the written and photographic materials. For example, will photographs always be removed to form a separate series within the collection or will a decision be made for each collection? The ideal approach from the viewpoint of the integrity of the collection and access to the materials would be to make a decision for each collection.

Original Order

A second major consideration is the registry principle or sanctity of original order. After consideration is given to provenance for overall collection-level organization, the order in which the materials within the collections are arranged within that framework must be considered. The registry principle requires that the materials be maintained in their original order below the collection level. The reasons for maintaining original order are similar to those for maintaining provenance and involve the accumulative informational value of the items themselves and the context of the items within a group. Like provenance, this principle is often compromised in an attempt to enhance access to the materials for various types of users. Materials may be rearranged to provide better access than does the original order. Alterations often include organization by subject, name, or geographical or other content-related element. Also, materials may be arranged to provide order where there was none, or in an attempt to recreate original order. Most often files are rearranged to provide new modes of access, particularly by subject.

Strict adherence to provenance and original order requires that the archivist develop indexes so that photographs can be found by subject, name, location, or date. Even when photographs are arranged by subject or name, only one content element can be accommodated by the physical arrangement.

Processing

Checklist

Once general planning and overall issues have been considered, processing can proceed with the aid of a checklist. The first steps involve gaining physical and intellectual control of the photographs and recording basic information about them. Information gathering for analysis and decision making is followed by the physical arrangement of the collection and the preparation of the appropriate descriptions. The following procedures are adaptable for individual photographs, a photographic collection, or a group of photographs that are part of a manuscript collection or record group.

A processing checklist helps bring together the various steps of planning, analysis, and decision making necessary to process a collection. As with any complex task, it is necessary to divide the task into manageable components that can be accomplished sequentially. Listing all the steps insures that they will all be considered for each collection, thus encouraging consistency. The thought given to making up a checklist will help foster an understanding of the various options for each step in processing and how they are interrelated. The processing checklist is also important to document the current status of the processing of a collection, who carried out each step, and when it was done.

The first sample checklist (see figure 4-1) is a simple framework that can become much more complex as it is adapted to the unique characteristics of individual repositories. This checklist will be used to discuss the steps in processing. The second sample (see figure 4-2) is more

fully developed in order to meet the needs of the archives of the Massachusetts Institute of Technology. This checklist contains many more steps and cross checks and was developed for all types of materials. With a wide variety of materials and many processors a checklist allows the archivist to exercise oversight and to insure consistency among processors. For individual photos that will be placed in a general file not all steps may be relevant.

Collection File

This file, sometimes referred to as a case file, contains all materials pertaining to an individual collection, including correspondence relating to its acquisition, legal documents, and any other information related to the collection and its creator. The formation of this file is covered in detail in Chapter 3, Appraisal and Collecting Policies, and Chapter 6, Legal Issues.

There should be a collection file for every unit of materials received into the repository, including individual photographs. If a group of photographs is part of a manuscript collection or record group, this file may document the larger collection. If the photographs are separated and placed in a centralized photographic archives, it may be desirable to duplicate parts of the larger file so that a collection file specifically on the photographs can be maintained. One photograph left on the doorstep of the repository requires a collection file, even if it only contains a note documenting when and how the photograph was received. This information may be essential to archivists who subsequently deal with the photographs when determining copyright ownership or for identification purposes.

Accessioning

All photographs should be entered in the accession log. This is the one place where the entrance of all materials into the repository can be traced. Basic information about the materials can be found here as can a record of the disposition of the materials as a collection. The log indicates whether a collection is stored as a collection or in a general file, was traded or sold to another institution, or was discarded. If the photographs are part of a manuscript collection, accessioning may be done for the whole collection elsewhere.

The accession record can be maintained in different formats; options include a log with preprinted forms in a notebook or a card file with an individual card for each collection. Regardless of the format, a minimum amount of information, as shown on the sample log sheet, must be recorded (see figure 4-3). An accession number, which is a unique number within the institution, must be assigned. It can be a strict sequential numbering, or a numerical code indicating the number of collections received within the year. For example 983-101, is the 101st collection received in 1983. A combination of numerals and letters can indicate a col-

PHOTOGRAPHIC ARCHIVES

PROCESSING CHECKLIST

TASK	PROCESSOR	DATE
1. COLLECTION FILE		
2. ACCESSION		
3. LABEL		
4. PRELIMINARY INVENTORY		
5. ARRANGEMENT		
6. STORAGE MATERIALS		
7. DESCRIPTIONS		
8. REPRODUCTION OR VISUAL ACCESS		
9. FILE COPY NEGATIVES AND PRINTS; MICROREPRODUCTION		

Figure 4-1. Processing checklist. A general list that may be adapted to the specific needs of individual institutions.

The Libraries
Massachusetts Institute of Technology
Cambridge, Massachusetts 02139

Institute Archives and Special Collections
Room 14N-118
(617) 253-5688

file: control file - accessions
       and processing

PROCESSING RECORD

Accession No. _____   Collection No. _____

MAIN ENTRY:

TITLE:

Inclusive Dates: Bulk Dates: Vital Dates:

Extent: in ___ linear ft. or ___ items; in ___ rc cartons, ___ ms. boxes, or _____

Prominent language: Other languages:

Donor/Donor Representative:

Creator Generated Lists (type, author, date):

Restrictions:

Circumstances of Transfer (how, when, and from where was the collection moved):

Date Collection Received:

Description:

Figure 4-2. Processing checklist used at MIT Archives for all archival materials. Courtesy of MIT Archives.

ACCESSIONING AND INITIAL PROCESSING	Work Done By	Date Completed
____ Assign accession number	_____	_____
____ Make blue card	_____	_____
____ Generate locater card	_____	_____
____ Establish control file	_____	_____
____ Generate provisional catalog card	_____	_____
____ Generate container list	_____	_____
____ Label boxes	_____	_____
____ Donor acknowledgement	_____	_____

Notes:

FURTHER PROCESSING		
____ Collection analysis (see attached)	_____	_____
____ Rearrange (describe in attached memo)	_____	_____
____ Flag security records	_____	_____
____ Separate illustrations	_____	_____
____ Separate minutes	_____	_____
____ Separate books or technical reports	_____	_____
____ Generate finding aid consisting of	_____	_____
____ cover sheet / card copy on letterhead		
____ biography / organizational history		
____ scope and content note		
____ series description		
____ container list		
____ folder list		
____ other special list (describe)		
____ index (describe)		
____ Write new catalog card based on further processing	_____	_____

PRESERVATION		
____ Re-box: ____ rc cartons or ___ ms boxes	_____	_____
____ Replace folders	_____	_____
____ Remove staples / Replace staples	_____	_____
____ Flattening	_____	_____
____ Cleaning	_____	_____
____ Photocopy Thermofax, clippings, _____	_____	_____
____ Encapsulate / Enclose fragile or acidic items	_____	_____
____ Keep log of special preservation problems	_____	_____

Figure 4-2 (reverse).

lection or section of a repository (for instance PA for Photographic Archives or MS for Manuscripts), with either a straight numerical sequence or a year and sequence number. Regardless of how the number is formed, it should be unique so that no other collection of any kind in the repository has the same number. The name of the collection also should be documented. Collections can be given names based on their content but are often named after the donor, the collector, or the creator of the materials. If the name of the collection is not that of the donor, the name of the donor and relevant information about the donor should also be documented. The date of the acquisition is critical and materials should be accessioned as soon as possible after they come into the repository. The volume of materials may be estimated initially. It is not always necessary to list the exact number of glass negatives and paper prints in a collection if they are all contained in a cubic-foot box. The purpose here is to indicate the relative quantity of materials in order to later locate the collection, or to plan for the purchase of storage materials or designate storage space. However, it is important to record whether the collection constitutes one shoebox or ten shipping crates. A general description of the photographs can be as brief or elaborate as the collection requires and time permits. Often a collection can be summed up in a few sentences which note the predominant subjects, the approximate inclusive dates, and the technical processes. Space should be left to indicate final disposition of the collection, although this probably

will not be done until a later date. Options under disposition include: 1) maintaining materials as a collection in the form received, 2) reforming the collection based on archival appraisal, 3) interfiling materials with other collections, 4) dispersal into general files, 5) transferring materials within the institution or to other institutions, or 6) discarding the materials. Even when the materials are discarded it is important to record that they were in the repository at one time and that they were destroyed. This can be critical information for researchers and archivists when trying to reassemble a collection, understand gaps in the record, or document the complete range of a photographer's work. Often it is helpful to give a brief explanation of how an individual disposition decision was made. This will help subsequent curators and patrons understand how the collection was formed as well as give valuable clues to someone tracking down particular materials. Many of the disposition options may be governed by the deed of gift (see Chapter 6, Legal Issues).

Label

Immediately after a collection is logged in and an accession number is assigned, the containers of the collection should be labeled. When dealing with an individual item, it should be marked in an inconspicuous place with a soft lead pencil as explained in Chapter 5, Preservation of Photographic Materials. For boxes it is often convenient to have labels printed on pressure-sensitive stock so that the blanks

ACCESSION LOG				
DATE	ACCESSION #	DESCRIPTION (subjects, volumes, dates, processes)		DISPOSITION

Figure 4-3. Basic form for accession records in log format.

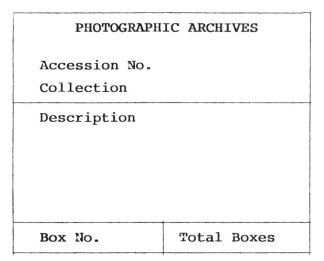

Figure 4-4. Self adhesive box label containing basic information may be applied to all types of containers.

can simply be filled in. Information contained on the label should include the accession number, the name of the collection, the volume of materials (box 1 of 1 box, box 1 of 2, etc.) and the dates of the collection, as seen in figure 4-4. The collection should be left in its original boxes and filing enclosures until a preliminary inventory is completed to avoid losing important information that is often written on or attached to the original enclosure materials (see figure 4-5). Consequently, unless the collection is contaminated or infested in some way, it should be labeled and retained in the original enclosure materials. Once this is done the archivist has begun two important processes: gaining intellectual control of the materials by the assigning of an accession number, and obtaining physical control of the materials by labeling the materials. These processes will establish a tie between intellectual and physical control.

Preliminary Inventory

The next step is to conduct a preliminary inventory of the collection. For groups of photographs that are part of a manuscript collection or record group, this must be coordinated with the overall processing of the collection. It is important that during the preliminary inventory nothing be changed about the collection, including its enclosure materials, physical arrangement, or the removal of any descriptive materials. The objective of the preliminary inventory is to gather information about the content and structure of the collection, the types of photographs it contains, and the collection's conservation needs (see figure 4-6). The preliminary inventory is a written record for both the staff and patrons. In addition this information often is needed for a deed of gift (see Chapter 6, Legal Issues), and for discussions and decisions about arranging and describing the collection. It is also at this time, based on the preliminary inventory, that a decision should be made on the degree of adherence to provenance and original order. Depending on

the resources and needs of the institution, a preliminary inventory can be done very quickly or it can involve great lengths of time. The more time spent, the better the archivist will understand the collection. Consequently, better decisions can be made about arrangement and description. Information recorded about conservation needs of the collection is also important. Even if there are no immediate plans to undertake conservation measures, it is helpful to maintain a conservation log so that conservation efforts can begin at a later date without again inventorying or surveying the collections. This allows the collection to be handled as few times as possible, which in itself is an important conservation concern.

While the specific format can vary, preliminary inventory sheets should be designed so that the processor can easily record the necessary information (see figures 4-7 and 4-8). The basic information that should be recorded includes:

1) Accession number
2) Name
3) Volume or size
4) Inclusive dates
5) Predominant dates
6) Types of processes
7) Photographers
8) Major subjects
9) Analysis of the collection
10) Related materials/cross reference

Figure 4-5. Unprocessed collections. Photographic collections can come into a repository in a variety of containers. Here a photographic archivist reviews a new collection. *Courtesy of Chicago Historical Society.*

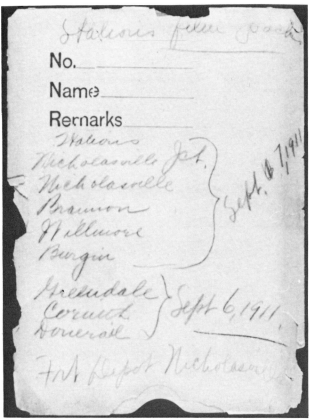

Figure 4-6. Original negative envelopes can contain a great deal of identifying information that must be recorded. *Courtesy of private collection.*

It should again be emphasized that the preliminary inventory is for gathering information only. Nothing about the physical arrangement or original enclosures should be changed. If the photographs are part of a manuscript collection or record group, the preliminary inventory should be done before any materials are separated. The information gathered will be used to decide how best to proceed with the subsequent steps on the checklist. To insure that adequate information is gathered the following points should be considered.

The accession number (1) and the name of the collection (2) should be the same as those listed in the accession log. The volume of the collection (3) should be more precisely calculated. For small collections the items might actually be counted. Measurements of linear feet and estimates of number of items per foot are appropriate for larger collections. This information will aid in calculating processing time and required storage materials and shelf space. The inclusive dates of the photographs (4) are the earliest and latest dates of materials. The predominant dates (5) are the dates within which the largest quantity of materials falls. For example, the inclusive dates of a collection may be 1840-1970. However, if there is one daguerreotype in the collection and one instant color print and the rest are silver gelatin prints, the predominant date might be 1920. Dates may be ascertained from labels on photographs, identifi-

cation of technical processes, and examination of internal evidence. Listing types of processes (6) included helps in dating, appraising, identifying, and interpreting the materials. In addition, noting specific processes can indicate the need for special handling or storage. The name of the photographer whose work is represented (7) is also important information. In some cases the photographer cannot be determined, while in others the entire collection may be the work of only one photographer. Often collections will have a mixture of work by a number of identified and unidentified photographers.

Major subjects represented (8) should not be a detailed listing but rather a list of a few predominant subjects. If no subjects are predominant, that fact should be recorded along with an indication of the variety found. The terms used for subjects should come from a controlled vocabulary or thesaurus selected for the repository's subject authority. The analysis of the collection (9) is perhaps the most important aspect of information gathering. The analysis should include a description of the overall nature of the collection, its various elements, and how they interrelate. Any existing order should be noted along with an evaluation of its adequacy for access. The lack of any discernible order also should be noted. The presence or absence of factors that determine the cohesiveness of a collection should be analyzed. If the photographs are part of a manuscript collection or record group, attention should be given to the extent of the relationship between the photographs and written materials, whether it should be retained and, if so, how best to do so. Other broad questions of provenance and original order should be addressed. If there is not an existing order or if the order is inappropriate for research, alternate organizations should be evaluated.

Finally, any related materials (10) in the repository or elsewhere should be listed. This may be other photography collections, manuscripts or records, or published materials. Collections in other repositories may be mentioned here, as may any other information that might assist in the processing of the collection or benefit researchers.

Arrangement

The basis of archival arrangement is to deal with groups of materials. With all three ways in which photographs are acquired—individually, in groups, and as part of larger collections—groups are maintained or created to effectively make them available for research. The preliminary inventory assembles information that allows the archivist to make informed decisions regarding the integration of new material into the repository.

Individual Photographs

Individual photographs are interfiled with other photographs to form various types of groups. One option is to form artificial collections. These are collections that are formed by the archivist according to some organizing principle. The organizing principle can be a content descriptor

```
┌─────────────────────────────────────────────────────────────────┐
│                                    Processed by_____         │
│  Photographic Archives             Date _____           │
│                                                                   │
│                        WORKSHEET                                  │
│              PRELIMINARY COLLECTION SURVEY                        │
│                                                                   │
│  ACCESSION #:                                                     │
│                                                                   │
│  NAME OF COLLECTION:                                              │
│                                                                   │
│  SIZE OF COLLECTION:                                              │
│                                                                   │
│  OVERSIZED MATERIAL:  _____ Yes _____ No                     │
│                                                                   │
│  DESCRIPTION & ANALYSIS:                                          │
│                                                                   │
│                                                                   │
│                                                                   │
│                                                                   │
│                                                                   │
│  PHYSICAL CONDITION:                                              │
│                                                                   │
│                                                                   │
│  PROPER STORAGE:    _____ Needs re-boxing                       │
│                     _____ Needs envelopes and interleaving      │
│                     _____ Archival storage completed            │
│                                                                   │
│  DATES OF MATERIAL:  (Inclusive & predominant)                    │
│                                                                   │
│  PHOTOGRAPHIC PROCESSES:   Check representative selection from    │
│                            collections;                           │
│                            Note number of items if quantity is    │
│                            small                                  │
│                                                                   │
│  Positive Processes    Negative Process    Size    Mounts         │
│                                                                   │
│  Daguerreotype         Glass negatives:            Album          │
│  Ambrotype             --Wet                       Carte-de-viste │
│  Tintype               --Dry                       Cabinet card   │
│  Salt Print                                        Stereograph    │
│  Albumen               Flexible negatives          Other          │
│  Printing-out paper                                               │
│  Developing-out paper                                             │
│  Carbon                INDEXES COMPLETED:          PREDOMINANT     │
│  Platinum                                          SUBJECTS:      │
│  Gum bichromate        Photographer   _____                     │
│  Cyanotype             Subject        _____                     │
│  Photomechanical       Conservation   _____                     │
│  Lantern Slide         Photo Process  _____                     │
│  35 mm Slide                                                      │
│  Other                                                            │
│                                                                   │
│  FOR ADDITIONAL INFORMATION SEE:                                  │
└─────────────────────────────────────────────────────────────────┘
```

Figure 4-7. Preliminary inventory. A general form that may be adapted to the specific needs of individual institutions.

```
┌─────────────────────────────────────────────────────────────────────────────┐
│                        COLLECTION INFORMATION FORM                            │
│                                                                               │
│   _____ PRELIM                                                                │
│                                                                               │
│   _____ FINAL                               1.  Catalog No. _____         │
│                                                                               │
│   CENTER _____      2.  Accession No. _____       │
│                                                                               │
│   3.  COLLECTION TITLE _____  │
│              and                                                              │
│           INCLUSIVE DATES _____  │
│                                                                               │
│   4.  DONOR (name & address) _____  │
│                                                                               │
│       _____│
│                                                                               │
│   5.  Date received _____     6.  Restrictions _____   │
│                                                                               │
│       _____│
│                                                                               │
│   7.  No. of Boxes _____        8.  No. of Volumes (in boxes) _____ │
│                                                                               │
│   9.  Linear inches or feet _____     10. No. of Volumes (outside boxes)_ │
│                                                                               │
│   11. Number of items (small collections) _____ │
│                                                                               │
│   12. Donor Agreement Form Signed (date) _____  │
│                                                                               │
│                                                                               │
│   ABSTRACT SUMMARY OF COLLECTION:                                             │
│                                                                               │
│                                                                               │
│                                                                               │
│                                                                               │
│                                                                               │
│                                                                               │
│                                                                               │
│                                                                               │
│                                                                               │
│                                                                               │
│                                                                               │
│                                                                               │
│                                                                               │
│                                                                               │
│   RCC-1 (72)                                                                  │
│   A/M: 6-20-77                                                                │
└─────────────────────────────────────────────────────────────────────────────┘
```

Figure 4-8. This preliminary inventory form is called a Collection Inventory Form (CIF). *Courtesy of Minnesota Historical Society.*

(subject, date, location, person) or an element of the photographic object (technical process, format, photographer). It should be remembered, however, that the purpose here is to organize individual photographs, not to gather in one location all photographs on a particular subject. To do so would involve destroying true collections with a loss of the informational value of the collection. Drawing together materials in various collections that have common content descriptors is done through description, particularly indexing.

Artificial collections are often arranged around a subject, such as logging, mining, or fishing; a location, such as a city, state, or region; or a person. Individual photographs from the nineteenth century are often arranged by technical process or format. Artificial collections are often made up of daguerreotypes, ambrotypes, tintypes, cartes de visite, cabinet cards, stereo cards, oversized materials, and albums. This type of collection is particularly useful for unidentified materials. When it is possible to identify a photographer's work, assembling his photographs received from various sources can be beneficial.

The other option for arranging individual photographs is in a general file. A general file is also an artificial collection, in that its contents did not come from a common source, but it is usually broader in scope than the previously described artificial collections. Usually general files are arranged by subject and can include geographic locations, proper names, and time periods. For larger collections it may be appropriate to have separate general collections for subjects, places, and people. Choosing proper subject headings is critical to the organization and retrieval of the photographs. Some repositories use published subject headings in an effort to encourage standardization.

Possible sources of subject headings are:

1) *List of Subject Headings for Small Libraries*, an abbreviated list of library subject headings used by smaller libraries, which is often useful for photographs because they are not as specific as other listings.

2) *Subject Headings Used in the Dictionary Catalog of the Library of Congress*, intended for books; it is comprehensive but may be too detailed and otherwise inappropriate for photographs.

3) *Subject Headings Used in the Library of Congress Prints and Photographs Division*, containing headings that were developed to be used for the photographic collections at the Library of Congress, the largest photograph collection in the world. Headings are consequently very complex and require revision for use in most repositories.

Often, the best solution is for an archivist to develop subject headings based on the content of the collections in the repository. However, while this has the advantage of being custom tailored to the needs of the repository, it can also be overly restrictive by being too narrowly focused and detailed. The system should be flexible, comprehensive, expandable, and simple. In an attempt to offer the best subject access, subject headings are often made very detailed. While at first this may appear to offer the best access, in fact it can cause fragmentation of the collection and makes it difficult to find images. Specialized or detailed subjects contained in a photograph are best revealed through indexes. An attempt to arrange a small number of photographs by headings related to the individual images, such as carriage, sled, stagecoach, and trolley, might not make them as accessible as would grouping them under a more general term like Transportation. This is especially true if only a few images are involved. For larger numbers a hierarchy of terms is helpful, again starting with a general term such as Transportation and adding a more specific secondary term—Stagecoach. Further terms or dates can be added to qualify the subject heading; for example, Transportation—Stagecoach—1880-90. However, all the transportation photographs will be in one place, including those not further identified. A study of subject headings used at other repositories is helpful in developing a system, but a system that is successful at one institution may be entirely inappropriate at another.

From an archival point of view this hierarchy of terms can be viewed as similar to arrangement by series, subseries, and folder, and standard archival methodology can be followed. The amount of materials and the time available for processing will dictate the level to which the photographs are arranged. A hierarchical approach also allows more specific arrangements to be done at a later date without necessarily destroying the order previously imposed. The previous example of "transportation" would be considered a series. If all transportation photographs are gathered together and not further arranged, an overall organization that will be useful to a researcher will have been imposed. As time permits, series that contain large amounts of photographs or frequently used photographs can be arranged in more detail to the subseries and folder level. Item-level arrangement is usually avoided in general files and may only be done on collections that contain especially important or valuable materials. At the subseries level the transportation photographs can be divided by types of transportation: trains, automobiles, horse-drawn vehicles, airplanes, etc. Further arrangement may involve separating the horse-drawn vehicles into stagecoaches, carriages, trollies, wagons, etc. However, it is best to have all collections arranged at the series level before giving more detailed attention to any particular collection.

It must also be remembered that general files and artificial collections, unlike other collections, are dynamic rather than static. Photographs will continually be added to them. The hierarchical arrangement best suits this situation because new folder or subseries headings can be added without disrupting the series level.

An important problem in arranging by subject either within

collections or in a general file is that an original photograph may be placed under only one subject heading arrangement unless multiple copies are made of that photograph. One way of overcoming this is by intellectual access, i.e., subject indexes and cross references. Thus, though a photograph may be categorized as being primarily about one subject, it can be indexed for any other subjects it contains.

Groups of Photographs

During the preliminary inventory of a group of photographs information will be gathered that will indicate if the photographs meet the criteria for a collection. If it is determined that the group does not constitute a collection, then the group may be dispersed and treated as are individual photographs. In addition to the criteria listed on p. 73, another consideration is volume. Will groups of photographs that meet the criteria of a collection but only contain twenty photographs be maintained as a collection? Some repositories set a number of items below which a collection will be placed in the general file and above which it will be retained as a collection. However, the final judgment should be made on the basis of the content of a collection, not of its quantity. Also, the ability to maintain small groups together (as with a hierarchical arrangement) may encourage placing smaller collections in the general file. For example, while a small group of ten photographs of a lumber camp could remain intact in a general file, a group of ten diverse images by one photographer would be dispersed by subject and lost as a collection unless detailed records were kept in the collection file.

The preliminary inventory should also indicate if there is an internal order to the photographs. If an internal order is discerned, it must be evaluated to determine whether it is appropriate for the collection and if it will serve the research demands placed on it. Common arrangements are alphabetical by subject, name, or location; by institutional structure; by chronological order; and by numerical order. There can be other arrangements that are esoteric and difficult to discern. Knowledgable collectors may use an arrangement based on their detailed understanding of a subject, and which may not be readily apparent to others, including the archivist. Consequently, the examination for original order should be intensive and should, if possible, involve subject experts and other archivists.

In institutional archives an internal order is rarely changed. For other types of collections there may be less objection to altering an existing order if the changes are documented in the finding aids. Collections of family photographs will often have no internal order. If there is no internal order or if the order is inadequate, then an organization must be imposed on the collection. The most common arrangement is by subject. Subject headings should be selected or developed as discussed for general files under Individual Pho-

tographs. There are often advantages of consistency and ease of access and processing if the collections use the same system of subject headings as the general file. The hierarchical arrangement can allow as detailed arrangements as are necessary even for a specialized collection.

Often a collection of the work of one photographer or studio will be numbered. Such photographs should be arranged in numerical sequence, even if some numbers are missing, rather than by subject.

Photographs in Manuscript Collections

In addition to gathering the previously discussed information during the preliminary inventory, particular attention must be paid to the relationship between the photographs and written materials. If the relationship so demands, the photographs may be interfiled with the written materials. If they are removed a separation sheet should be used (see figure 4-9). More often the photographs will be separate from the written materials when the collection is acquired, often with no internal arrangement for the photographs. In this case the photographs may comprise a separate series of the larger collection. The arrangement may need to parallel the arrangement of the written documents. If the preliminary inventory shows that such a coordination is not necessary, then the photographs may be arranged similarly to collections of photographs.

Numbering

Each item in a repository may be assigned a unique number. This gives additional physical control over the photographs, assuring that each item is properly filed. Item numbers may also be integral to intellectual control through written descriptions and indexes. For photographs retained in collections, the numbering system should be developed from the accession number. The simplest way is to number the prints in sequence after they are arranged, using the accession number followed by the item number. For example, a collection of 239 items that was the twelfth collection accessioned into the photographic archives in 1982 could use the number 982PA012-1 through 982PA012-239.

In a general file or an artificial collection sequential numbering does not work, because materials are continually being added. For this reason many repositories do not number these items. Often only the series (Transportation, Architecture, Industry, etc.) is written on the item. However, more specific labeling can help refile photographs. The photographs can be labeled with the series, subseries, and folder headings, or numbers can be assigned to these and used on the photos. If the number of items in each file is restricted, then an item number can also be assigned without need of alteration when materials are added. For example, a photograph might be labeled GF–Architecture–Churches–Boston–#16. If patrons are allowed to use only one folder

PHOTOGRAPHS

SEPARATION SHEET

Photographs originally contained in this collection:

COLLECTION NAME:

ACCESSION NUMBER:

     Series:

     Box:

     Folder:

Have been removed and are now located in:

COLLECTION NAME:

ACCESSION NUMBER:

     Series:

     Box:

     Folder:

Figure 4-9. A separation sheet provides one way of recording the removal of photographs from written materials.

at a time, labeling the items is less important. Such a restriction is not practical, however, for many repositories.

Negatives

Negatives should be filed separately from prints and access to them should be restricted. Many researches find negatives difficult to view and interpret and require a positive image to inspect. Negatives are often considered the archival original in that they are the first reproduction of the object photographed. Negatives can be more fragile than prints and require different storage and handling procedures.

Negatives should be filed separately either within individual collections or in a repository negative file. If the primary access to the collection is through the prints, the negatives should be labeled with the print number or headings followed by the letter "N." If the photographer numbered the negatives, this number should be kept. If it is necessary to renumber the negatives, the original number should still be retained and can follow the item number in parentheses. For example, in the number 982PA012-104 (#176), 982 refers to the year of accessioning: 1982; PA indicates Photographic Archives; 012 identifies this as the twelfth collection accessioned in 1982; 104 is the sequential number assigned to the negative after arrangement; and #176 is the photographer's original number. If a collection is primarily negatives of one photographer's work, the original numbers can be used for the item numbers following the accession number. Copy and duplicate negatives can constitute their own files numbered to correspond to the original of which they are a copy. The addition of a C for copy and a D for duplicate is one way of differentiating between types of negatives.

Description

The physical arrangement of a collection will influence the detail and format of its description. In archival arrangement descriptions usually apply to a group of materials at the collection, box, or folder level and not to individual items. However, the level at which a collection is described should be based on the size and scope of the collection, its historical importance, its potential research use, its artifactual value, its uniqueness, and how it relates to the institutional profile. Only the most important collections can justify the time and expense of item-level descriptions. Often collections may already have item-level descriptions prepared by a photographer, family member, collector, or processor. These descriptions should be labeled as to source and preserved to supplement the group-level description and analysis for the collection, with the realization that they may need further verification by the researcher or the archivist if time permits.

During the preliminary inventory and arrangement of the collection the appropriate level of description will be determined. The level of description will match that of arrangement with each level being more specific and building upon the previous level. The most general description is at the collection level. This will be similar to the preliminary inventory but should refer to the final organization of the collection and give a more detailed analysis of it. Since the collection description is written after all other operations have been completed, the processor should have a thorough knowledge of the collection and be able to report not only the characteristics of the collection but some interpretation of it as well. For many collections this level of description is more than adequate to service most researchers. Very often, by simply knowing the dates of the materials, the subjects it contains, and a brief analysis of its research value, researchers will know if the collection may be excluded from their inquiries or if they need to investigate it more closely. All collections should be described at this level, including general files and artificial collections (see figure 4-10).

General files are considered "self indexing" and are usually not accompanied by written descriptions. Because the photographs are readily accessible and all photographs determined to belong under the same subject heading are brought together, it is often felt that finding aids are unnecessary. The ongoing addition of new material also makes it difficult to construct finding aids. Nevertheless, a general file has overall characteristics, weaknesses, and strengths that can be described at least at the collection level. Series-level descriptions may also be helpful. Descriptions at the subseries level and below may easily become inaccurate due to the addition of material. The collection description gives the researcher an overall orientation to the collection by listing the series and general subjects, photographers, inclusive and predominate dates, and significant strengths and weaknesses, similar to the preliminary inventory.

Descriptions of photographic collections and photographic series in manuscript collections should follow standard archival formats.[3] The description should be at the same level as the arrangement of the collection (see figure 4-11).

Identification

To assist in the use of internal evidence in determining content identifiers (subject, person, geography, date), it is helpful for the archivist to compile an identification directory. The information compiled will be dictated by the type of repository and the photographic holdings, but most repositories will benefit from a listing of dates, people, places, and events important to the collections. The content of the directory should be drawn directly from the collections. For a general local history collection, it is important to document the dates of occurrence of man-made objects com-

---

[3] Society of American Archivists Committee on Finding Aids, *Inventories and Registers: A Handbook of Techniques and Examples* (Chicago: Society of American Archivists, 1976); Gracy, *Arrangement & Description*, p. 19-40.

```
                    PHOTOGRAPHIC ARCHIVES
                 UNIVERSITY OF KENTUCKY LIBRARIES
                        COLLECTION GUIDE


ACCESSION NUMBER:  PA 56M307        MICROFILM NUMBER:  M PA 56M307

NAME OF COLLECTION:  SEATON COLLECTION

SIZE OF COLLECTION:  176 ITEMS IN 3 BOXES; 15 ALBUMS IN 15 BOXES; 7 OVERSIZE ITEMS
                                                               IN 1 BOX
NUMBERED FRAMES:  882


OVERSIZE MATERIAL:    X  YES ____ NO __7 ITEMS_____

NEGATIVES:          ____ YES  X  NO _____

NEGATIVES PRINTED:  ____ YES  X  NO _____

DATES OF MATERIAL:  CA. 1854-1954

SUBJECTS INDEXED:   ARCHITECTURE  GEOGRAPHICAL   PORTRAIT
                    ARTIFACT      INDUSTRY       STILL LIFE
                    BLACKS        LANDSCAPE      STREET SCENE
                    CITYSCAPE     OCCUPATION     TRANSPORTATION
                    EVENT         PEOPLE


PHOTOGRAPHIC PROCESSES:   DAGUERREOTYPE     ALBUMEN PRINT
                          AMBROTYPE         CYANOTYPE
                          TINTYPE           PAPER PRINT
                          CARTE-DE-VISITE   SILVER GELATIN PRINT
                          CABINET CARD
                          STEREOVIEW


SELECTED PHOTOGRAPHERS:   SAVAGE      W & D DOWNEY      SAYRE
                          TABER       VAN LOO          EVICK
                          WATKINS     LANDY
                          MUYBRIDGE   SCHMIDT
                          HOUSEWORTH  A.J. MELHUISH
```

DESCRIPTION: THE MEANS AND SEATON FAMILY PAPERS ARE INTERRELATED THROUGH THE MARRIAGE OF ELIZA ISABELLA MEANS TO WILLIAM B. SEATON, HOWEVER THE DONORS REQUESTED THAT THE TWO BRANCHES OF THE FAMILY BE KEPT SEPARATE AND CATALOGED AS TWO DISTINCT MANUSCRIPT COLLECTIONS. WHILE THE PHOTOGRAPHS WERE PULLED FROM THE SEATON FAMILY PAPERS, THEY INCLUDE IMAGES OF BOTH SEATON AND MEANS FAMILIES AND PROVIDE DOCUMENTATION OF AN IMPORTANT KENTUCKY FAMILY. THE MEANS PLAYED A KEY ROLE IN THE DEVELOPMENT OF THE IRON AND STEEL INDUSTRY IN OHIO, VIRGINIA, AND ASHLAND, KENTUCKY AND PHOTOGRAPHS OF 19TH CENTURY INDUSTRIAL ARCHITECTURE ARE OF SPECIAL INTEREST. THE MANY ALBUMS IN THE COLLECTION RECORD TRIPS TAKEN ABROAD AND THROUGHOUT THE UNITED STATES (CABINET CARD AND STEREOVIEWS ARE ABUNDANT), FORMAL AND INFORMAL FAMILY PORTRAITS, AND SNAPSHOTS POSSIBLY TAKEN BY E.C. MEANS, BELIEVED TO BE A PROFICIENT AMATEUR PHOTOGRAPHER. THE SCOPE AND VARIETY OF SUBJECTS, PHOTOGRAPHIC PROCESSES, AND PHOTOGRAPHERS REPRESENTED IN THE COLLECTION MAKE IT A SIGNIFICANT RESOURCE FOR STUDY.

FOR ADDITIONAL INFORMATION SEE: MANUSCRIPT COLLECTION 56M307
                                 MANUSCRIPT COLLECTION 56M301

Figure 4-10. Finding aid. This is one format for a collection level description. *Courtesy of Special Collections, University of Kentucky Libraries.*

PHOTOGRAPHIC ARCHIVES
UNIVERSITY OF KENTUCKY LIBRARIES
COLLECTION GUIDE

ACCESSION NUMBER: 81PA101   MICROFILM NUMBER: M 81PA101

NAME OF COLLECTION: LOUIS EDWARD NOLLAU RAILROAD GLASS NEGATIVE COL-
                    LECTION

SIZE OF COLLECTION: 2963 ITEMS CONTAINED IN 143 BOXES

NUMBERED FRAMES: 2963

OVERSIZE MATERIAL: _____YES __X__NO   _____

NEGATIVES: __X__YES _____NO   ___ENTIRE COLLECTION_____

NEGATIVES PRINTED: _____YES __X__NO   _____

DATES OF MATERIAL: CA. 1909-1917

SUBJECTS INDEXED: ENGINES   GENERAL
                    RIGHT OF WAY
                    STRUCTURES
                    MACHINERY
                    EVENT

PHOTOGRAPHIC PROCESSES: GLASS PLATE NEGATIVE
                          FLEXIBLE NEGATIVES

SELECTED PHOTOGRAPHERS: LOUIS EDWARD NOLLAU

DESCRIPTION: A PROFESSOR OF ENGINEERING DRAWING AT THE UNIVERSITY
                OF KENTUCKY FOR FORTY-NINE YEARS, LOUIS EDWARD NOLLAU WAS
                ALSO A PROLIFIC PHOTOGRAPHER. THIS EXTENSIVE COLLECTION
                OF HIS RAILROAD NEGATIVES PROVIDES EXCELLENT DOCUMENTATION
                OF THE SOUTHERN RAILWAY SYSTEM. IN ADDITION TO STANDARD
                VIEWS OF ROLLING STOCK AND RIGHT OF WAYS, NOLLAU PHOTO-
                GRAPHED THE RECONSTRUCTION OF HIGH BRIDGE, INSPECTION TRIPS,
                RAILROAD PERSONNEL, RAILROAD STATIONS, TOWERS, WATER TANKS,
                STORE ROOMS, AND WORKSHOPS. PLEASE CONSULT THE ACCOMPANY-
                ING INVENTORY FOR MORE DETAILED INFORMATION.

FOR ADDITIONAL INFORMATION SEE: UNIVERSITY ARCHIVES COLLECTION OF
                                 RAILROAD PHOTOGRAPHS BY NOLLAU.

Figure 4-11. Finding aid. The collection level guide can be supplemented with standard series, box, and folder descriptions if the collection warrants. *Courtesy of Special Collections, University of Kentucky Libraries.*

```
                              81PA101
              NOLLAU RAILROAD GLASS NEGATIVE COLLECTION
                             INVENTORY



                             ENGINES
                            Boxes 1-2

Engines are arranged numerically by engine number, sequence is incomplete.

Box 1      1-24           Engines 114-814



Box 2      25-34          Engines 816-6691
           35-48          Engines, unidentified


                          ROLLING STOCK
                            Boxes 3-5

Rolling stock is arranged alphabetically by type of car.  For additional
images of Rolling Stock, please consult EVENT--Inspection trips, boxes 120-125.

Box 3      49             Baggage car
           50-51          Box car
           52             Caboose
           53-54          Coupler
           55-56          Crane
           57             Dining car
           58-65          Ditcher
           66-71          Flat car

Box 4      72-81          Gondola
           82-85          Hand car
           86-92          Observation car
           93-99          Passenger car

Box 5      100            Side dumping car
           101-117        Trains


                          STRUCTURES
                      Stations and Depots
                          Boxes 6-26

Stations and depots are arranged alphabetically by location of station or
depot and chronologically.  For additional views please consult EVENT--
Inspection Trips, boxes 120-125.

Box 6      118-119        Akron, Alabama
           120            Allen            8-16-16
           121            Alpine           8-14-13
           122            Annadel          7-9-13
           123            Arklet           7-15-15
           124-132        Attalla          1916
           133            Avondale         10-4-14
```

Figure 4-11, continued.

```
                              81PA101
               NOLLAU RAILROAD GLASS NEGATIVE COLLECTION
                              INVENTORY


                             STRUCTURES
                         Stations and Depots
                            Boxes 6-26

    Box 7       134        Babhatchie             7-3-12
                135        Bear Creek Junction    12-22-14
                136-155    Bessemer, Alabama      1915-1917

    Box 8       156        Bibbville              7-13-15
                157-158    Blanchet               9-6-11, 6-22-15
                159        Blocton                8-21-15
                160        Boligee                11-14-12
                161        Bowen                  10-15-15
                162-166    Boyce                  4-23-12, 7-31-13
                167-168    Bracht                 9-6-11, 6-5-15
                169        Brannon                9-7-11
                170-176    Brighton               4-30-14
                177        Buffington             1-25-13
                178        Burgin                 9-7-11
                179        Burnside               7-15-13
                180        Burstall               7-13-15

    Box 9       181        Caldwell               7-24-12
                182        Cardiff                4-25-12
                183-184    Chattanooga            8-10-15
                185        Cincinnati Freight Depot
                186-192    Cincinnati, Lincoln Park
                           Freight Depot          5-2-14
                193-202    Cincinnati, Vine Street
                           Station                1914

    Box 10      203-220    Cincinnati, Vine Street
                           Station, detail of doors, 1914
                221        Coalfield              8-29-16
                222        Coaling                8-18-14
                223        Collbran
                224        Collinsville           12-3-12
                225-227    Corinth                9-6-11, 6-22-15, 6-28-15

    Box 11      228-229    Cottondale             11-3-16
                230        Coulterville           4-24-12
                231        Crescent Springs       1-25-13
                232-234    Crittenden             6-5-15
                235        Crudup                 12-3-12
                236        Cumberland Falls       11-30-12
                237        Cypress                7-14-15
                238-244    Danville               8-10-14
                245        Dayton, Tennessee      11-21-11
                246        DeArmond               8-29-16
                247        Deermont               8-12-16
                248-250    Delaplain              6-11-15
```

Figure 4-11, continued.

monly found in photographs. Usually the dates of construction or installation and demolition or removal of various buildings and objects in the area are helpful. Such objects may include: local landmarks; gas and electric streetlights, noting if their use overlapped; telegraphs and telephones and the required wiring; horse- or mule-drawn trollies, and the use of tracks; electric trollies; and automobiles. In addition, the identification directory should list names and dates for local events and people. Included should be birth and death dates for public or prominent figures who often appear in photographs, together with important dates in their lives, such as a term of office. Events such as celebrations of various anniversaries of a town or city and political or social events also should be noted, along with the date of each. Disasters such as floods, fires, earthquakes, tornadoes, or storms should be listed with dates.

Specialized collections require additional information. For example, if the collection relates to a religious order, founding dates, opening and closing dates of regional houses, and names and dates of members of the order are important. A directory for collections relating to a business should include information on organizational structure, dates of products, advertisement campaigns, and other information relevant to the particular business. Other specialized collections, such as those documenting the history of science, labor, and material culture, should list dates relevant to their particular collections as well as those that will help place the collections in a larger social, political, and cultural context.

After the turn of the nineteenth century most prints were silver gelatin and identification of the process will not be very helpful in assigning a date more specific than 1900 to the present. The internal evidence thus becomes even more important for dating such photographs. Consequently, the directory must include twentieth-century information such as dates for electricity in homes, televisions, television antennas, motorized buses and fire trucks, the placing of utility wires underground, modern shapes of electric streetlights, and any other information relevant to the local area.

This type of information will not only give specifics that will aid in identifying photographs, but while gathering the information the archivist will necessarily gain a better understanding of local history that will enhance interpretations of individual photographs or groups of photographs. The information in the directory will grow gradually as a collection is analyzed and used. Information found while researching one collection may be relevant to others in the repository and should be recorded.

Information for the identification directory as well as other relevant data for the area can be obtained from a number of sources. City directories published from the late 1700s to the present offer a wealth of information on a city's economic and social history, including the development of photography. Such directories list businesses, individuals, and residences as well as offering informative advertisements and profiles of the city and its prominent citizens. The advertisements for photographers sometimes give biographical information and list the range of processes offered. The movement of citizens and photographers in the city can be traced from year to year, as can the history of a particular site. The classified headings will reveal the local terminology for various professions, including when the term "photographer" began to replace that of "daguerreotypist" or "ambrotypist" (usually in the mid-1850s).

Many directories contain maps, which are particularly important for cities that changed the names of streets or renumbered street addresses. Telephone directories can be important supplements to city and regional directories. Contemporary newspapers offer important information, as do contemporary local histories. City histories are often published to commemorate anniversaries of foundings and can be in book or pamphlet format. Transportation schedules and route maps also can offer valuable information on street names and numbers as well as dating technological advances in transportation, such as changes from horse-drawn and electric trolleys to buses powered by various means and with various body styles.

Visual Access

Regardless of the design of the physical arrangement or the detail of the descriptions of photographs, at some point researchers must see individual photographs in order to use them. How to give access to the images and in what form relates to the overall arrangement and description systems, conservation needs, costs, types of researchers, and value of the collections. The quickest method of access that requires the least initial expense is to make the original photographs available to researchers. However, continued handling of prints can damage them and other formats, such as negatives and cased images, are even more fragile. Xerographic copies of prints can be made available to researchers fairly inexpensively. An additional advantage is that numerous copies of the same print can be made and then be filed under many different subject headings. There are now copiers available that make very faithful copies of original photographs. (For cautions on photocopying see Chapter 5, Preservation of Photographic Materials). A more expensive alternative is to produce copy negatives of prints and make appropriately sized copy prints. 8″ × 10″ prints can easily be filed, and small prints, such as contact prints of 35-mm negatives, can be mounted on cards along with bibliographic information if item cataloging is done. This procedure is often used for fine print or museum collections. More appropriate for archival collections is copying on 35-mm or 16-mm continuous-tone microfilm or microfiche. This allows visual access to entire collections while maintaining their integrity as collections. Large negative collections particularly can benefit from microfilming. The negatives can be backlighted and filmed often less expen-

Figure 4-12. Microfilm copies of negatives or prints can be made for research use. These are positive images of glass plate negatives. *Courtesy of private collection.*

sively than a paper print can be made. A positive film image can be placed in service for researchers, thus diminishing the usual problems of conservation and interpretation of negatives (see figure 4-12).

Indexes

The physical arrangement of photographs cannot provide direct access by all avenues of inquiry. Most photographs will contain numerous content identifiers (subject, person, geography, date) but yet the original photograph can only be filed under one of these. Even when a photograph is filed by a subject descriptor it is usually filed only under its primary subject and not under the many other subjects it contains. Intellectual access by the use of indexes can help overcome the limitations of physical arrangement. Like other written descriptions, indexes can be generated at the collection, series, file, or item level. For example, on the collection level an index for agriculture could list all collections that contain photographs classified as agriculture. Below the collection level indexes can list series classified as ''agriculture,'' but they also can list other series and subseries classified otherwise but containing materials on ''agriculture.'' For example, the series Architecture in some

collections may contain farmhouses and barns that would be indexed under agriculture.

Ideally, every photograph in a repository could be assigned dozens of content classifications for subjects, names, places, photographer, technical process, etc. In the past this has been attempted with card files and manual systems. The amount of detailed work involved is overwhelming and often the system cannot be maintained. This approach is not recommended as a manual system. More valuable information for researchers can be given in analytical descriptions of groups of photographs and indexes at the collection, series, and folder levels. However, extensive indexing and item-level descriptions may be possible with the use of new technology.

Automation

Although not proceeding at the pace predicted some years ago, automation is surely becoming an integral part of archives. Electronic technology is relevant to photographic archives in two areas: manipulation of written descriptions and reproduction of visual images. In some cases the coordination of the two aspects is possible.

In an attempt to establish conventions for describing photographs, Elisabeth Betz has published rules for describing photographs and other graphic materials.[4] The rules are very useful for manual systems and should be consulted. They are particularly important for automation systems. With the proliferation of affordable personal computers, more repositories will be moving toward automation. Even those repositories not now considering automation should devise manual systems that are compatible with and easily converted to an automated system. One goal of automation is the widest possible sharing of information. In order to achieve this goal, standards must be followed for the format of the descriptive information. Betz's *Graphic Materials* provides those standards for describing both individual items and collections. The system also has a great deal of flexibility as to the amount of information given for each entry. Based on these rules a new Machine Readable Catalog (MARC) format for photographs has been developed and will soon be published. Currently, a number of larger photographic repositories are planning projects using these standards on personal computers. The intent of at least one project is to offer for sale software to be used for photographic collections. The next few years will bring significant developments in this area. Photographic archivists should become knowledgable in this area and keep abreast of current developments. Before beginning any new arrangement and description projects, computer specialists within the institution or at a neighboring archival repository should be consulted.

---

[4]Elisabeth Betz, comp., *Graphic Materials: Rules for Describing Original Items and Historical Collections* (Washington, D.C.: Library of Congress, 1982).

Videotape and video disks are currently being used to reproduce visual images. Reproduction is desirable both for preservation (less handling of originals) and ease of access. A video transfer process that takes slides, negatives, and film, in either black-and-white or color, and places the images on videotape is now available through some commercial photographic processors. The transfer takes approximately seven seconds per image and costs about $.40 per image. Electronic enhancement of the image is possible, as are titles and captions. Although intended for mass marketing to amateur photographers, the service has many implications for photographic archives.

The Library of Congress is conducting a far-reaching experiment with video disk reproduction. The video disk is probably more stable than videotape and allows selected viewing of 54,000 single frames on each side of a disk. In addition, the Library of Congress is also experimenting with integrating the retrieval of descriptive information, stored in a data base in a minicomputer, with the video disk images. Thus a researcher can use the data base to search written descriptions to identify the image or group of images desired, and call up those images from the video disk. The International Museum of Photography at the George Eastman House in Rochester, New York, is also involved in an important video disk project with minicomputer interface.

The pervasiveness of photographic images in our lives has prompted concerns for visual literacy—an understanding of what and how images communicate and how to use them. People who have been widely exposed to visual images view them as an integral part of the broad universe of information. Good systems of arrangement and description allow photographs to take their place among information resources that contribute to knowledge of ourselves, our culture, and our world.

5 Preservation of Photographic Materials
Mary Lynn Ritzenthaler

Conservation encompasses the three functions of examination, preservation, and restoration. Examination includes actions undertaken to determine original structures and materials and the extent of deterioration or loss. Preservation procedures are designed to stabilize existing conditions and prevent deterioration by controlling the environment, providing suitable housing and storage, and monitoring use and handling. Restoration involves actions to stabilize and return a deteriorated or damaged artifact as nearly as possible to its original condition.

In the context of administering photographic collections, the first two elements—examination and preservation—are pertinent. It is mandatory that archivists and curators be able to identify at least the most common types of photographic processes in order to devise appropriate storage systems and use policies. Certain categories of photographic materials are known to be inherently unstable because of their chemical composition, and some photographs have very specific storage requirements. Following examination and identification, appropriate preservation steps may be taken to enhance the useful life of photographic materials. Archivists must be able to recognize unstable or sensitive photographs in order to create the correct storage environment, initiate necessary copying procedures, or limit handling and use.

Restoration of photographs is a complex field that requires specialized training and knowledge. There are a small number of practicing photographic conservators who are highly qualified to carry out treatments designed to stabilize and preserve photographic materials. Unfortunately, however, what is sometimes called ''restoration'' is oftentimes little more than copying, stain removal, and touch-up work, using techniques that are damaging or that may have unknown consequences. Also, unknowing practitioners may attempt to apply techniques gained from paper conservation directly to photographs without fully understanding the unpredictable ways in which photosensitive emulsions can respond to treatments.

Archival institutions should focus their energies on examination and preservation and avoid restoration in most instances. In addition to the fact that there are very few qualified photographic conservators, most institutions face the problem of large masses of photographic materials requiring identification and storage. In such situations, especially where resources are limited, it is best to focus energy toward the preservation of the entire collection, rather than toward the expensive individual treatment of a few

images. Some situations, however, require that technically demanding or sophisticated work be carried out on historically or artifactually valuable materials. It is the responsibility of the archivist to recognize these instances and to make sure that the work is set aside until it can be referred to a qualified conservator (see page 128). Within archival contexts, the approach to conservation properly falls within the area of preventive maintenance. Restoration should be left to fully-trained and qualified photographic conservators.

Record keeping is an important part of any preservation program. As will be discussed later in this chapter, preservation concerns should be integrated with standard archival procedures, and important information on technical processes and condition should be recorded during accessioning and arrangement and description activities. In addition, it is important to record any preservation actions or restoration treatments that are carried out on the photographic materials, such as copying unstable cellulose nitrate negatives, making prints from glass plate negatives, or removing photographs from destructive mounts and mat boards. Such record keeping ensures that all pertinent data regarding the photographs and their provenance, condition, and manner of treatment and handling is permanently available in collection files for future reference. Records should be maintained at the collection level unless individual items have high intrinsic value. When undertaking copy work, it is important to record information regarding the type of film used and attendant processing, as well as to note who carried out the work. Information on supplies and suppliers also should be documented. For example, when undertaking a project to replace original enclosures with conservation-quality envelopes or sleeves, information regarding the materials used, including technical specifications, manufacturer, and supplier, should be recorded. If problems ever arise with the products, it is then easier to backtrack to locate the source of the difficulty. Systematic records also should be kept on environmental conditions within the repository. Temperature and relative humidity should be monitored daily, and prevailing conditions should be recorded; data also should be compiled regarding light sources and air quality. Record keeping is an important tool in the preservation of photographic collections; the process should not be considered burdensome, but, rather, should be accepted as integral to ongoing archival and administrative tasks. Forms described throughout this chapter can expedite the gathering of information.

Material Nature of the Photographic Record

Photographs are complex chemical and physical structures. Historically, a great many substances and materials have been used to create photographic images. If any one of the component parts or elements suffers damage or alteration, this could lead to the eventual loss of the image.

Figure 5–1. This print has suffered much damage over the years. It is bent, dirty, and a portion of the image is missing on the right side. Both the base and the emulsion are cracked and broken in a number of places, due to previous rolling and improper storage and handling. The photograph contains much useful information, and should be copied and retired to flat, supported storage with future handling severely limited. *Courtesy of Special Collections, University of Illinois at Chicago.*

A photograph may be defined very simply as having a base or support upon which an emulsion or image-bearing layer is coated. Subbing and adhesive layers adhere the emulsion to the base (see figure 2-4). As photography has evolved, different materials have been used in varying combinations to compose the layers of a photograph. For example, the photographic emulsion in most common use today consists of a suspension of light-sensitive silver salts, known as silver halides, in gelatin. However, other image-forming substances have been used, such as platinum, pigments, and dyes; and carriers besides gelatin, such as collodion and albumen, have been used as well. A wide number of support materials have also been used, including metal, glass, paper, and plastic film, as well as less common materials, such as silk, leather, ceramics, and oilcloth.

With such a diversity of materials and substances, it is no wonder that photographs are subject to damage and deterioration. Metals can corrode or rust, glass can break, paper can tear, and film can shrink. Photographs are also subject to damage through careless handling or well-intentioned but hazardous remedies to such problems as dirt, tears, abrasion, fingerprints, stains, and flaking emulsions.

Chemical instability, either inherent or due to processing, is also a factor in the loss of some photographic materials (see figures 5-1 and 5-2).

The emulsion is the most critical layer in the photograph, for it is in the emulsion layer that the image is captured and held. The emulsion is also the most susceptible to damage or loss due to adverse environmental conditions, breakage or degradation of the support, or mishandling or abuse. Perhaps the most important thing to remember about photographs is that they often consist of several dissimilar materials, each of which will react somewhat differently—and perhaps in opposition to one another—in response to changes in the environmental conditions. This can result in stress and dimensional instability, and perhaps in the loss of the image. Further, each structural element in a photograph is susceptible to different kinds of chemical or physical damage; the whole artifact is thus very dependent upon the structural integrity of its parts. Archivists and curators must be able to respond to the preservation needs of the entire assemblage in order to assure the preservation of the image.

Two primary archival concerns are the preservation of original photographs as well as the information they contain. Also important, however, is preservation of mounts, cases, albums, and similar artifacts that help to identify and define the photographic record. When devising preservation systems, the archivist must consider the image, structural materials, and artifacts that are integral to a complete understanding of the history of photography.

Causes of Deterioration

A number of factors affect the preservation of photographic materials. Environmental conditions are among the most important and include temperature, relative humidity, light, airborne pollution, and biological agents.

Temperature and relative humidity are interdependent. At high temperatures the air will contain considerable moisture; sudden cooling will precipitate this moisture, causing damage. Temperatures above 75°F and a relative humidity above 60% will accelerate harmful chemical reactions. These moisture and temperature levels also will promote softening of gelatin emulsions, causing them to stick to other surfaces, and will encourage mold growth. Since many chemical reactions are dependent on both temperature and water, the deteriorative effect of residual processing chemicals are dramatically increased under conditions of high temperature and relative humidity. Under conditions of very low (below 15%) or fluctuating humidity, emulsion layers may crack or peel and become embrittled. Frequent fluctuations in temperature and relative humidity are most damaging, as emulsion and base materials expand and contract at different rates in response to changes in the environmental conditions. Such fluctuations result in instability and separation of the emulsion and base layers.

Atmospheric pollutants, including acidic fumes, hydrogen sulfide, ammonia, oxides of nitrogen, ozone, peroxides, and sulfur dioxide, affect the stability and permanence

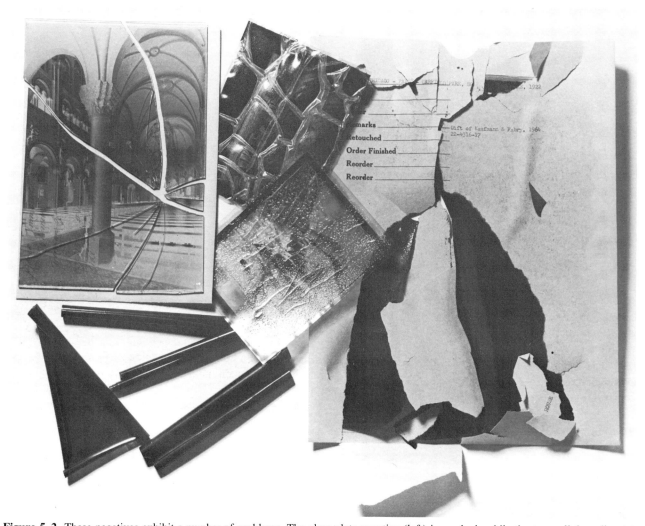

Figure 5–2. These negatives exhibit a number of problems. The glass plate negative (left) is cracked, while the two cellulose diacetate negatives (center) exhibit buckling emulsions due to the shrinking of the film bases. The very thin cellulose nitrate negatives (lower left) are tightly rolled, while the decomposition gases being emitted as the cellolose nitrate negative (right) deteriorates are causing the paper sleeve to break and fracture. *Photograph courtesy of the Chicago Historical Society.*

of photographic materials. Such contaminants are especially prevalent in industrial areas or regions with high concentrations of automobile exhaust, and, unfortunately, are becoming broadly diffused throughout the world. They initiate deteriorative chemical reactions that can stain and degrade the base materials and accelerate fading, staining, or loss of the image. Ozone, a by-product of combustion that initiates oxidation-reduction reactions, is also emitted by electrostatic filtering systems and some photocopy machines, and is thus created internally within some archives and libraries. Paint fumes, another source of oxidizing contaminants, are also damaging, as are the gases that are emitted as cellulose nitrate-base film decomposes. Photographs also must be protected from solid particles, such as gritty dirt and dust, which can abrade image layers, hold moisture, and deposit acidic compounds.

Exposure to visible light is potentially damaging to photographic materials, but visible light in the violet-blue-green area (400–500 nanometers) and ultraviolet radiation at the short end of the light spectrum (300–400 nanometers) are most active and thus most damaging (see figure 5-3). Ul-

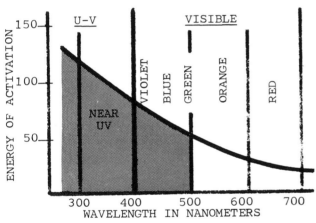

Figure 5–3. Short-wave radiation (300–500 nanometers) is most damaging. *Chart drawn by Edward R. Gilbert.*

traviolet radiation is most prevalent in unfiltered sunlight and fluorescent light. Light does not affect the metallic silver image if the photograph has been properly fixed, but light does speed up the detrimental effects of oxidation and other deteriorative chemical reactions, especially to paper or film bases. Light also causes fading, which is especially damaging to color prints and other light-sensitive images. Damage caused by light is cumulative; it depends upon intensity and length of exposure. Further, harmful chemical reactions that are initiated during exposure to light will continue even after photographs have been placed in dark storage.

Biological agents that are attracted to photographic materials include mold, fungi, insects, rodents, and similar pests. Under warm, humid environmental conditions (usually temperature above 75°F and relative humidity above

60%), mold spores in the air will begin to grow on surfaces that provide nutrients. Paper and gelatin emulsions serve as ideal hosts, with the result that images can be obliterated or lost. Temperature and relative humidity threshold limits for mold activity vary with the type of mold and depending on whether or not the material has been infested before; pockets of stagnant air also encourage mold growth. Insects (including silverfish, cockroaches, and beetles) and rodents (such as mice, rats, and squirrels) also are attracted to gelatin emulsions and paper, using both as a nutrient; many rodents also like to use shredded paper as a nesting material. Damage caused by such pests is irreversible, and their droppings are corrosive and leave permanent stains.

Another major cause of deterioration of photographs is the presence of residual processing chemicals (sulfur-containing substances used for fixing—sodium thiosulfate or ammonium thiosulfate—and silver compounds formed as a result of the fixing reaction). These chemical compounds react with the silver in the emulsion to form silver sulfide, which turns the image a brownish-yellow. Yellowish stains on prints or negatives are usually caused by the decomposition of residual silver compounds, which also form silver sulfide. The deteriorative effects of residual processing chemicals are intensified by high temperature and relative humidity.

Contact with harmful materials and fumes also hastens the deterioration of photographs. Historical mounting and storage materials will generally be unstable. Many new materials—from enclosures to adhesives and mounting or backing boards—even though they may be designed and advertised as appropriate for photographic materials, can be very damaging as well because they are chemically unstable and/or have mechanical properties that may prove damaging over time. For example, many commercially available paper folders, sleeves, and envelopes are acidic because they contain groundwood and alum-rosin sizing. Plastic materials may be directly contaminating or have harmful coatings or plasticizers that emit decomposition by-products that accelerate the aging of photographic materials. Adhesives are often acidic and eventually leave permanent stains. Fumes from cleaning supplies, solvents, and paint may contain ammonia, peroxide, or other oxidizing agents.

Disasters, whether of natural origin or caused by human or mechanical error, can result in tremendous loss and damage if precautions are not taken and salvage techniques are not considered beforehand. Disasters often involve fire—which could be catastrophic with such highly flammable materials as nitrate negatives—as well as water, which can be extremely damaging to emulsions (especially collodion, see page 129), hand-colored prints, and photographic artifacts such as cases, mounts, or albums.

Abuse and mismanagement caused by carelessness or neglect by well-intentioned but uninformed archivists and curators poses additional threats to photographic materials. Improper storage and handling, destructive exhibition techniques, mending tears with pressure-sensitive tape, writing on the backs of prints with felt-tip or ballpoint pens, and similar activities may all be considered mismanagement. A broader example of mismanagement is the institution that does not have intellectual control over its photographic holdings, thus subjecting photographs to unnecessary handling and browsing that should be alleviated by the use of guides and finding aids. The failure to implement programs for preservation, security, and disaster preparedness is an equally threatening example of mismanagement that endangers entire photographic collections.

Preservation Actions

Environmental Controls

It is recommended that photographic materials be stored and used at a temperature of 68°F ± 2°F with a constant relative humidity of 35–40%. These are compromise figures, based on the fact that repositories are likely to have a diverse group of photographic processes represented in their holdings, each of which—under optimum conditions—would be maintained within slightly different ranges. The suggested fluctuation of ± 2 degrees is intentionally narrow as an aid in more closely achieving building conditions within target goals. The figure ± 5 is often cited in the literature as an allowable fluctuation, but this actually allows a latitude of 10 degrees or percentage points, which is excessive for archival storage. At all times, the temperature should be kept below 70°F.

Ideally, conditions should be kept within these ranges, with a minimum of cycling, 24 hours a day, 365 days a year. Air conditioning systems must be kept operational after office hours and over weekends and holidays. Fluctuating temperature and relative humidity result in much structural damage to photographic materials as the various layers respond to changes in the environment. Major fluctuations, which occur when rapid cooling follows a shut-down that causes high temperatures, generally result in serious and irreparable damage. When compared to the possible loss of historical photographs due to an unstable environment, the shut-down of heating, cooling, and ventilating systems to save energy dollars is false economy.

Room-sized air conditioners, humidifiers, and dehumidifiers can be used within moderately sized storage areas when major installations are not feasible. Any form of air conditioning that can be maintained on a 24-hour basis is better than nothing, and many portable units are very efficient. If air conditioning is not feasible, photographic collections should be stored in a cool part of the repository.

Since the recommended relative humidity for photographs is somewhat lower than that advised for the storage of paper-based records, storage for photographic materials should be separate from other archival and manuscript material, if at all possible. Such conditions would generally be easiest to achieve and maintain within a vault or similar enclosed space. Given the difficulty most institutions have in maintaining any environmental controls, it may be too optimistic to suggest that separate environmentally correct storage areas be maintained for photographs and other archival materials. If such records must be stored together, a temperature of 68°F with a relative humidity of about 40% should be satisfactory. The primary goal is a stable temperature and relative humidity; this is even more important than maintaining conditions precisely within the recommended ranges.

Temperature and relative humidity should be monitored on a continuous basis to determine conditions and gather data in order to make necessary corrections. The most efficient means of monitoring is with a hygrothermograph (see figure 5-4), which plots an ongoing record of changes in the temperature and relative humidity on a graph. Conditions can thus be monitored whether or not staff are present to take readings. Depending on the size of the repository, one or more hygrothermographs may be necessary to monitor conditions in various rooms and storage areas. If a hygrothermograph cannot be acquired because of the expense, non-recording devices—a sling psychrometer or a thermometer and hygrometer—are available that can give very accurate readings.[1] The drawback with such non-recording devices is that readings can only be taken when staff are present, and thus data cannot be acquired when system shut-downs are most likely; they also require the manual compilation of a log or chart of prevailing conditions (see figure 5-5). Despite these drawbacks, such devices can be used very effectively to initiate a monitoring program. A sling psychrometer is required to calibrate recording devices such as the hygrothermograph.

Sources of ultraviolet and high-energy visible radiation must be controlled. Ultraviolet (UV) filtering sleeves may be placed over fluorescent tubes, or low-UV emission fluorescent tubes may be used. Ultraviolet filters are available in rigid sheet form (such as Plexiglas® UF3) as well as in thin sheets, which may be placed directly on windows. The filters effectively screen the UV and the violet-blue visible light without affecting the apparent color value of the lighting. Such filters also can be used in glass exhibit cases and as a glazing for framed items. It is recommended that UV filters be changed every seven to ten years; they will not retain indefinitely their ability to inhibit or absorb ultraviolet light. It is important to record both installation dates and the types of filters used. Incandescent lights emit negligible amounts of ultraviolet radiation and from this per-

---

[1]A large number of instruments are available for monitoring environmental conditions. Good hygrothermographs can be purchased in the $400–$600 range, while sling psychrometers are available for much less ($40–$100). Catalogs and price lists are available from suppliers (see Appendix C).

Figure 5–4. The hygrothermograph measures, and through a series of gears and linkages records, temperature and relative humidity on charts that incorporate a time scale. The standard recording period is weekly, although daily or monthly capabilities are also available. Note flat storage system for photographic materials. *Courtesy of the Chicago Historical Society.*

and exhibition areas. In some instances, when it is aesthetically acceptable architecturally, sunlight can be eliminated entirely by boarding up or blocking windows.

Air filtration will remove gaseous and particulate pollutants from the incoming air. Repositories should be outfitted with mechanical filters employing cellulose or fiberglass to remove particulate matter, as well as adsorption systems using charcoal to filter out gaseous contaminants. Charcoal and fiberglass filters can be easily retrofitted into existing air filtration systems. To be effective, filters must be monitored and changed on a regular basis. Electrostatic filtering systems should be avoided because they generate ozone. Ventilation is important to ensure that there are no pockets of stagnant air, which could encourage the growth of mold; shelving and cabinets should be positioned to avoid air pockets. Also, it should be determined whether a shared ventilation system is leaking such contaminants as sewer gas, ozone, or illuminating gas into the archives from other parts of the building.

Storage

Photographic collections should be stored in a cool, dry area within the repository, away from overhead steam or water pipes, washrooms, or other sources of water. The storage environment should be secure, with access allowed only by specifically designated staff. Distribution of keys and vault combinations should be limited and monitored.

Storage furniture should be constructed of noncombustible and noncorrosive materials, such as anodized aluminum, stainless steel, or steel with a baked-on enamel finish. Surfaces should be smooth, nonabrasive, and durable. Cabinets or drawers should have no mechanical features, such as spring clamps, that could damage or place undue pressure on their contents. Wooden shelves, cabinets, or drawers should be avoided because of the presence of lignin (naturally occurring organic acid), peroxide, and formic acid, which can leach out and initiate deteriorative chemical reactions in photographic materials. If wood must be used, it should at least be sealed with several coats of polyurethane varnish. Before sealing the wood, photographs should be removed from the area, and the freshly sealed surface should be allowed to air for several weeks before the material is refiled. Wooden boxes and filing cabinets are especially dangerous because the interiors of such containers are often raw wood; when closed, the decomposition byproducts are concentrated within the enclosed space, rather than dispersed in the surrounding air. Photographs should never be stored in such environments.

Optimally, all photographs—paper prints, glass and film negatives, etc.—should be stored within individual paper or plastic enclosures. Envelopes and sleeves made of paper should have a high alpha-cellulose content and should contain no lignin, groundwood, or alum-rosin sizing. The pH should be neutral (about 7.0), and the paper should not have

spective are the preferable light source in archival storage areas, although incandescent lights also can raise heat levels. Many institutions have installed fluorescent lights as a means of conserving energy and money, but from a preservation point of view, careful consideration should be given to the possibility of retrofitting incandescent lights. Savings could be effected over time just by eliminating the necessity of purchasing filters or special fluorescent tubes. Many institutions are illuminated to the .point of excess; when possible, ranges of lights should be shut off or reduced when they are not in use, and timed shut-off switches should be considered as well. Lights in stack or storage areas should be on only when there is need to have access to material. A further inexpensive means of controlling light is to close window curtains and shades in storage, processing, reading,

TEMPERATURE/RELATIVE HUMIDITY LOG

Date	Day	Time	Temp.	RH	Location	Remarks	Staff
	Monday						
	Tuesday						
	Wednesday						
	Thursday						
	Friday						
	Saturday						
	Sunday						

Average conditions for week:

Measuring devices used:

Figure 5–5. A manual record of temperature and relative humidity must be compiled if non-recording instruments are used to monitor the environment.

an alkaline reserve.[2] Plastic enclosures should be constructed of an inert plastic, such as polyester,[3] polyethylene, polypropylene, or cellulose triacetate, which contains no surface coatings or UV absorbers or inhibitors. Paper enclosures are opaque and require either opening flaps or sliding the photograph out in order to view the image, whereas plastic enclosures are transparent and allow immediate visual access to the image. When deciding which type of enclosure to use, a number of factors must be considered, including institutional resources, access needs, and storage requirements of specific photographic processes.

If paper enclosures are to be used, a four-flap design (see figure 5-6) is recommended, as no adhesives are employed in its construction and photographs can be accessed with no danger of abrasion.[4] Such storage enclosures may not be feasible for large collections, given problems of added bulk and weight. At a minimum, however, photographs with flaking or chipping emulsions or cracked cardboard mounts should be placed in flapped enclosures to allow safe, non-damaging access. With traditional paper envelopes, not only is there considerable danger of abrading the emulsion as the photograph is slipped in and out of the enclosure, but the adhesives used to construct the envelope can be damaging to photographs, sometimes leaving permanent stains. If paper envelopes are used, they should have a side rather than a center seam, and photographs should be inserted with the emulsion side away from the seam.

A number of factors also should be considered when selecting plastic enclosures. First is the possibility of the build-up of static electricity with some plastics (notably polyethylene and polyester): the static electricity attracts dirt and dust that can abrade the surfaces of images. Also, under conditions of high humidity, the image may ferrotype

[2]A number of conservators are questioning the advisability of storing photographs in an alkaline environment (i.e., in paper enclosures having a pH in the decidedly alkaline range, 8.5–10.2). For example, recent research indicates that storing albumen prints in alkaline enclosures accelerates the yellowing of these photographs. Neutral pH paper or inert plastic enclosures are thus recommended for albumen prints, and this recommendation is being extended to other photographic materials. See James M. Reilly, "Albumen Prints: A Summary of New Research about their Preservation," *Picturescope* 30 (Spring 1982): 36; and Klaus B. Hendriks, *The Preservation and Restoration of Photographic Materials in Archives and Libraries: A RAMP Study with Guidelines* (Paris: UNESCO, 1984), 85–86. It is not proposed that archivists immediately resleeve photographs currently stored in alkaline paper, but when purchasing new supplies neutral pH enclosures should be acquired.

[3]Polyester is available under the following trade names: Mylar® (Dupont), Scotchpar® (3M), and Melinex® (I.C.I. America, Inc.). For information on grades of polyester suitable for conservation purposes, see *Polyester Film Encapsulation* (Washington, D.C.: Library of Congress, 1980), 21–23.

[4]A number of suppliers offer such enclosures (see Appendix C). Also see Hilda Bohem, "A Seam-Free Envelope for Archival Storage and Photographic Negatives," *American Archivist* (July 1975): 403–405.

Figure 5–6. Paper enclosures designed with three or four flaps are recommended, especially for fragile photographs or those that have great value. *Drawing by Pamela Spitzmueller.*

from the smooth plastic surface of the enclosure, leaving shiny areas on the emulsion. Thus, when considering plastic enclosures, the environmental conditions within the repository should be evaluated; if the humidity reaches high levels on occasion or if there is a great deal of airborne dirt and particulate matter, paper enclosures may be a better choice. Plastic enclosures should not be used for photographs that have flaking or lifting emulsions because the static electricity will exacerbate the problem, possibly resulting in greater loss of the image. Further, some plastic sleeves have one surface that is slightly matted or roughed-up to avoid ferrotyping. Although the likelihood of damage may be minimal, matte surfaces are too abrasive for safe contact with photographic emulsions. If such enclosures are already in use, it is a simple matter to insert the photographs with the emulsion side away from the matte surface.

A number of storage materials should be expressly avoided because they are known to damage photographic materials. Kraft paper and manila envelopes and folders are acidic and become brittle and weak; they are not capable of providing long-term protection to photographic materials. Glassine envelopes are generally quite acidic, and are also hygroscopic; thus, under humid conditions they attract moisture and can stick to emulsion surfaces. For this reason, even neutral pH glassine is not recommended. Polyvinylchloride enclosures emit plasticizer and decomposition by-products that are very damaging to photographs; they should not be used. Rubber bands (which contain sulfur) and pressure-sensitive tapes should be banned as well.

When acquiring supplies for the long-term storage of photographic materials, it is important to purchase storage enclosures directly from reputable archival and conservation suppliers (see Appendix C). Unknown products should be avoided, and manufacturers' claims should be disregarded unless there is independent evidence to verify such claims. Local photographic supply stores should not be relied upon as an outlet for storage materials; most often sales people will not know product lines well enough to provide generic names or precise product specifications. Also, advertising literature and packaging can be misleading and incomplete. When purchasing paper supplies, it is possible to undertake simple and fairly accurate in-house testing to determine pH level and the presence of alum and groundwood.[5] Questions that arise regarding plastic materials, however, are not so easily answered. Inquiries, along with samples, may be sent to the supplier and manufacturer, and the product data sheet can also be requested. When in doubt, a product should not be used with valuable photographic records until all questions regarding its safety and stability can be resolved; new products should be used very cautiously.

Once placed in individual enclosures, paper prints and film negatives may be placed within stable file folders and document cases that contain no lignin, alum-rosin sizing, or groundwood. It is acceptable for paper and board stock used for such secondary storage materials to have an alkaline reserve. Flat storage in document cases or clamshell boxes is recommended, especially for fragile images and those that are affixed to brittle mounts (see figure 5-4). Upright storage in boxes (with photographs filed standing on edge, perpendicular to the shelves) is satisfactory for photographs that are intact and in good condition. Boxes should be neither overfilled nor underfilled; the former condition will result in damage as photographs are forced in and out of tight boxes. Conversely, boxes that are not completely filled will encourage slumping and the natural tendency of photographs to curl. If photographs are to be stored in filing cabinets, hanging or suspended filing systems should be employed to avoid damage that would be caused by folders (and thus the enclosed prints and negatives) slumping, moving about, and sliding under one another. Folders that can be scored to accommodate varying thicknesses of material should be used, rather than single-fold file folders.

No single storage system is ideal for all materials, and individual decisions must be made based upon the format, condition, and value of the photographs. As indicated above, optimum practice prescribes a separate storage enclosure for every photograph. This may not be feasible for every collection and compromises may be necessary. The establishment of priorities will help to govern the application of necessary departure from ideal practice. For example, if

[5]Mary Lynn Ritzenthaler, *Archives & Manuscripts: Conservation* (Chicago: Society of American Archivists, 1983), 99–100.

not every photograph can be placed in its own enclosure, attempts should be made to at least enclose original prints of high value and those that are in fragile condition. Of equal importance are negatives, both originals and copies, which must be protected from handling and contact with harmful materials. On an interim basis, it may be necessary to store less valuable prints together within a folder, sleeve, or portfolio; indeed, many repositories handle all of their photographs in this manner. If such practice is required because of limited staff or financial resources, it should be realized that it is not optimum practice, and priorities should be established for the ultimate transfer of the images to a more satisfactory storage system. As an interim step, interleaving sheets of neutral pH paper or polyester could be employed to separate items within a single enclosure.

Decisions regarding flat or upright storage also must be made with the understanding that either method poses potential problems. In flat storage, the pressure on items at the bottom of even a small stack of photographs in a document case could damage mounted prints that have a slight curvature, or could exacerbate the possibility of ferrotyping of images within plastic sleeves. On the other hand, with upright storage the weight of the photographs must be borne by a single edge, which is sometimes weak and fragile. In every instance, sound decisions must be based upon knowledge of the physical needs and condition of the material, and necessary compromises should be balanced by appropriate use and handling procedures that will minimize threats to the photographs.

Related to these concerns are issues pertaining to the storage of photographic materials of various formats and composition. For example, a single collection might contain a number of photographs that have precise and very different storage requirements. From a preservation point of view, it is necessary to separate such items and to rely upon intellectual controls (i.e., finding aids and location indexes) to unite materials as necessary. Cellulose nitrate negatives provide perhaps the most compelling example of the need to provide separate storage for various materials. Other examples relate to physical format. Cased photographs are often in fragile condition; for this reason alone, safe separate storage is desirable. Beyond this, however, is the fact that cased photographs stored in a file with paper prints would cause distortion and buckling in the latter. Ideally, small format paper prints, cased images, negatives, and oversized photographs all should be given separate secure storage (see figure 5-7). Recommendations for specific processes and formats appear in the following section.

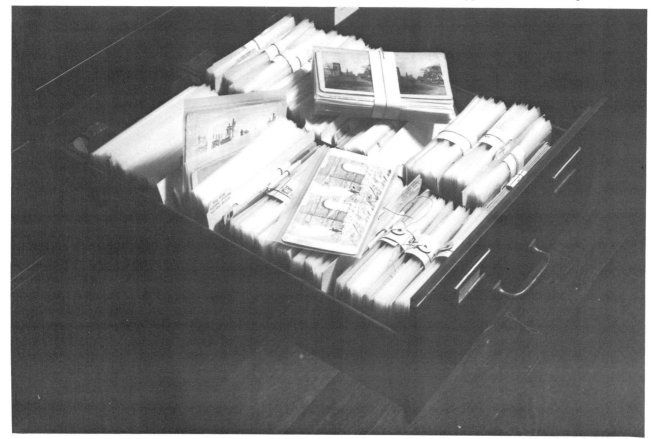

Figure 5–7. This photograph illustrates storage by single format in steel cabinets with a baked-on enamel finish. These stereograph cards are individually sleeved in polyester enclosures; subject groupings are held together by microfilm ties. *Courtesy of the Chicago Historical Society.*

Storage Requirements of Specific Formats and Processes

Cased Photographs

Daguerreotypes, ambrotypes, and—very often—tintypes are found in decorative cases constructed of wood, leather, plastic, or papier-maché (see figure 2-8). These cases not only protect the images from air, dirt, handling, and abrasion, but also were intended as beautiful and decorative presentation pieces. The cases and the historical images they contain have artifactual and monetary value and are avidly sought by collectors; archivists must devise security and preservation measures to protect both.

Many cases are quite fragile; hinges are often broken and exterior surfaces and corners are often scratched and abraded. Unqualified personnel should not attempt to repair or restore damaged cases. Cases usually contain one image, although there are examples of double mounts. The left side of the interior of the case is usually lined with a soft fabric such as velvet or silk. The photographic plate is protected by the following sequence: mat, cover glass, and preserver frame (see figure 2-7). The plate, mat, and glass are held together with binding tape within the preserver, and the whole assembly is placed in the case. On occasion it is necessary to remove a daguerreotype or other photographic plate from its case, such as when the cover glass is missing or broken. From an archival perspective, removal for the purpose of examination may be desirable, as identifying information may be recorded behind the plate. In rare instances a second image will be found within the case, generally floating loosely behind the matted plate. Removing a photographic plate from its case is often the only way to positively identify the photographic process (i.e., whether it is an ambrotype or a tintype—daguerreotypes are distinctly recognizable). It should be realized, however, that there is a great difference between slipping a unit out of its case and leaving it intact, and the further separation of the matted unit into its component parts. Simple removal of the plate from the case with no further disassembly should suffice for purposes of identification, and does not affect the integrity of the unit.

The problems posed by cased photographs exemplify the range of issues and considerations that must be addressed in the context of preservation. Artifactual value and preservation needs must both be evaluated before undertaking any alteration of the original mount and case. In dealing with such images, as in all conservation treatment, it is important to document all actions and findings as a permanent record. All pertinent data should be recorded at the time of initial examination to reduce the need for future handling or dismantling. An examination sheet may be devised expressly for cased photographs (see figure 5-8).

CASED PHOTOGRAPH DOCUMENTATION FORM

Collection: Location:

Accession Number:

Subject: Photographer:

Photographic Process:

Condition:

Assembly (description, condition, physical evidence):

    Case
    Preserver frame
    Cover glass
    Mat
    Binding tape

Markings/notations:

Observations:

Preservation actions:

    carried out:

Recommendations (handling, storage, exhibition):

Examined by_____   Date_____

Figure 5–8. Sample examination and documentation record for cased photographs.

Figure 5–9. A clean, flat work surface is required when removing a photograph from its case; and the hinged cover of the case must be supported to avoid damaging it. If the cover glass is broken or cracked, work must proceed very cautiously to avoid having the glass shift and thus possibly damaging the emulsion surface. *Drawing by Pamela Spitzmueller.*

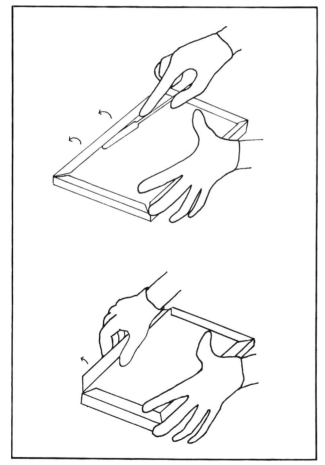

Figure 5–10. Usually, the preserver frame can be gently lifted with the fingers, but on occasion it will be necessary to carefully lift the metal by inserting a microspatula between the frame and the back of the photographic plate. *Drawing by Pamela Spitzmueller.*

A photographic plate may be removed from its case by gently slipping the rounded end of a microspatula between the long side of the case and the metal preserver frame (see figure 5-9). If too much pressure is applied, the wall of the case could collapse or the matted unit could be damaged. Once one side of the matted photographic plate is slightly raised, it may be lifted out of the case and placed on a clean flat surface. Thin, white cotton gloves should be worn during this procedure. If it is necessary to disassemble the unit (generally this should be done only if the cover glass is missing, cracked, or broken), the metal frame must be removed by gently lifting the lips that extend around to the back of the unit (see figure 5-10). Because the preserver frame is made of a soft thin metal, it can withstand a very limited number of openings and closings.

Before further disassembly, the matted unit should be carefully examined. In many instances, elements of the frame assembly as well as cases have been interchanged, either by the original owner or by a dealer who wished to create a saleable unit by combining an appealing image with an attractive case. Since the cases and the elements of the frame assembly evolved in identifiable ways that can be dated, such tampering can alter their usefulness in accurately dating and identifying the encased photograph. Thus, if the binding tape is intact and appears to be original, this is evidence to support the assumption that the image is in its original frame assembly. Out-of-sequence assembly of the framed unit indicates previous disassembly. Original binding tape generally should not be removed (see p. 106 for specific recommendations regarding daguerreotypes). If it is not intact, however, the tape will not fulfill its function of keeping air from reaching the plate and should be replaced even if it is original. Filmoplast® tape can be used to replace the binding tape, as illustrated in figure 5-11.[6] Careful documentation of such actions ensures that the evidence offered by the original binding tape and assembly sequence is not lost for future archivists or scholars.

If the cover glass is broken or missing, it can be replaced with modern window glass of similar thickness. Dirty glass can be cleaned with mild soap and water and thoroughly rinsed and dried. Such cleaning can radically improve the appearance of the image. Cleaning solutions containing ammonium hydroxide should not be used to clean cover glass. No attempt should be made to clean the surfaces of daguerreotypes, ambrotypes, or tintypes because emulsion surfaces are very delicate and susceptible to mechanical abrasion as well as disfiguring fingerprints.

Cases in poor condition should be wrapped individually and stored flat in a single layer in a shallow drawer or flat

---

[6]Filmoplast® pressure-sensitive tapes are available in various weights; the adhesive is in the neutral pH range and is carried either by thin transparent paper or flexible white cloth. Available from archival suppliers (see Appendix C).

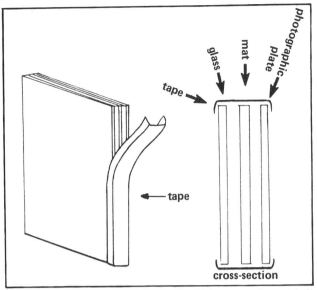

Figure 5–11. The Filmoplast® tape should be wrapped around all four sides, thereby holding the glass, the mat, and the photographic plate together as a unit. The tape does not come into contact with the emulsion. *Drawing by Pamela Spitzmueller.*

document case. Neutral pH tissue paper may be used to wrap the cases, which may then be placed in small envelopes or boxes. Microfilm boxes are useful for separating cased photographs when several are stored in a single container. A 35-mm photograph of the cased image can be affixed to the outside of the envelope or box containing the case to reduce unnecessary handling (see figure 5-12).

Loose daguerreotypes and ambrotypes that have been separated from their cases must be protected. A narrow mat ·should be constructed of four-ply neutral pH museum board to protect the emulsion from the cover glass, and the whole unit (cover glass, mat, and plate) should then be supported by a piece of four-ply museum board cut to the same size as the photographic plate. The side edges should be sealed with Filmoplast® tape (see figure 5-13).

The above procedures should not be undertaken casually. They require experience, care, and manual dexterity. All work on historically significant photographs or those having high artifactual value should be referred to a qualified conservator.

Figure 5–12. Storage for cased photographs separate from other formats provides the greatest protection for all materials. Early methods of marking cases with white ink and paper labels may be seen. Plans call for individual packaging to avoid abrasion and to provide increased physical protection for each cased photograph. *Courtesy of the Chicago Historical Society.*

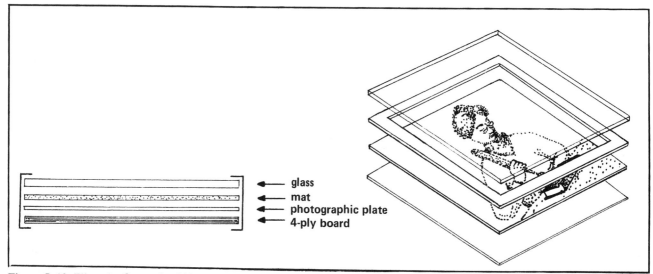

glass
mat
photographic plate
4-ply board

Figure 5–13. Filmoplast® tape should be wrapped around the four edges to keep the unit intact. The neutral pH museum board provides an extra measure of support, and the extra thickness it adds to the unit poses no problem as the plate will not be placed in a case. *Drawing by Pamela Spitzmueller.*

Daguerreotypes

Surfaces of daguerreotypes are extremely fragile and never should be touched; the image can be removed or permanently damaged with the touch of a finger, cloth, or brush. Air sprays are also a problem as the dirt and dust particles may leave a track as they are blown across the surface of the image. Recent research by Susan Barger indicates that the nineteenth-century cover glass used as glazing for daguerreotypes is inherently unstable. Glass decomposition products fall on the surface of the daguerreotype and initiate corrosion; also, air and water vapor that enter the daguerreotype unit combine with alkalies present in the glass and become oxidative and caustic. Resulting damage to the plate cannot be reversed, and washing and reusing the original glass cover will not solve the problem. Barger recommends replacing nineteenth-century cover glass with modern window glass. Filmoplast® tape can be used to reseal the unit.[7]

No preservation activities beyond replacing the cover glass or supporting loose plates as described in the previous section should be undertaken. No attempt should be made to clean daguerreotypes or remove tarnish. It was formerly recommended in the photographic conservation literature that daguerreotypes be cleaned with various solvents; most recently a thiourea phosphoric acid cleaning solution was in fairly common use. However, it has been determined that this method leaves permanent spots on the image, removes image silver, and thus should not be used. A technique known as sputter cleaning is now being studied and may have useful application in the future.[8]

Ambrotypes

Ambrotypes are collodion negatives on a glass support and are thus very fragile. An opaque black backing (fabric, paint, or lacquer) converts the image from a negative to a positive; if any of this backing is missing or not intact, the image will appear as a negative in those areas. This can be easily remedied by replacing the backing with a new piece of neutral pH black paper (see figure 5-14). This simple

Figure 5–14. A piece of neutral pH black paper slipped behind an ambrotype that exhibits chipping or flaking of its original black paint or lacquer will visually fill-in the missing areas, and make the image appear intact. *Drawing by Pamela Spitzmueller.*

---

[7]M. Susan Barger, "Devitrification of Cover Glasses: The Relation to the Corrosion of Daguerreotypes," reported in *American Institute for Conservation/Photographic Materials Group 1984 Louisville Abstracts*, 7–8.
[8]M. Susan Barger, S.V. Krishnaswamy, and R. Messier, "The Cleaning of Daguerreotypes: Comparison of Cleaning Methods," *Journal of the American Institute for Conservation* 22 (Fall 1982): 13–24.

Figure 5–15. These cabinet cards are individually sleeved in polyester. Storage of the same-sized photographs together ensures that they all will be given equal support. *Courtesy of the Chicago Historical Society.*

procedure can often radically improve the appearance of ambrotypes. Ambrotypes were assembled in many different ways (see page 36); sometimes the glass support was simply turned over and lacquer or paint was applied directly over the emulsion. Thus, care must be taken during handling to avoid scraping off original paint or lacquer, and possibly part of the emulsion as well. Repainting should be undertaken only by a conservator.

Tintypes

Tintypes were often placed in cases, but presentation in thin paper folders, cardboard mounts, or loose without any protective packaging was also common. All original mounts should be preserved. Today, tintypes are often found loose, and many are bent because of the malleability of the thin iron base. No attempt should be made to flatten bent tintypes, as this would likely cause the emulsion to lift and crack. Loose tintypes may be lightly positioned between two pieces of neutral pH museum board and placed in an envelope. If extra support is not required, tintypes may be placed singly in neutral pH paper or inert plastic enclosures. No pressure should be exerted on them. Also, despite earlier prescriptions in the photographic literature, tintypes should not be washed. Water can cause rusting in any exposed areas of the iron base, and also can cause emulsions

to lift away. Tintypes can be gently dusted with a soft brush or air bulb if the emulsion is intact.

Paper Prints

Mounted and unmounted paper prints—salt, albumen, collodion, and gelatin—that meet the size requirement may be stored in individual paper or plastic enclosures and then filed in letter- or legal-sized folders and placed in document cases or filing cabinets (see figure 5-15). Enclosures should be slightly larger than the photographs, should exert no pressure on them during insertion or storage, and should not distort their shape. Enclosures are available in a wide range of standard sizes and formats, or they may be fabricated in-house or custom ordered. Prints with flaking or chipping emulsions should not be stored in plastic enclosures because of the static charge. Extra support may be required for unmounted prints on very thin paper or prints mounted on brittle boards that are breaking and chipping away to the point that the image is endangered (see figure 5-16). Such support may be provided by cutting pieces of neutral pH museum board slightly larger than the print or mount (two-ply is satisfactory for unmounted prints, four-ply should be used for mounted photographs), to serve as a support for fragile images. Adhesives neither should be used nor are required, as the enclosure will keep the prints and supports together (see figure 5-17).

Figure 5–16. The brittle mount is chipping away to the degree that the print is no longer adequately supported; there is already some loss of image in the lower left corner. This photograph is a likely candidate for perservation copying, after which it should be supported by a piece of neutral pH museum board and stored flat. *Courtesy of Special Collections, University of Illinois at Chicago.*

Figure 5–17. Neutral pH museum board will provide necessary support for fragile unmounted prints as well as those with brittle mounts. *Drawing by Pamela Spitzmueller.*

Many mounted prints have acquired a definite bow or curvature, and any attempt to flatten them could result in the cracking of both the emulsion and the mount. Flat storage that will exert no pressure must be devised for such materials. Some card stereographs were fabricated with an intentional slight curvature, and this shape, too, must be respected. No attempt should be made to remove a print from its mount, even if the mount is acidic and brittle. Such a task not only requires exacting skill if the image is not to be threatened, but also raises questions about the historical integrity and artifactual value of the object. Such questions are not easily answered, but it is certain that removing prints from original mounts should not be approached casually. In many instances, mounts known to be of poor quality are intact and seemingly have not adversely affected the condition of the image. When there is no discernible damage and the artifact has survived decades or even a century, there seems to be no good reason to tamper with the mount, especially in archival repositories that house hundreds or thousands of such artifacts. However, if the mount is brittle, it is not possible to know exactly how much more handling it can withstand before both the photograph and the mount break. To prevent such damage, a piece of museum board may be placed within a plastic enclosure with the mounted print. This would provide rigid support and also would allow viewing without handling or removal of the photograph from its enclosure. If the mount is cracked and the emulsion is already damaged or clearly endangered, a copy print should be made and the original retired to safe storage after providing support by placing it between two pieces of museum board (see figure 5-18).

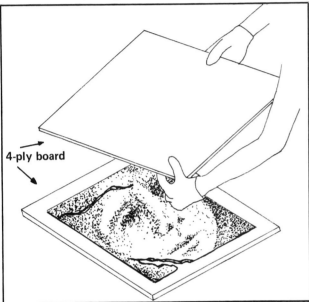

Figure 5–18. Such damaged photographs require flat storage in addition to the support provided by the neutral pH museum board. *Drawing by Pamela Spitzmueller.*

Salt Prints

The image in salt prints rests on or near the top layer of the paper, making the texture of the paper very obvious in the print. Salt prints are thus very vulnerable to surface abrasion, which could remove paper fibers and image areas simultaneously. For this reason, salt prints should not be surface cleaned, even with a soft brush. Because of their scarcity and value, salt prints require special handling and storage. They should be protected from light and maintained in a low-humidity environment. Salt prints require rigid support and adequate surface protection. They should be stored in four-flap enclosures that allow non-abrasive access, and interleaving sheets of polyester should be placed over the prints with museum board underneath to provide rigid support. Salt prints should be inspected on a regular basis and any observable signs of deterioration should be referred to a qualified conservator.

Albumen Prints

A characteristic of albumen prints are fissures or cupping in the albumen layer. These breaks in the emulsion layer are visible, often without magnification, especially in poorly preserved prints. In extreme cases, these fissures can result in loss of portions of the image and also can hasten the loss of physical strength in the print. Fluctuating temperature and relative humidity exacerbates this problem, as does any flexing of the prints during handling. Unmounted albumen prints have a tendency to curl tightly and also are very susceptible to tearing and creasing if they are not handled properly. Thus, all unmounted albumen prints as well as those exhibiting fissures (which may or may not be mounted) or those affixed to fragile mounts require rigid support; they should be placed in enclosures with a piece of neutral pH museum board. Enclosures should be constructed of an inert plastic or paper with a neutral pH. Surfaces of albumen prints may be gently dusted with a soft brush, although this step should be omitted if the emulsion exhibits fissuring or cupping.

Collodion Prints

Collodion prints require rigid support, which may be provided by paper or inert plastic enclosures and the use of museum board as necessary. Collodion prints are very susceptible to abrasion, and also are very sensitive to solvents, including water. The latter factor requires special consideration when developing disaster preparedness and recovery plans.

Gelatin Prints

The structural composition of gelatin prints has implications for their storage and handling. The several layers comprising gelatin prints are essentially a laminate structure; the layers expand and contract in response to fluctuations in the temperature and relative humidity, resulting in cockling and curling of the prints. Under hot, dry conditions, gelatin emulsions can become brittle, while the gelatin can become soft and stick to other surfaces under humid conditions. The laminate structure is also very susceptible to flexing and bending, which can result in cracks and breaks, and thus permanent damage, in the emulsion. Gelatin prints pose additional problems. During processing, hardening agents are generally added as a supercoat to protect the emulsion surface. These have not been studied thoroughly, but an excess of hardening agents seem to result in brittle emulsions, and too light an application appears to cause the gelatin to swell when moist and stick to nearby surfaces.[9] Gelatin prints require a controlled and very stable environment. Enclosures may be constructed either of neutral pH paper or inert plastic and should provide rigid, non-flexible support.

[9]Alice Swan, "Conservation of Photographic Print Collections," *Library Trends* 30 (Fall 1981): 267–96.

Resin-Coated Papers

Most contemporary gelatin prints—unless specified otherwise—are processed on resin-coated (RC) papers. These papers have been coated on both sides with polyethylene to limit absorption of processing chemicals and thereby speed up washing and drying times. They are thus a boon to the photographic processing industry. A number of problems have been observed with RC papers, however, including crazing of the emulsion surface. Since they have not been subjected to long-term evaluation and have undergone very little testing, RC papers are not considered acceptable as archival copies. Any prints being created to form part of the permanent archival collection should be processed on traditional fiber-based paper. (The term "fiber-based paper" is a technical misnomer since all paper is composed of fibers. However, it is the term used in the photographic trade to designate non-resin-coated papers.)

Oversized Prints

Oversized photographs should be stored flat in folders and filed in map cases. The number of prints placed in a folder should relate to the value and condition of the images and the weight of the paper supports plus any mount boards. Given the awkwardness of handling oversized photographs and their potential fragility, the maximum number should be approximately twelve, although one item per folder may be appropriate for very valuable photographs or those in very poor condition. Interleaving sheets of neutral pH paper or polyester should be layered between the photographs to protect the emulsion surfaces; thin museum board (two-ply) may also be used for interleaving if additional support is required. If map cases are unavailable, oversized photographs may be placed in large document cases and stored flat on industrial shelving units.

Extremely large photographs, such as some panorama landscapes or group portraits, may not fit in map cases or on industrial shelving. If such images are framed, the best solution may be to keep them in their frames, after first examining and disassembling the units and rematting the photographs to conservation standards. It also may be possible to devise flat storage by placing oversized prints between pieces of museum board that have been hinged together to the required dimensions. Carefully rolling oversized photographs may be the best storage solution for some very large unframed prints. Large-diameter neutral pH tubes (or cardboard tubes that have been wrapped with polyester) should be secured, as well as a supply of neutral pH tissue paper. The larger the diameter of the tubes, the better (within reason). Large-diameter tubes will allow the photographs to be rolled gently and loosely rather than in a small, tight roll. The tissue paper is used as an interleaving material, to protect the emulsion layer. Very carefully, the photograph (with its protective sheet of tissue paper) is rolled onto the *outside* of the tube, emulsion side in toward the center. Additional tissue paper should be added as required. After the photograph is completely rolled, the unit should be wrapped in a piece of neutral pH paper, which is lightly held in place with a piece of flat unbleached cotton or linen

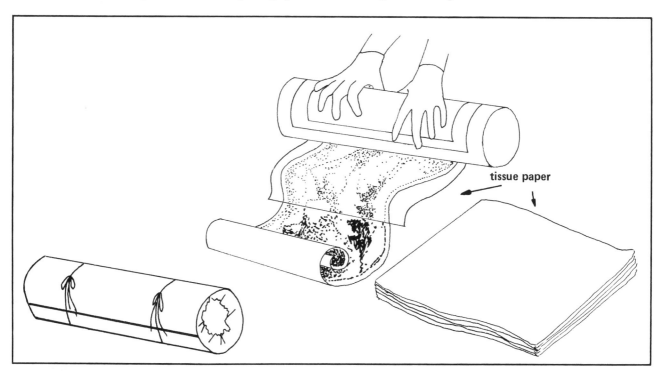

tissue paper

Figure 5–19. Prints with chipped or flaking emulsions should not be rolled, as the action of rolling and the curved storage position would exacerbate the problem. Flat storage must be devised for damaged photographs. *Drawing by Pamela Spitzmueller.*

tape used as a tie (see figure 5-19). Rolled photographs should be placed flat on shelves, not stood upright in bins. Photographs should never be rolled and placed *within* tubes; they will expand to fill the space and will suffer much damage in attempts to remove them. Maintenance of proper ranges of temperature and relative humidity will keep rolled photographs flexible enough that they may be unrolled and used without damage or the need for humidification. To reduce handling and enhance access, it is recommended that copy negatives and prints be made before rolling oversized photographs.

Framed Photographs

All framed photographs should be removed from their frames for the purpose of examination and, depending on their size, filed in individual enclosures as described above. It is safe to assume that most framing was not done to conservation standards, and it is important to remove acidic matting materials and inappropriate mounts, which will only accelerate the deterioration of the photographs. Information is often recorded on the backs of prints or mounts, which will help to identify or date the images, and this serves as further impetus to disassemble framed units. Accession records or work sheets should be used to record information regarding formats, disposition of frames, and any written notations found within the units. Depending on the significance of any written notations on dust covers or backing materials, it may be advisable to retain or photocopy them for collection files.

Photographs must be removed from their frames very carefully.[10] In most instances, the image and its frame do not have great intrinsic value as a unit. If framed items do have association value, however, or if the frame is integral to an accurate understanding of a photograph, it is necessary either to reassemble the unit to conservation standards (see figure 5-20) or to keep a cross-reference file so that the items may be reunited as necessary for exhibition or similar purposes. As noted above, it may be necessary to store some oversized photographs in their original frames once they have been examined and rematted as necessary.

Scrapbooks and Albums

Scrapbooks and albums can pose many preservation and handling problems, depending upon the quality of the mounting paper or board, type of mount and adhesive used, and overall condition or stability. It was formerly common practice to remove photographs from scrapbooks and albums; collectors and dealers often did this because they were concerned only with the images (and often their monetary value), not with their context. Curators and conservators often felt compelled to dismantle scrapbooks and albums over concern for physical and chemical stability of the photographs. In fact, a great number of photographs seem to survive quite well within scrapbooks and albums, despite surroundings that would appear to be very threatening.

Photographic albums and scrapbooks are now seen to possess greatest historical and artifactual value as whole

[10]Ritzenthaler, *Conservation*, 113–15.

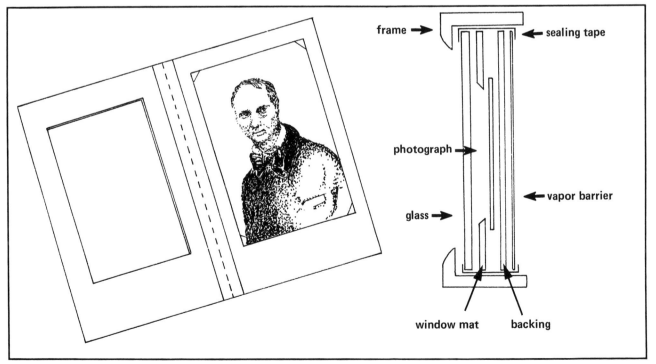

Figure 5–20. Proper framing requires non-adhesive mounting techniques and the use of neutral pH museum board and non-acidic backing materials. The window mat should protect the photograph from the cover glass, as shown in the cross-section of the frame assembly. *Drawing by Pamela Spitzmueller.*

objects; the photographs should be seen in the sequence and context that was imposed by the creator. While each album and scrapbook must be assessed individually on the basis of condition, value, and use, archivists and curators should make every attempt to maintain them as whole artifacts in their original form (see figure 5-21).

Albums that receive heavy use or that are in such poor condition that the photographs are endangered, should be reproduced photographically, and the copy should be used to protect the original from handling or damage. Scrapbooks and albums should not be photocopied; attempts to do so probably will damage the material because of the condition of the pages, the method of mounting or tipping in, and, oftentimes, size constraints. If physical condition demands the dismantling of a scrapbook, such work should be referred to a qualified conservator, given the diverse photographic processes and adhesives that are likely to be present in a single volume. Scrapbooks should be photographed before treatment is undertaken.

Scrapbooks and albums should be individually wrapped in alkaline paper or placed in document cases and stored flat on shelves. Volumes containing brittle pages that are breaking at the edges to the point that images are endan-

gered may benefit from the insertion of neutral pH paper or polyester as interleaving sheets (see figures 5-22 and 5-23). Such sheets will support and bear the weight of brittle pages as they are turned. Some binding structures, however, are so tight that they cannot accept the strain of added sheets; interleaving sheets should not be used if they will cause structural damage. The string or ribbon ties on some scrapbooks may be loosened to allow the insertion of interleaving sheets.

Glass Plate Negatives

Collodion and gelatin glass plate negatives are very susceptible to damage and breakage. Careful examination should precede removal of glass plates from original storage envelopes. Except in the most obvious cases of breakage, it is not always easy to determine the condition of the plates through opaque paper envelopes. It is not unusual for the emulsion to be lifting at the edges, or for the emulsion to be intact while the glass exhibits cracks. Careless removal of such plates would result in much damage. Rather than pulling the glass plates from their enclosures, it is best to cut or slit the paper away while the plates are resting on a flat work surface. The plate should be placed emulsion side down on the work table in its original envelope (it may be

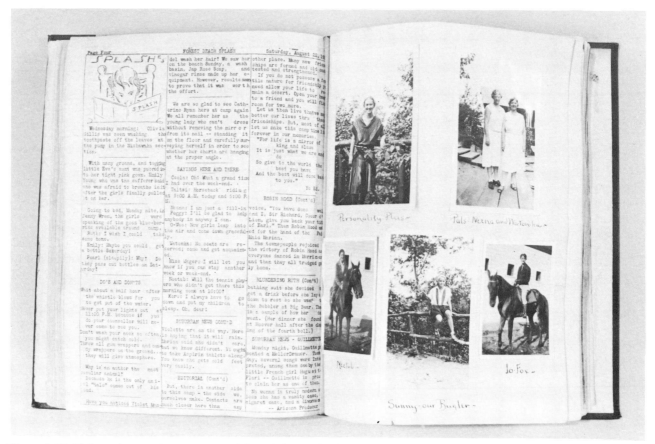

Figure 5–21. If these photographs were removed from their scrapbook mounts, their context and some information would be lost, not to mention the charm of their presentation. *Courtesy of Special Collections, University of Illinois at Chicago.*

Figure 5–22. After recording names and captions, removal of the photographs from this scrapbook may be the best preservation solution. The pages are so weak that even the use of interleaving sheets would provide minimal assistance in using the volume in a non-damaging fashion. Fortunately, the photographs can be easily and safely removed from the pages. However, rather than flexing the prints out of the photo corners, two corners along one side should be carefully lifted from the scrapbook page using a microspatula. The photograph then can be safely slipped out of the mount with no danger of cracking or breaking the emulsion. *Courtesy of Special Collections, University of Illinois at Chicago.*

necessary to slightly cut or tear the paper to determine which side of the plate carries the emulsion). A microspatula or a scalpel may then be used to slit open two sides of the envelope, thus allowing it to be lifted to expose the plate. As the emulsion is face down on the table, it is not endangered should the microspatula or blade slip. A supply of appropriately-sized pieces of glass or museum board should be available to aid in lifting and supporting damaged negatives. Gloves should be worn when undertaking these procedures.

Plates that are cracked or broken should be placed between two pieces of clear window glass cut to the same size as the plate for rigid support (see figure 5-24). Filmoplast® tape should be wrapped around the pieces of glass to keep the unit intact, and the plate should be stored flat until copying can be undertaken. If plates have missing corners or pieces, a "plug" cut from museum board to match the shape and thickness of the missing area can be positioned with the plate on its support to help provide stability. If glass plate negatives have lifting emulsions but are otherwise intact, they may be placed emulsion side down on a single piece of glass and taped around the edges with Filmoplast® to keep the unit immobile. Following stabilization on glass supports, negatives can be copied or contact printed directly through the glass. If copying is not imminent, four-ply museum board may be substituted for the glass to reduce problems of excessive storage weight.

The non-emulsion side of glass plates may be cleaned with a soft water-dampened cloth; the cloth should be nearly dry to avoid any possibility of water seeping around and damaging the emulsion. The emulsion side, if it exhibits no breaks or edge frills, may be gently dusted with a soft brush or air bulb. Glass plates that are intact should be stored in individual strong paper enclosures and placed vertically on their long edges (for added support) within strong boxes or containers. The plates should not be allowed to slant, and must be maintained in a perfectly vertical orientation. Boxes with grooved separations that keep plates from coming into contact with one another are best; they should be constructed of steel with a baked-on enamel finish, an inert plastic, or alkaline board. Traditional wooden grooved boxes do not provide safe storage unless the raw

Figure 5–23. These album pages are heavy and board-like. The top layer of paper, which carries the captions, is brittle and breaking away. It would be advisable to correctly position all of the loose pieces and make a good photographic copy of the pages before important information is permanently lost. The copy could then be used to meet access requirements. *Courtesy of Special Collections, University of Illinois at Chicago.*

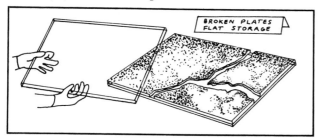

Figure 5–24. Support between two pieces of glass will protect cracked or broken glass plate negatives from further damage or loss. *Drawing by Pamela Spitzmueller.*

wooden interiors have been sealed with protective coats of polyurethane varnish. Although tedious, the task can be accomplished with a small brush. Once coated, the boxes must be allowed to thoroughly dry and cure for several weeks before refiling the plates. If grooved boxes are not available, pieces of four-ply museum board should be cut to the size of the plates and used as rigid dividers between every five to ten plates. The dividers will help to support and bear the weight of the plates, and keep them upright (see figure 5-25). Glass plates should be stored according to size, i.e., 4″ × 5″, 5″ × 7″, and 8″ × 10″ plates, etc., should each be stored separately. If random sizes were stored together, they would not all receive equal support and the

resulting pressure could cause breakage (see figure 5-26). Glass plates should never be stacked; because of the weight on top of them, the plates near the bottom of a pile would likely crack or break.

All folders and boxes containing glass plates should be marked clearly with the word "GLASS" to help ensure their safe handling. Glass plates are very heavy, and appropriate markings will serve to warn staff to expect substantial weight when handling boxes that contain them. It may be useful to have a storage area specifically designated for glass materials; and they should never be stored on the top ranges of shelves (see figure 5-27). Contact prints and, if possible, duplicate negatives should be made of all glass plates to minimize their handling. As they represent unique archival resources and pose no threat to other materials in the collection, they should not be discarded after copying.

Lantern Slides

Lantern slides are transparencies that were intended to be projected for viewing. Often confused with glass negatives, lantern slides are positive images on glass. The emulsion is protected by a second piece of thin glass, and the unit is secured around all four edges with black paper tape. They share similar storage and handling requirements with glass plate negatives.

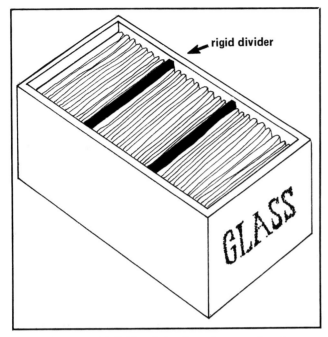

Figure 5–25. Rigid dividers keep glass plate negatives in a perfectly vertical orientation and provide support that otherwise would have to be borne by the glass plates themselves. Each negative should be sleeved in a strong paper enclosure. *Drawing by Pamela Spitzmueller.*

The exterior glass (which carries no photographic emulsion) may be gently cleaned with a damp cloth. If the binding tape is missing or partially detached, it may be replaced with strips of strong Japanese paper and polyvinyl acetate adhesive. The adhesive does not come into contact with the emulsion and thus poses no threat to it. Filmoplast® tape also may be used to replace original binding tape. If it is necessary to replace broken cover glass, lantern slides may be disassembled by lightly running a microspatula or scalpel along the line of tape between the two pieces of glass. Cracked or broken cover glass should be replaced with thin clear window glass (see figures 5-28 and 5-29). Any mats or captions form part of the artifact and should be retained.

Lantern slides often have their own specially grooved cases that provide upright storage with no danger of contact with other plates (see figures 5-30 and 5-31). These may be retained if any raw wooden interiors are treated with protective coats of polyurethane varnish. Otherwise, an alternative storage system similar to that described above for glass plate negatives should be devised. Steel cabinets with a baked enamel finish and slots for individual filing of lantern slides are also available from archival suppliers.

Figure 5–26. This collection of negatives is in the process of being re-housed. Glass and flexible film negatives are being segregated for separate storage, and all are being individually sleeved. *Courtesy of the Chicago Historical Society.*

Figure 5–27. Large rubber stamp notations provide warning that caution must be exercised when handling these boxes containing heavy, fragile glass plate negatives. *Courtesy of the Chicago Historical Society.*

Figure 5–28. The cover glass on this lantern slide should be replaced before the emulsion is further damaged. *Courtesy of Special Collections, University of Illinois at Chicago.*

Lantern slides should never be stacked and should be protected against breakage by individual strong paper envelopes if vertical storage in non-grooved boxes is necessary. All boxes containing lantern slides should be labeled "GLASS." As a precaution, given their susceptibility to cracking, copy negatives and prints should be made of lantern slides.

Film Negatives

The storage system devised for film negatives depends on the manner in which they must be used. Optimally, negatives should be used for reproduction only and not as the point of access to the collection. Prints should be made to serve the needs of researchers. When researchers will not be handling negatives, opaque paper four-flap enclosures are recommended as they provide protection from light and allow non-abrasive access to the image. Damaged negatives that exhibit cracked, flaking, or chipping emulsions should be stored in paper since the static charge present in plastic sleeves could aggravate such problems. If negatives must be used for research access, transparent plastic sleeves are recommended as the negatives can be viewed with no need to remove them from their enclosures. Negatives that are in poor condition, however, should not be handled by researchers.

Cellulose Nitrate Film

Cellulose nitrate film was produced between 1889 and 1951 in both sheet and roll formats. Nitrate film is inherently unstable; it will ultimately self-destruct, resulting in the loss of the image. Of equal importance is the fact that the gaseous by-products of deteriorating cellulose nitrate

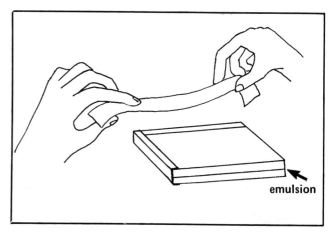

Figure 5–29. The emulsion is protected by two pieces of glass: the base upon which it rests and the cover glass. *Drawing by Pamela Spitzmueller.*

film will damage other photographic materials and paper-based records stored in the same vicinity. As cellulose nitrate film decomposes, nitrogen dioxide is released; moisture in the film (determined by the relative humidity of the storage environment) converts the nitrogen dioxide to nitric acid. The necessity of identifying cellulose nitrate film in repositories is thus two-fold: the cellulose nitrate film must be placed under optimum storage conditions in order to prolong its life while copying options are explored, and it must be isolated to keep it from contaminating other record materials (see figure 5-32).

Nitrate film is highly flammable, but its susceptibility to spontaneous combustion has been overemphasized. Cellulose nitrate (i.e., celluloid) film is indeed capable of spon-

Figure 5–30. Original grooved cases often contain descriptive notes that identify the lantern slides. All raw wooden interiors should be sealed. *Courtesy of Special Collections, University of Illinois at Chicago.*

taneous combustion under certain high temperature conditions, but concern in this area is more reasonably directed toward motion picture film, where there is a high concentration of film packed together in a reel, rather than toward individual sheet negatives, which are generally separated from one another by paper envelopes. Known fires involving cellulose nitrate film have involved motion picture and x-ray film.

Cellulose nitrate film sometimes has the term "nitrate" or, less frequently, "cellulose nitrate" printed on the border (see figure 5-33). Such a clue will be valid identification, however, only if the film is an original negative; if at some point the negative was duplicated onto safety film, the notation might have been captured as well. However, the notation in the duplicate negative would be a photographic image, and would not be embossed as on the original.

Two tests are available to aid in identifying cellulose nitrate film.[11] They involve removing small pieces of film from the border edge, which will result in no loss of image. In the first test, a thin sliver is cut from the border of the negative. The sliver of film is held horizontally by a pair of tweezers at arm's length and is lit with a match. Cellulose nitrate film will flare and will give off a distinctive acrid odor; safety film will not flare and will only burn slowly

---

[11]Ric Haynes, "A Temporary Storage Method to Retard the Deterioration of Cellulose Nitrate Flat Film Negatives," *American Institute for Conservation Preprints* (May 1981): 76–78.

Figure 5–31. These lantern slides are endangered because they are stacked and have no protective enclosures. Upright storage with rigid dividers and paper sleeves would provide a safer environment. *Photograph courtesy of Special Collections, University of Illinois at Chicago.*

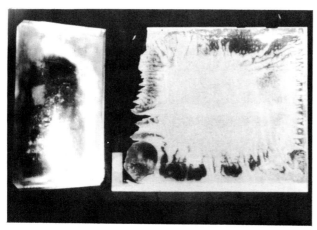

Figure 5–32. The cellulose nitrate negative on the left is in an advanced stage of deterioration and exhibits a total loss of image. The cellulose nitrate negative on the right is tacky and is sticking to its paper enclosure. *Courtesy of private collection.*

while the match is held directly to it. Preliminary to testing the actual sample of unknown film, it is helpful to conduct this test on known samples of nitrate and safety film to differentiate between the burning characteristics of each. The flame test can be inconclusive, because safety film that has been stored with nitrate film or that has a subbing layer of cellulose nitrate will exhibit burning characteristics similar to, though somewhat less dramatic than, those of nitrate film. This is important information, however, as such safety film should be handled in the same fashion as nitrate film. It is recommended that the flame test be undertaken out-of-doors or in a fume hood well away from other archival materials.

In the specific gravity test, or float test, a ¼″ chip of film, which may be removed from the border with a hole punch, is placed in a small bottle or test tube containing 25 cc trichloroethane to which 43 cc trichloroethylene has been added. The stoppered bottle should be shaken to thoroughly wet the film sample. The test will indicate the relative densities of various film bases. If the sample sinks to the bottom of the bottle, it is cellulose nitrate film. If it floats to

Figure 5–33. Border notations help to differentiate between cellulose nitrate and safety film. *Courtesy of Photographic Archives, University of Louisville.*

the top it is cellulose triacetate film, while polyester film floats at various mid-levels during a ten-second test period (see figure 5-34). The vapors from trichloroethane and trichloroethylene are toxic, and this test should be conducted in a fume hood.

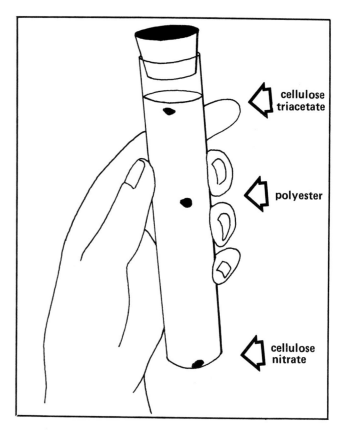

Figure 5–34. The specific gravity test is a relative measure of the densities of cellulose nitrate, acetate-based, and polyester films. *Drawing by Pamela Spitzmueller.*

Safety film was introduced in about 1934, and while it gradually replaced cellulose nitrate film, there is no arbitrary cut-off date beyond which cellulose nitrate film was no longer used. Its continued use was dependent to some degree on photographers' inclinations, technical requirements, and film supplies. Nitrate film was produced in a number of formats until 1951 and any film negatives made before this date should be considered suspect. Also, during the transition period from cellulose nitrate to safety film and up through the early 1960s, cellulose nitrate was sometimes used as the adhesive layer between the gelatin emulsion and the film base. Such negatives should be handled as cellulose nitrate, as should safety film that has been exposed to nitric acid fumes that are emitted as cellulose nitrate film deteriorates.

Cellulose nitrate negatives may go through the following identifiable stages of deterioration:

1. Film base turns yellow-brown, accompanied by staining and fading of the image.

2. Emulsion becomes soft and tacky, causing the film to stick to other surfaces.

3. Film base contains gas bubbles and emits nitric acid.

4. Film softens and welds to adjacent film and is frequently covered with a viscous froth.

5. Finally, film degenerates entirely or partially into a brownish acid powder.[12]

The nitric acid emitted during the third stage is an oxidizing agent that can cause yellowing and fading of silver images and softening of gelatin emulsions in photographic materials stored nearby.

Although it is certain that nitrate negatives will ultimately self-destruct due to inherent chemical instability, there is no definite timetable for this action. Nitrate film is unpredictable and the rate of deterioration depends on many factors, including original processing of the film and subsequent storage conditions. Many nitrate negatives survive fifty years or longer in seemingly stable condition; others begin to deteriorate much more quickly. Since the time element is so uncertain, it is important to identify and segregate nitrate film as speedily as possible. Once it is placed in safe separate storage, resources and copying options can be explored. Regular inspection is important during this period to ensure that copying can take place before images become distorted. While awaiting copying, nitrate film should be stored at a temperature below 50°F with a relative humidity between 30% and 40%. The storage area should be well ventilated, and nitrate negatives should be stored in paper rather than plastic sleeves in order to discourage the buildup of decomposition gases. Nitrate films should be stored where there is no opportunity for the decomposition gases to invade the general archives storage area, through, for example, a common ventilating system. Envelopes and sleeves that have been used to store nitrate negatives should be considered contaminated and should not be recycled for use with other photographic materials.

The following factors should be considered when exploring options to duplicate nitrate film: value and use of the collection, financial resources, and technical capabilities. Appraisal decisions are very important in this context, given the likelihood of large numbers of nitrate negatives and limited resources. The informational content and quality of the images should be considered very carefully; it is quite likely that judicious weeding will reduce the number of negatives requiring duplication. Specific copying options are discussed in Chapter 7, Managing a Photographic Copy Service, p. 147.

Once nitrate negatives have been duplicated, the issue of whether to discard the originals must be addressed. This decision should be based in part on whether there is visible evidence of deterioration, and whether separate, secure storage capable of maintaining recommended environmental conditions is available. Another important factor to consider is the potential long-term stability of the copy film. Given the fact that materials and procedures do not always fulfill expectations, it is advisable to retain original nitrate negatives under controlled conditions for as long as possible, should recopying prove necessary. For long-term storage, a temperature of 0°F is recommended; if refrigerated storage is not available, preservation will be enhanced in low-temperature storage with relative humidity in the 40% range. Nitrate film should not be disposed of casually. Safety officers or local fire marshalls should be consulted. It is important to be aware of local fire laws that govern the storage and disposition of nitrate film. Also, it is wise to be aware of any clauses in insurance policies pertaining to possession and storage of nitrate film that might affect coverage in the event of fire.

Cellulose Acetate Film

Cellulose acetate, or safety, film was developed in a number of formulations in response to the flammability and chemical instability of cellulose nitrate film and the subsequent need for a stable recording medium. Early cellulose acetate film (diacetate), however, has proved unstable because the base shrinks, causing the emulsion to buckle and separate from the base (see figure 5-2). Cellulose diacetate was replaced by cellulose triacetate film, which is stable. It is important to be able to differentiate between stable and unstable materials given the fact that it is impossible to plot exactly the rates of deterioration. As with cellulose nitrate film, cellulose diacetate film must be identified and copied before important images are lost through distortion.

Cellulose acetate film normally has the word "safety" imprinted along its edge. The flame test described in the preceding section will provide further confirmation; safety film will only burn with difficulty as a match is held directly to it. Once the match is removed, the flame will extinguish. The float test, also described above, will differentiate between cellulose diacetate and cellulose triacetate film. Cellulose triacetate film will float to the top, while cellulose diacetate film will float in the solution, at mid-level, as does polyester film. The latter two films can be differentiated by examining the border areas, where the word "safety" will appear on diacetate film, and "ester" (or the Kodak name, Estar®) will appear on polyester film. Analysis of subject content and subsequent dating also may help to differentiate between cellulose diacetate and polyester film.

Cellulose acetate negatives may be stored either in neutral pH paper or inert plastic enclosures. Given their instability, cellulose diacetate negatives should rank high among the priorities for copying. Until copying can be undertaken, the negatives should be placed in cold storage and inspected regularly for signs of shrinkage and increased deterioration.

---

[12]Haynes, 76

Polyester Film

Polyester (polyethylene terephthalate) film is strong and chemically stable and is being used increasingly as a replacement for cellulose triacetate film. Either neutral pH paper or inert plastic enclosures should be used for storage.

Color Photographs

Color photographs created by chemical processes are inherently unstable. Color images are made up of dyes that vary in their stability over time; temperature, relative humidity, and light all affect the longevity of color photographs, as do original manufacturing and subsequent processing. Black-and-white images that have been hand-colored with various pigments are not generally classified as color photographs. Although the colors applied to black-and-white prints may alter or fade over time, the informational content of such photographs remains intact. Chemically-produced color images, on the other hand, can alter radically over time as the three dyes (yellow, cyan, and magenta) comprising color photographs fade. Unstable dyes can result in changes in both density and color, and thus in the informational content of the images and their usefulness for reproduction purposes. While color photographs do not meet archival criteria for permanence, they are found increasingly in repositories, and steps must be taken to preserve them for as long as possible.

The permanence of the dyes varies with the process and is also dependent on conditions of storage and use. Fading is accelerated under conditions of high temperature and high relative humidity, and color photographs are also very susceptible to damage from violet-blue visible light and ultra-violet radiation. Color materials should be stored in the dark, and original items should not be exhibited except for short periods under carefully controlled conditions. Color photographs stored under temperature and relative humidity conditions recommended for black-and-white images will exhibit a much greater degree of deterioration than the latter during a given time period. For maximum permanence, color photographs require cold storage. Temperature should be maintained between 0° and 10°F with a relative humidity of 25% to 30%. Such storage requires the use of a freezer or refrigerator, and the photographs must be packaged carefully to maintain proper moisture levels. Materials must be preconditioned before sealing packages for low temperature storage, and they must be carefully brought through warm-up stages to prevent condensation before they are made available for use under normal room conditions.[13] Low temperature storage is neither recommended nor intended for photographs accessed on a regular basis.

A proven way to preserve color information is to have three-color separation master negatives made on black-and-white film, including a gray scale. These master negatives should be processed to archival standards and stored under optimum conditions. This method preserves in silver the dye layers of the original color image, and allows its later reconstruction. The process is costly, however, and requires skillful and exacting photographic work. Given the expense, it is probable that very few color images in a repository would justify this approach. A more feasible preservation response would be to make black-and-white negatives from original color photographs. This will preserve the informational content of the images to some degree and at a reasonable cost, although it can be a complex process because different colors will reproduce as the same shade of gray, thus resulting in loss of contrast and possibly of information.

Preservation Procedures and Cautions

Archival photographic collections often contain a broad sampling of technical processes that present a wide range of preservation problems. In reading the archival and conservation literature, as well as the technical literature of the photographic industry, it will be obvious that a large number of treatments and procedures have been advocated to meet the preservation needs of specific processes and formats. Many of the "breakthroughs" have later been found to pose problems and have sometimes resulted in irreversible damage to valuable photographic materials. The field of photographic conservation is relatively new, and much research and study is required before the chemical and physical properties of the photographic record in all its diversity are fully understood, let alone how various materials (that have been processed and stored differently) will react to various treatments. Extreme caution is urged, therefore, before undertaking any procedures that involve photographs and chemicals or water. Archivists should limit their activities to copying, to physical stabilization, and, especially, to providing a suitable environment and should leave actual treatments to qualified personnel. Copying is a very important preservation tool and is advisable before any restoration treatment is initiated.

In the context of treatments, there are a number of actions that should be expressly avoided. No attempt should be made to mend photographic materials, either with archival pressure-sensitive tape or traditional methods of mending paper using Japanese tissue and wheat-starch adhesive. Torn prints should be copied and then protected in an appropriate enclosure; rigid support is necessary to prevent further tearing.

Residual processing chemicals are the major cause of staining and ongoing deterioration of photographic images. Spot tests to determine the presence of residual silver (silver thiosulfate) and residual thiosulfate leave stains that are not acceptable on valuable prints; further, after the tests, prints

---

[13]For further information see Henry Wilhelm, "Storing Color Materials," *Industrial Photography* 27 (October 1978): 32–35; and *Preservation of Photographs* (Rochester, N.Y.: Eastman Kodak Company, 1979), 39.

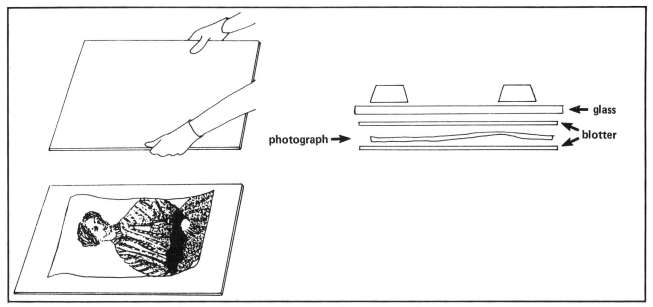

Figure 5–35. This means of flattening involves only pressure; no moisture is induced. Flat storage under the constraint of enclosures and folders will help to keep photographs from reverting to a rolled or curled position. *Drawing by Pamela Spitzmueller.*

must be thoroughly washed to remove the test solutions, which can pose problems with some materials. Refixing and rewashing are often recommended in the literature as the appropriate means of dealing with problems posed by residual processing chemicals. However, it is impossible to know the exact conditions under which most photographs were originally processed, and chemical tests, treatments, and washing may prove ineffectual or result in further degradation of the images. While such procedures may be satisfactory for newspaper photographs that are relatively recent and most certainly were originally processed quickly and without concern for permanence, older processes or images that have high individual value may not fare so well. Any testing and reprocessing that is deemed necessary for historical materials should be carried out by trained photographic conservators and technicians. The most effective archival response to problems posed by residual chemicals is to control the environment. Humidity is the most critical factor, as high humidity promotes the oxidation of the silver image; relative humidity of the storage environment should not exceed 40%.

Opening and Flattening Rolled Prints

A loosely rolled print that does not resist gentle attempts at opening may be flattened by placing it between two pieces of clean, dry, white blotting paper under weights (see figure 5-35). The pressure exerted by the weights must be evenly distributed over the entire surface of the photograph to avoid cockling; pressing boards or pieces of plate glass with smoothed edges may be used satisfactorily. Photographs should be checked periodically while undergoing flattening; usually twelve to twenty-four hours should suffice. Because the emulsion layer is coated on only one side of the base,

prints have a natural tendency to curl. Further, since paper retains a "memory", it will easily revert to the rolled state. Thus, it may be necessary to repeat the procedure before the materials can be stored flat in folders and boxes.

Prints that have a more pronounced curl and that resist gentle attempts at opening require humidification. If they are forced open, the emulsion layer can crack (and may separate from the base) and the paper support may break into pieces (see figure 5-36). An acceptable means of introducing moisture is to place rolled prints in a humidity chamber (see figure 5-37); with this approach, the prints are not actually wetted, but the moisture level is raised to the degree that the paper fibers relax and thus can be safely unrolled.[14] When using a humidity chamber, photographs must be watched closely for signs of mold growth. Following humidification, relaxed prints should be placed between weighted blotters to dry.

Before attempting to humidify photographic materials it is necessary to apply several appraisal criteria. To the degree possible, the photographic process should be identified. Consideration also must be given to the value of the print; dealing with a long series of similar group portraits is an entirely different matter from treating the work of a master photographer. Finally, the skill level of the archivist or technician must be balanced against the value, uniqueness, and condition of the images. If there is uncertainty about any of these factors, it is best not to undertake the procedure. Work requiring a high level of skill and any treatments to be carried out on important photographs should be done by a photographic conservator who has the requisite

---

[14]Ritzenthaler, 90–92.

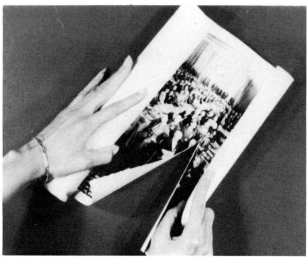

Figure 5–36. This rolled print is being irreversibly damaged as it is being forced open. Humidification prior to opening would have prevented this loss. *Courtesy of the Archives of Labor and Urban Affairs, Wayne State University.*

experience and knowledge of how various materials will respond to treatments. Rolled film negatives are not likely to respond to humidification, because film bases are relatively impervious to moisture.

Cleaning and Stain Removal

The emulsion surfaces of prints and negatives may be gently dusted with a soft brush or air bulb to remove surface dirt and dust. Before proceeding, it is important to critically examine the photographs to determine whether they can withstand even gentle dusting. Emulsions that are cracked

or exhibit edge frills should not be dusted, since even gentle action could further damage the emulsion. As stated previously, the surfaces of daguerreotypes should never be touched, even with a soft brush or stream of air. If it is determined that the photograph can withstand surface dusting, work should begin in the center of the image and continue outward toward the edges (see figure 5-38). Camel's hair photographic negative dusting brushes or soft Oriental brushes may be used (similar to those used for surface cleaning paper); light-colored bristles are best since it is easy to see when they become soiled. A number of brushes should be kept on hand so that a clean, dry brush is always available; dirty brushes may be washed in water and a mild soap (such as Ivory®) and hung with bristles downward to dry. If air bulbs or syringes are used in surface dusting, care must be taken to assure there is no build-up of moisture in the bulb that could be transferred to the photographs. Nothing more abrasive than a gentle brushing or flow of air should be used to dust emulsion surfaces. Erasers are much too abrasive and could easily remove portions of the emulsion. Paper and cardboard mounts and mats may be surface cleaned with a Magic Rub® vinyl eraser or with crumbled eraser particles (such as Skum-X®); care must be taken, however, that all eraser particles are removed after cleaning and are not left to move onto the emulsion, where they could become permanently affixed over time and become abrasive as they harden with age.

Mold resting on the surface of photographs may be carefully dusted away with a soft brush. This should be done well away from other collection materials. No attempt should

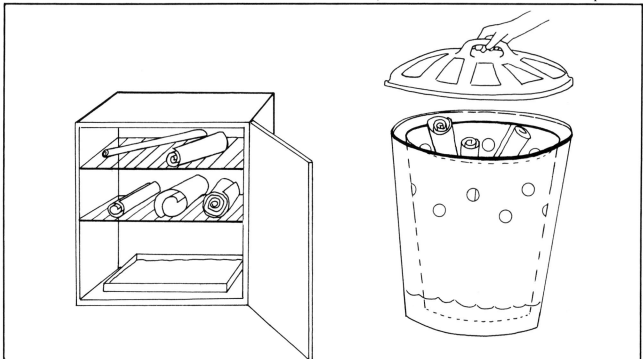

Figure 5–37. A humidity chamber may be fabricated out of a non-corrosive, air-tight chamber, such as an old refrigerator or plastic garbage cans. *Drawing by Pamela Spitzmueller.*

Figure 5–38. Prints must be held stationary when undergoing surface dusting; a light weight on a clean blotter or a gloved hand may be used satisfactorily. Damaged photographs, or those that have sooty, oily dirt that will streak and become imbedded in the surface rather than respond to gentle brushing, should be referred to a qualified technician for cleaning. *Drawing by Pamela Spitzmueller.*

be made, however, to remove stains resulting from mold, residual processing chemicals, or other sources. Photographs exhibiting such stains should be copied, using filters to reduce or eliminate stains in the copy prints. Removal of fungal and other stains through washing or use of solvents is potentially hazardous and can result in the loss of the emulsion. Such procedures should only be undertaken by qualified personnel.

Setting Up a Work Space

It is important to set aside a work area specifically for the examination and handling of photographic materials (see figure 5-39). It should be in a secure area that is not exposed to casual traffic by staff, since valuable and/or fragile images will often be visible on work surfaces and thus susceptible to accidents if handled by curious but uninitiated personnel. The size of the work space should be determined by the size of the photographic collection and the number of staff working with it. Each work station, however, should consist of a large flat table or desk, good light sources, and easy access to supplies and storage materials. Glass-topped tables are often recommended as they encourage careful work practices, and they also provide perfectly flat surfaces upon which to examine photographic materials. Ideally, each work station should have a light table to expedite viewing of negative images, transparencies, and lantern slides. Useful supplies and tools include microspatulas, scalpels and blades, brushes, white cotton gloves, magnifiers, as well as necessary hand tools for dismantling frames

(see Appendix C). The work area should be kept scrupulously clean, and chemicals, solvents, and cleaning supplies should not be stored nearby.

Integrating Preservation and Archival Procedures

At virtually every stage of administering a photographic collection, preservation needs should be considered. Each task should be evaluated to determine where opportunities exist to survey and evaluate the collection and whether existing procedures pose threats to the materials. Staff training and orientation should be undertaken as necessary. Not every function described will be applicable to every archival situation.

Field Work

During the initial survey of a collection before it is brought into the repository, the type and approximate number of photographs should be determined. The environmental factors to which materials have been exposed should be noted, as they will provide good clues to the resulting physical condition of collection items. For example, if materials have been stored in a damp basement, gelatin emulsions may be sticking together, and mold infestation is a possibility. Conversely, materials stored in a hot, dry attic may be brittle and quite fragile. Evidence of insect or rodent infestation should be noted as well.

Physical condition of the images should be evaluated. Oversized or rolled items, framed photographs, brittle prints,

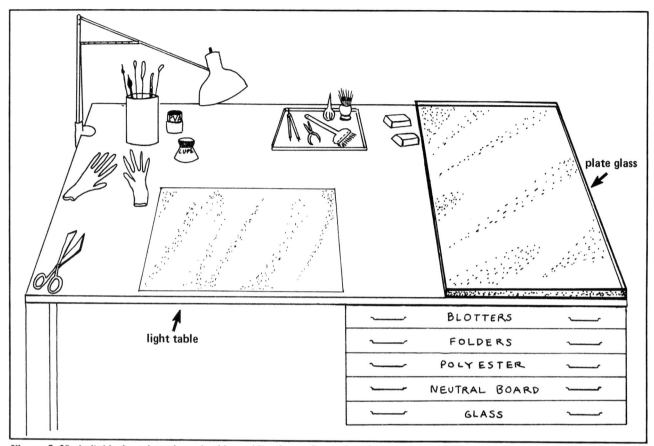

Figure 5–39. Individual work stations should provide a large, flat surface for examining and housing photographs, and all necessary supplies should be readily accessible. *Drawing by Pamela Spitzmueller.*

Condition Notes

Collection:

Donor: Location:

Estimated size:

    boxed   loose
    filing cabinets   other

Special formats/processes/condition:

    Description of photographs   Amount   Location

Water damage:
Mold or insect infestation:
Packing supplies: Special equipment:
Approx. # of packing days: Personnel:
Transportation:
Additional comments:

Archivist_____   Date_____

Figure 5–40. The condition and special handling and packing requirements of photographs should be recorded during the field survey.

and glass plates all will require special handling. A checklist may be devised to assist in recording field notes (see figure 5-40). Appropriate packing supplies should be available: strong boxes, paper envelopes for loose prints and negatives, stiff binder's board for supporting glass plates, plastic bubble wrap for padding framed items, etc. The archivist must supervise packing and transport, considering physical condition of the photographs, staff orientation, as well as external factors such as the weather. Security of the material also must be considered, and all boxes and containers should be clearly marked with the names of the collection and the repository before they leave the site.

Accessioning

As collections are received in the archives, the field inventory should be checked to make sure that all containers and boxes have arrived intact. Collections infested with insects or mold should be kept isolated from the rest of the holdings until treatment can be undertaken. Recent research indicates that most photographic materials can be exposed to common fumigants (ethylene oxide, methyl bromide, thymol, and p-dichlorobenzene) with no resultant change in gelatin stability or image density.[15]

During accessioning procedures it is possible to get a much more thorough sense of the content and condition of a collection than is usually feasible during the field survey. Staff should be trained to recognize preservation problems, including fragile photographs, flaking emulsions, broken glass plates, and cellulose nitrate and cellulose diacetate negatives. Photographs that are too fragile to handle or that require physical stabilization should be set aside until appropriate action can be taken; such images should not be made available to researchers. Record keeping is very important, both to note the nature and location of the preservation problems and to assign accession and similar control numbers to the images. During accessioning, decisions are made regarding physical condition and whether or not photographs can withstand handling; initial intellectual controls are imposed as well. Thus, from both security and conservation perspectives, an institutional policy should be established to prohibit access to photographs that have been received but not yet accessioned.

Arrangement and Description

During arrangement and description activities, a number of preservation procedures should be carried out. These include removing foreign materials, humidifying to open rolled photographs, cleaning, marking, and providing a proper storage environment. Issues pertaining to physical condition and need for stabilization or copying should be further evaluated by the archivist during this stage of processing, considering, among other factors, the intrinsic value of the

[15]Hendriks, *Preservation and Restoration of Photographic Materials in Archives and Libraries*, 88.

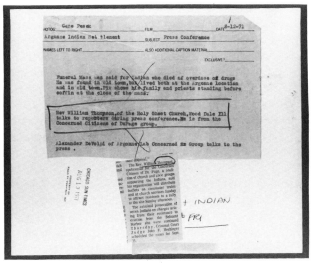

Figure 5–41. The back of this photograph illustrates several marking and recording techniques that can prove damaging over time: rubber stamp and ballpoint pen ink, pencil and crayon notations, and a pasted label and newspaper clipping. While the information provided can be very helpful in identifying the photograph, the inks and adhesives can result in permanent staining of the print. The pressure of writing also can cause breaks and indentations in the emulsion. Depending on the value of this photograph, preservation copying may be advised. *Courtesy of the Chicago Historical Society.*

images. Priorities for necessary copying should begin to evolve, based upon relative values (scarcity; historical, evidentiary, or monetary value; uniqueness) assigned to a collection and its physical condition. Photographic processes should be identified at this time as well, and appropriate enclosures and storage systems designated.

As stated previously, no attempt should be made to force open tightly rolled photographs that resist gentle attempts at unrolling. Humidification under controlled conditions is required to safely open such photographs and thus proceed with evaluation and other archival tasks.

After gaining necessary information regarding the relationships among photographs and any accompanying archival records, harmful means of attachment (staples, paper clips, rubber bands, etc.) should be carefully removed. All pertinent data (such as names, dates, captions, and job numbers) from original folders, envelopes, and similar enclosures should be recorded before they are discarded. Before photographs are placed in new enclosures, they should be gently cleaned following the procedure described on page 122 to remove any dust or abrasive dirt.

Non-destructive means of marking photographs must be employed (see figure 5-41). As little information as possible should be recorded on the backs of paper prints; normally the accession and image numbers will suffice. Notations should be written lightly with a lead pencil (#2 or softer) while the photographs are supported on a clean hard surface. If too much pressure is exerted when writing, an impression or indentation will be forced into the emulsion layer, thus damaging it. Additional identifying information may be recorded on the enclosure (all data should be written or typed on the enclosure *before* the photograph is placed inside); extensive data, such as the names of individuals in a large group shot, should be listed on a cross-reference sheet. Inks (ballpoint pen, felt-tip, manuscript, and rubber stamp) should be avoided because they may be acidic and can thus cause fading of the silver image. Since resin-coated (RC) papers do not readily accept pencil, a small patch within the border area on the backs of RC prints may be gently abraded with a piece of emery paper to permit written notations. No attempt should be made to mark film negatives (which may, however, already bear photographers' file numbers). Because of their artifactual value cased photographs should not be marked either, though pertinent data can be recorded on strips of neutral pH paper that can be placed within the cases. All enclosures should be marked, however, and the practice of keeping materials in or with their enclosures at all times should be strictly enforced.

For reasons of security, some institutions find it desirable to mark photographic prints with ownership marks. If such practice is followed, it is recommended that a small rubber stamp bearing the name of the institution be designed; this image may be stamped on the backs of prints using the non-acidic, non-bleeding ink that is available at no charge from the Preservation Office, Library of Congress.

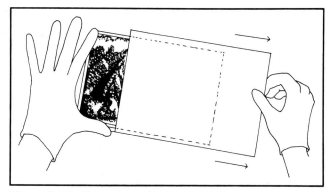

Figure 5–43. The paper enclosure should be carefully removed from the photograph, rather than pulling the print out of its sleeve. *Drawing by Pamela Spitzmueller.*

Research Handling of Photographic Materials

Access and use policies must be established to govern the use of photographs. Access to stack and storage areas by researchers should be prohibited, and, as with other archival records, photographs should not be allowed to circulate, even to institutional or administrative staff or other special categories of users. Reading room policies governing eating, smoking, drinking, and handling materials should be posted and strictly enforced. Also, policies on access to fragile photographs, collections that are not accessioned or otherwise protected by intellectual controls, and original prints and negatives must be adopted and thoroughly understood by everyone on staff. Access systems that employ copy prints, microfilm copies, or, in some instances, even xerographic copies, will reduce wear and tear on original images. The reading room must be monitored at all times, and researchers should be required to provide positive identification, sign a daily register, and complete collection request and use forms. The number of items provided at a given time to a single researcher should be strictly limited to several folders or a single box. In some instances, depending upon the value and condition of the items, perhaps only one or two photographs should be made available, and their use should be closely supervised by the archivist.

Researchers should be instructed in the proper ways to handle photographic materials. Prints and negatives should be held with two hands by the border edges (see figure 5-42). A light table should be available in the reading room for the safe viewing of transparencies, negatives, and lantern slides that patrons are permitted to handle; use of such original materials by researchers must be closely monitored. If images are housed in paper enclosures, researchers should be shown how to correctly remove them in a non-damaging, non-abrasive fashion (see figure 5-43). White cotton gloves should be worn when handling photographic materials; gloves should be mandatory when accessing images that are not protected by any type of enclosure, as well as when hand-

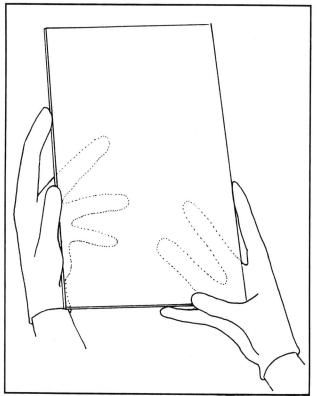

Figure 5–42. Handling photographs with two hands provides rigid, non-flexible support. *Drawing by Pamela Spitzmueller.*

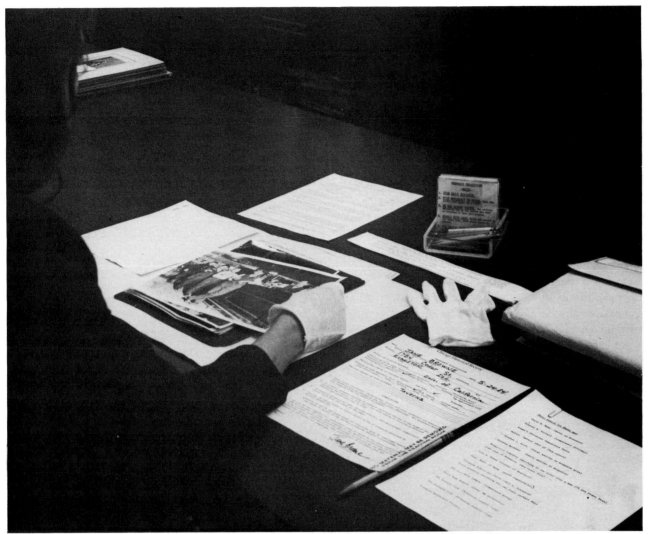

Figure 5–44. This researcher is set up to study the photographs in a safe and efficient fashion: gloves are being worn, inventory and conditions of use forms are at hand, and a pencil rather than a pen is available for note-taking. *Courtesy of the Chicago Historical Society.*

ling photographs that must be removed from paper sleeves or those mounted in scrapbooks or albums. When researchers and staff are required to wear gloves when working with photographs, they will generally approach the materials with an added measure of care and respect (see figure 5-44).

Exhibition

There are several preservation and security concerns that should be addressed when exhibiting photographic materials. First is the decision whether to use original prints or good reproductions. Factors to evaluate in making this decision include condition and value of the photographs; environmental conditions, location, and security of the exhibition site; and nature of the exhibition. In many instances reproductions are not only satisfactory, but are the only viable solution, especially when exhibition space and conditions do not meet conservation or security standards.

Exhibit cases should have locks. Environmental conditions within cases should meet recommended storage re-quirements for temperature and relative humidity; the most economical means to accomplish this is to make sure that exhibit cases are placed in areas that are temperature and humidity controlled. Cases should not be airtight, but should allow for ventilation so that conditions within the cases will equal those in the exhibition hall. Filters may be placed over air holes to prevent dirt and dust from entering exhibit cases.

Generally, light sources within exhibit cases are not necessary and should be kept off, or the units should be removed entirely, since they often emit too much light and can contribute to an excessive build-up of heat. If conditions within the exhibit area require lights within cases, however, fluorescent tubes are recommended because they will not give off as much heat as incandescent bulbs. Fluorescent tubes must be covered with ultraviolet filters (or low UV emission tubes should be used). Diffusion panels also should be incorporated into the light units to ensure even illumination of the entire case and to keep any one object from receiving too much light. Lights within cases should be on only when viewers are present. Other light sources in the exhibit gallery must be evaluated as well. Windows should be glazed with UV filtering sheets, and filters should be placed over all fluorescent tubes. Beams from spotlights or track lighting should not be aimed to fall directly on photographic images. To diminish problems posed by light within the exhibition gallery, exhibit cases can be glazed with UV filters. The recommended light level for museum exhibits is a maximum of five footcandles. While it may not be feasible to achieve such a low light level for exhibits in archival reception areas or reading rooms, it is likely that light levels could be lowered substantially without affecting other activities. Notes posted in exhibition areas explaining the reasons for reduced light levels will help to generate understanding and support on the part of visitors.

Security within the exhibition area is equally important, especially if original photographs are to be framed and hung on gallery walls. Such images will be more vulnerable to vandalism and theft than photographs displayed within exhibit cases, and it may be necessary to have staff present in the exhibit gallery at all times. Framed items should be firmly attached to the walls with screws and brackets.

Original photographs should not be placed on permanent display. The actual length of exhibition should be determined by the value and condition of the images and a thorough evaluation of the exhibition environment from conservation and security perspectives. Three months is the maximum period recommended for exhibiting museum objects and highly valuable library and archival materials. While this may not always be a realistic figure, given the time and expense devoted to installing an exhibit and the often limited resources available for such activities in archival institutions, it should be borne in mind when selecting items for exhibition. In some instances, it is possible to rotate similar images, or those that evoke similar reactions, within the overall exhibition period, so that no single photograph is on display for too great a time.

All mounting and matting of photographs should be done to conservation standards. Neutral pH mat board should be used and mounting techniques should be reversible (see figure 5-45). Adhesives should not come into contact with original photographs, and dry mounting, which is potentially irreversible, is acceptable only for expendable copy prints. Polyester corners are ideal for mounting photographs, as such mounts are easily reversible and readily allow mats, which can be expensive and time-consuming to construct, to be recycled for other uses. Polyester corners must be used with caution, however; photographs should not be flexed to position a print within the corners, since such action could break emulsions and possibly crack brittle supports. The safest approach is to attach two polyester corners to the mount board and then to slip the photograph

into place; the final two corners should be slipped onto the photograph while it is supported flat on the mount. The polyester corners should not fit the photograph too snugly, as this could cause the print to buckle. Very often three rather than four corners will suffice to hold the photograph in place. When dismantling the unit, the corners should be removed from the mount board; no attempt should be made to flex the photograph out of the corners.

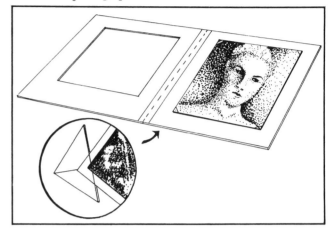

Figure 5–45. Polyester photo corners are unobtrusive and ensure that no adhesives come into contact with the photograph. *Drawing by Pamela Spitzmueller.*

Treatment Services

Photographic conservators may be required on occasion to treat images of high intrinsic value or to undertake such sophisticated and technically demanding work as cleaning daguerreotypes or removing prints from mounts or scrapbooks. Since there are very few trained and fully qualified photographic conservators (especially in private practice), it is of the utmost importance to gather information on potential conservators before entrusting them with institutional treasures. Discussion with colleagues at other repositories may prove helpful in locating a suitable conservator. A number of regional conservation centers offer treatment services for photographs, and information also may be sought from the American Institute for Conservation (AIC), which maintains a list of members of its Photographic Materials Group. While the latter does not constitute an AIC endorsement, it at least provides a point of departure for further gathering of data. References should be sought from potential conservators, and their adherence to the AIC Code of Ethics should be assured.[16]

Archivists must become knowledgeable consumers of contractual services and learn to compare and evaluate the

---

[16]See José Orraca, *"Shopping for a Conservator," Museum News* (January/February 1981): 60–66. For information regarding members and the AIC Code of Ethics, contact: American Institute for Conservation of Historic and Artistic Works, 3545 Williamsburg Lane, N.W., Washington, DC 20008.

quality of work produced. They also must have an understanding of technical processes in order to talk knowledgeably with conservators, technicians, and darkroom personnel. Ultimate responsibility for the preservation of photographic collections rests with archivists and curators, and this charge should not be taken lightly, nor should it be given over to others who do not have a broad understanding of archival concerns or the nature of the photographic record. Archivists must develop wide knowledge of the history of photography, in addition to a very detailed and precise understanding of where and how their collections fit into the greater whole.

Disaster Preparedness

Every archival repository should have a written disaster preparedness and recovery plan.[17] This plan should take into account potential natural disasters as well as possible disasters posed by human or mechanical error. Since many disasters are accompanied by fire and/or water, disaster and salvage plans should clearly address procedures to be undertaken in the event of damage from these elements. Planning efforts also should uncover sources of supplies and equipment as well as necessary technical expertise that may be obtained from conservators, regional conservation centers, or state library and archival agencies. Staff at all levels should be involved in the planning process (in part because knowledge regarding collection treasures or structural or mechanical building quirks is often quite localized). Once adopted and operational, the disaster plan should be widely distributed among staff and discussed periodically at meetings; it should also be made available to appropriate local officials, including police and fire departments.

Accurate information regarding the scope, character, and value of archival records is mandatory during the planning process. The physical and chemical make-up of various materials and their susceptibility to various kinds of disaster-related conditions (fire, smoke, water, dampness, etc.) must be taken into account when planning salvage operations. Priorities for salvage and recovery efforts must be planned in advance and the location of highly valuable or vulnerable materials must be carefully mapped out along with access routes. It is equally important to realize that not all materials can be treated in the same way during salvage operations; different approaches must be planned for various archival materials.

Photographic materials pose a variety of special problems in the context of disaster recovery. Given their great diversity in chemical and physical composition, as well as in original processing, various photographic materials will respond quite differently to salvage techniques. It was for-merly thought that water-damaged photographs should be immersed in water to keep them from drying out before they could be reprocessed and dried. Excellent work by Klaus Hendriks and Brian Lesser has dispelled many previous notions regarding appropriate means of handling specific photographic processes during recovery operations. Salvage methods that have proved satisfactory for recovering paper-based textual records should not automatically be applied to photographs. Hendriks and Lesser developed the following recommendations based on their experiments:

—Keep immersion time to a minimum.

—Keep water temperature low.

—Freezing of photographs retards further deterioration.

—As films appear to be more stable, salvage prints first.

—If personnel and time are available, proceed in this order:

    a. air dry (without freezing)

    b. freeze—thaw—air dry

    c. freeze-dry in vacuum chamber

—Freeze—thaw—vacuum drying, as is done with books, is not recommended for photographs, due to blocking or sticking of gelatin layers.

—Protect wet collodion glass plate negatives completely from being immersed in water.

—Wet collodion glass plate negatives must never be freeze-dried; none will survive.[18]

Wet collodion glass plate negatives as well as ambrotypes and tintypes (collodion positives) are very susceptible to water damage and will not survive freeze-drying; watertight storage containers should thus be devised for them. Vulnerability of silver gelatin prints to water and immersion varies depending upon whether or not hardening agents were used during original processing; non-hardened gelatin emulsions are likely to slip off their bases or dissolve into solution.

Identification of photographic processes represented in the collection is extremely important in the context of developing disaster preparedness and recovery plans to ensure that well-meaning salvage attempts do not result in the inadvertent loss of valuable images. When a disaster involving photographs occurs, it is highly advisable to bring in a photographic conservator to direct salvage operations. Regional conservation centers are good sources of technical information, and many also provide emergency services.

Implementing a Conservation Program

Preservation is an archival responsibility that must be integrated into all aspects of administering a photographic

---

[17]Good planning guides include: Hilda Bohem, *Disaster Prevention and Disaster Preparedness* (Berkeley: University of California, 1978); and Peter Waters, *Procedures for Salvage of Water-Damaged Library Materials*, 2d ed. (Washington, D.C.: Library of Congress, 1979).

[18]Klaus B. Hendriks and Brian Lesser, "Disaster Preparedness and Recovery: Photographic Materials," *American Archivist* 46 (Winter 1983): 67.

collection. Priorities for treatment and stabilization must be established, based upon need, relative values of collections, and institutional resources. Many preservation activities are relatively easy to implement, yield significant results, and have the added benefit of creating a sense of progress, which ideally will generate more enthusiasm for preservation. Preservation activity can begin in the following areas:

—Monitor and upgrade environmental conditions.

—Improve housekeeping practices.

—Upgrade handling procedures.

—Replace damaging enclosures and storage furniture.

—Isolate cellulose nitrate film.

—Initiate a regular inspection program for all photographic materials.

—Initiate a copying program.

—Establish priorities for copying, based on stability, condition, and access requirements.

Much can be done to enhance the useful life of photographic materials. Staff orientation and training is a cost-effective means of implementing a number of the above recommendations. The photographic record is an irreplaceable resource, and much can be done to preserve it. It is important to begin.

6 Legal Issues

Mary Lynn Ritzenthaler

A number of legal concerns must be addressed when administering a collection of photographic materials. Some of these issues, pertaining to such matters as acquisitions and ownership, reproduction, copyright, publication, and privacy rights, are broadly applicable to archival and manuscript materials. However, given the unique character of the photographic record, its manner of creation, and the uses to which photographs are put, a number of specific legal rights and obligations must be considered when developing systems to manage photographic collections.

Because of the complicated issues involved and the potential for litigation, every archival repository should have access to good legal counsel. Whether a lawyer is on retainer or actually on staff of larger institutions, legal advice should be sought when developing access and use policies as well as security controls, especially as they relate to possible theft or vandalism of archival materials. In addition, all forms that are created by an institution to document a transaction with another party should be reviewed by a lawyer. Such forms include deeds of gift, deposit agreements, loan agreements, transfers of copyright or other rights, and publication agreements. It must be determined that such forms and the actions they record fall properly within the law, do not compromise the parties involved, and actually accomplish what is intended. The archives must protect itself and its collections in all situations and must neither unknowingly give up rights or privileges nor place the parent institution in jeopardy.

A lawyer should be sought who has experience in the areas that are most pertinent to the administration of an archives. Working knowledge of copyright, local and state laws regarding shoplifting (which are important in developing security policies), tax laws as they affect the donation of gifts to institutions, and contract law is important. While it may not be possible to secure a lawyer who has worked in these areas specifically in the context of manuscript or archival materials, let alone photographs, it should be possible to locate a lawyer who is interested in and sensitive to the specialized needs of a repository. Referrals may be sought from local bar associations or arts groups. Increasingly, artists and studios are seeking legal advice as they develop their careers and/or educational programs. Since such groups share a number of concerns that are also pertinent to archival repositories, lawyers who have developed a specialty in this area would form a good pool from which to seek legal counsel. In some cases, trustees or officers of local historical societies are competent to provide legal advice and services, often without charge.

Ownership of Photographic Materials

All photographs placed in a repository should be documented as to source and ownership status. Normally, the archives will wish only to retain materials it actually owns, although there may be occasions when deposits or permanent loans will be found acceptable if that is the only way to gain access to valuable information or to preserve a collection from loss or destruction. Repositories will generally acquire photographic materials by gift or donation (often as part of a manuscript or archival collection), or by purchase. In every instance, the transaction, whether gift, purchase, or deposit, must be documented either by a formal legal agreement or a binding letter of transfer that specifies the materials acquired, terms of the transaction, provenance (if known), and owner or seller. When undertaking any of these transactions, the repository must be certain that the person or organization offering the materials to the archives actually has the right to do so; only the legal owner of the photographic materials can donate or offer them for sale. Physical possession does not necessarily guarantee ownership, nor does the legal owner of the physical property (i.e., photographic materials) necessarily own or have the power to transfer the legal rights to them; ownership of the actual photographs is separate from the legal right to use or reproduce them. Put simply, the owner of the photographs might be someone other than the copyright holder. These matters will be discussed fully in the section on copyright.

Many repositories and historical agencies have collections that were acquired at an early date and for which the documentation regarding the donor and the assignment of rights is either scanty or nonexistent. Even if the donor is unknown, in most instances it can be assumed that the photographs are held by the archives by intent of the donor, to be used in fulfilling the mission of the repository. Despite the lack of legal agreements, undocumented photographs probably are in the archives not by accident, but, rather, because they were donated to the repository for safe-keeping as well as for research, exhibition, and similar purposes. In such instances, as much supporting documentation as can be pieced together regarding original source should be recorded, and the institution should proceed judiciously in making the materials available for research use and publication.

In corporate, governmental, college and university, or similar institutional archives, the issue of ownership of materials is governed by law, institutional mandate, or tradition. Unless negotiated otherwise, the institution (i.e., creating agency), and not the employee, owns the materials and the rights to them. In volunteer associations in which the creations would not be considered works for hire, tradition—and the natural desire to document one's place in history—may benefit the archives. In all such instances, the archivist should determine the procedures and policies regarding the ownership and disposition of materials created during the normal course of conducting institutional business. Plans should be made to acquire legally by systematic transfer all important materials that do not automatically accrue to the archives. It is wise to develop acquisition policies and records retention schedules that are accepted by the institution and understood by all personnel. Such policies and procedures will assure an uninterrupted transfer of materials to the archives and can prevent confusion or misunderstandings regarding ownership of materials.

Copies of original photographs also may be acquired by a repository as part of a concerted effort during copy clinics or because a donor is unwilling to part with the original items. Such transactions also must be documented and reproduction rights must be acquired if possible.

Deed of Gift

A deed of gift should be drawn up to document gifts of photographic materials to the repository. This agreement should cover donations of either individual photographs, entire collections of photographs, or manuscript or archival collections containing photographic materials. The deed of gift should clearly and precisely transfer ownership of the material from the donor to the repository. The implications of the transaction should be perfectly clear to the donor, and the deed of gift should be worded in simple language to avoid confusion or misunderstandings.

Ideally, the repository will wish to acquire unrestricted gifts, which will make it much easier to administer the collection and will often make the collection more readily available for research use. However, in many instances restricted gifts must be accepted, and when negotiating such agreements the archivist must seek a balance between the needs of the institution and the needs and rights of the donor. Instances in which sensitive materials are involved, for example, or in which the donor stands to gain monetarily from materials in the collection through future publication, should be fully explored. Donors should not be pressured into making agreements with which they will be unhappy over the long term. Conversely, institutions should not accept complicated or unreasonable restrictions that will consume too much staff time to administer, or that will inhibit eventual use of the collections. Actual terms of the restriction may relate to such matters as closing all or portions of a collection for a specified time period, or requesting that researchers seek permission from the donor to publish sensitive or copyrighted material. The archives should not accept restrictions that will compromise its stance as a research institution. For example, donors who wish to control who may use their collections, or donors who wish to review manuscripts before publication, raise issues relating to censorship and preferential treatment of researchers. Repositories should avoid such compromising situations. Once agreements are negotiated and reasonable compromises are

reached, however, the terms and duration of any restrictions must be spelled out specifically in the deed of gift. The archives must then initiate controls to ensure that the terms of the agreement will be met as the collection is accessioned, cataloged, and made available for research use. To avoid lapses in institutional memory, it may be useful to shelve restricted collections in a special area, to mark such boxes and folders appropriately, and to list any restrictions in finding aids.

In addition to gaining physical ownership of materials, the repository should try to gain copyright or reproduction rights in order to expedite the actual use of the collection for research and publication purposes. However, the donor can transfer only such rights that he actually owns. Many collections consist of a wide range of materials created by other than the donor, and the donor has no authority to assign away rights except to those materials he created or owns through legal transfer. A donor who is neither the photographer nor the photographer's heir might not own the copyright to the photographs in question and thus might not be able to transfer rights governing their use. Optimally, all applicable copyright will be assigned to the archives. This may be accomplished in the deed of gift by one of the following two phrases: "transfer of all copyrights" or "grant of exclusive rights." One of these phrases must explicitly appear in the deed of gift, and as the issue of copyright can be confusing, it is important that the archivist explain the basic provisions of the copyright law to the donor during the process of negotiation. If complete rights cannot be secured by the institution, the archivist should at least try to acquire reproduction rights that will make it possible for the institution to fulfill its goals as a research institution. Depending upon the mission and functions of the repository, it also may be useful to acquire specific permission to display photographs and to use them for instructional purposes.

The deed of gift should transfer ownership of the material to the repository, outline any restrictions, and specify copyright status. In addition, it should include the legal name of the donor(s), address, and date of transaction. The gift should be described accurately in a brief, narrative fashion; on occasion—for purposes of appraisal if the materials have high monetary value, for example—it may be necessary to append a detailed list of items covered in the gift. Such a detailed inventory, however, is normally compiled during the accessioning process (see Chapter 4, Arrangement and Description); it then serves as a record of the gift and becomes part of the permanent file maintained on the collection. A staff member who is authorized to enter into legal agreements on behalf of the institution should sign the deed of gift, and copies of the agreement should be held by the donor and the archives.

It may not always be feasible to get a signed deed of gift

Deed of Gift

I, _____ , hereby donate the materials described below to the State Historical Society to become its permanent property and to be administered in accordance with its established policies. I assign and transfer all copyrights that I possess to the State Historical Society. Further, I agree that this material may be made available for research on an unrestricted basis, subject only to those restrictions which may be specified below.

Description of Materials:

Items not retained by the State Historical Society shall be:

_____ discarded
_____ returned to donor
_____ other (describe):

Restrictions:

Dated:_____   Signed:_____
                                                             Donor

                                                 _____
                                                             Address

                                                 _____

The State Historical Society hereby accepts the above property under the conditions specified.

Dated:_____   Signed:_____

Figure 6-1. The deed of gift should transfer both property rights and copyrights to the archives. In addition, the agreement should specify any restrictions governing the use of the collection, and provide for the disposition of unwanted or out-of-scope items.

because some donors are frightened of legal documents and are unwilling to sign them. In such instances, a letter of agreement should be written in lieu of a deed of gift. Letters of agreement are legally acceptable and can serve as non-threatening transfer documents; they should spell out the intent of the donor as well as any negotiated agreements or understandings.

Prior to the Copyright Act of 1976, common law doctrine governed literary property rights and the manner in which unpublished works could be used. The 1976 legislation brought unpublished works under statute for the first time and also changed the operating terminology. The term "literary property rights" has been replaced by the word "copyright" under the new law; legal forms should be revised accordingly. A sample deed of gift may be found in figure 6-1.

Deposit Agreement

A deposit agreement should be negotiated if the donor is unwilling to make a permanent gift to the repository, and if the institution feels that the collection is important enough to accept, given the fact that it may someday be withdrawn from the archives. Factors to weigh in making such a decision include the importance of the photographic materials, whether their preservation is endangered if they are not placed on deposit, potential research use, and institutional resources that will be expended on storage and organization. In negotiating a deposit agreement, some institutions find it advantageous—and necessary—to work out a financial agreement whereby the owner will reimburse the institution for storage and services rendered if the collection is eventually removed from the archives. The deposit agreement should specify the terms of the deposit, including reproduction rights, the length of the deposit, and provisions for renewal of the agreement or eventual transfer of ownership to the repository (see figure 6-2).

Bill of Sale

When purchasing photographic materials from a dealer or private individual, it is essential to gain as much information as possible regarding the provenance of the items to ensure that the seller has a legal right to transfer ownership of the materials. Further, information on provenance is also of great importance when analyzing and identifying photographs and subsequently making them available for research, publication, and exhibition; all information on the origin and ownership of the materials should be maintained in the collection file, and pertinent data should be presented in the finding aid as well. The archives should be familiar with the reputation of dealers or auction houses, and should under no circumstances purchase materials that entered the marketplace through unethical means. A proper bill of sale should be written up in legal form (see figure 6-3), and its format and language should be reviewed by the archives'

legal counsel. The bill of sale should adequately describe the materials purchased and their provenance and should include a written statement regarding the copyright status of the materials following the sale. Archivists should be aware that sellers or dealers often will neither know the copyright status of photographs they offer for sale nor be able to transfer or sell the rights to the photographs. Unless the repository is interested in building up a study collection that cannot be reproduced, it should purchase only well-documented photographs for which there is no question that both physical ownership and all copyright will be transferred to the archives following the sale. Otherwise, it may find itself in the unhappy position of having purchased a collection that it cannot fully use, and that also may be duplicated in a number of institutions.

Copyright

Copyright is an important issue in managing photographic collections because, under the law, only the copyright holder has the legal right to reproduce, publish, exhibit, or otherwise make available to the public materials that are protected by copyright. Photographs require special attention in this context. Unlike written materials, photographs cannot be easily summarized or paraphrased if their reproduction would violate copyright law. Further, because photographs are frequently used in books and magazines that return profits to authors and publishers, they are more likely than most written records to occasion complaints or lawsuits over violation of copyright. Thus, archivists must familiarize themselves with the copyright law and the ways it affects the use of photographic collections.

The Copyright Act of 1976 became effective on 1 January 1978 and superseded all earlier copyright legislation. It is clear that many aspects of the law require interpretation and that this body of knowledge will evolve over a number of years as these issues are examined by the courts. In the meantime, archival repositories must develop reasonable procedures to make their collections available for use within the spirit of the law.

Copyright is a public legal statement of proof of ownership of an artistic or literary property, which enables the legal owner to enter into legal agreements involving the assignment, sale, lease, or other commercial use of the property. To be eligible for copyright protection, a work must be original and must be fixed in a tangible form of expression. Photographs meet these criteria. The intent of copyright is to give a photographer, author, or artist exclusive rights to the rewards of his work for a limited period of time. Copyright thus encourages creativity by protecting original creative works against unauthorized reproduction or distribution. The needs of the creator are balanced against the needs of the user, freedom of the press, and freedom of information. A copyright owner enjoys the following

---

Deposit Agreement

I, _____ , hereby place the materials described below on deposit with the State University Library for a _____ year period, ending _____ . It is my intention that these materials be made available for research on an unrestricted basis, subject only to those restrictions which may be specified below. The State University Library has permission to publicly display the materials and to make single copies available for research purposes.

Description of Materials:

Restrictions:

Dated: _____   Signed: _____

_____
Address

_____

The State University Library hereby accepts the deposit of the above described materials under the conditions specified.

Dated: _____   Signed: _____

Figure 6-2. An agreement should be drawn up to meet the specific requirements of each deposit. If appropriate, provisions for renewal or converting the deposit to a permanent gift should be incorporated into the agreement. On some occasions, a continuing deposit (sometimes referred to as permanent loan) may be negotiated. To reduce problems in administering such collections, and to ensure their on-going usefulness, specific agreements should be reached regarding copyright and publication rights for all collections placed on deposit.

---

exclusive rights, which apply to all works eligible for copyright protection:

1. Right to reproduce work
2. Right to prepare derivative works
3. Right to distribute work
4. Right to publicly perform work
5. Right to publicly display work

As a number of these rights have a direct bearing on the use of photographs in archival repositories, it is clear that repositories must be aware of the copyright status of collection materials and attempt to gain these rights by transfer when possible.

Under the copyright law of 1909 the term of copyright was twenty-eight years, with an option to renew for another period of twenty-eight years, for a total of fifty-six years, at which point copyright was no longer renewable. Upon expiration of copyright, the property automatically entered the public domain. When a property is in the public domain, it is no longer protected by copyright law and may be used freely by anyone without paying the owner or estate for that right.

As mentioned previously, copyright laws prior to 1976 did not cover the manner in which unpublished works could be used. These rights were protected by common law doctrine. Common law protection extended indefinitely, until the point of publication, at which time the property was protected by copyright, providing correct procedures were followed. Common law protection was replaced by the Copyright Act of 1976. Under the new legislation, distinctions between published and unpublished works were removed and both were given statutory protection.

Provision was made for a transition period between the old and new copyright laws. Photographs in their first twenty-eight-year term of copyright as of 1 January 1978 need to be renewed at the end of that term to secure additional protection for a total of seventy-five years from the year of original copyright. Photographs that were in their second term of copyright (that is, they had been renewed for a second term of twenty-eight years) as of 1 January 1978 automatically had their copyright extended for seventy-five years from the end of the year in which copyright was originally secured, without the need for further renewal.

Under the 1976 copyright law, the following terms of copyright apply:

—Newly created photographs and those neither published nor registered for copyright by 1 January 1978 are protected by a copyright term of the photographer's life plus fifty years. The new law thus requires that biographical information on photographers be compiled in order to determine copyright expiration of photographic materials.

—Photographs published before 1978 are protected for twenty-eight years from the date copyright was first secured, with an option of renewal for an additional forty-seven years.

The following two categories, anonymous photographs and those created under corporate authorship (or for hire), are protected by a term of copyright extending seventy-five years from the date of first publication or 100 years from the date of creation, whichever comes first. Copyright originally secured between 1950 and 1977 must still be renewed; if it is not, protection expires at the end of the twenty-eighth calendar year. Works already in the public domain cannot be protected under the new law. That is, works whose copyright protection had expired do not gain copyright protection under the new law; if they had already entered the public domain, they retain that status.

E. G. Star Gallery
300 W. Superior
Chicago, IL   60602
(312) 555-1212

Sold to: *Lakeview Historical Society*   Date: *6 August 1984*
           600 Grant Street
           Chicago Ill   60657

Description: *One album containing 20 cabinet cards (all albumen prints), ca. 1890, depicting members of the Grant family. Photographs by J. Schmidtke, Chicago. 10 pages empty. Excellent condition. Album exhibits slight abrasion on back cover; all mounts intact; all photographs identified. #125.*

Provenance: *Owned by Grant family (Laurie Ann Grant) until 1981; acquired by Gallery at estate sale.*

Copyright status: *unknown*   Total due: *# 125.00*

                                                   Signed: *E S Star*
                                                            E. G. Star

Figure 6-3. Sample bill of sale. In this instance, the archives would have to attempt to uncover pertinent information regarding copyright ownership, although it is likely that these photographs are protected by copyright until 31 December 2002.

Perhaps most pertinent to archives and historical agencies are the provisions pertaining to photographs neither published nor copyrighted before the new law went into effect (that is, photographs formerly protected by common law) or photographs that are anonymous. Photographs created before the new law went into effect but never copyrighted nor published were automatically brought under statute for either the lifetime of the photographer plus fifty years or 100 years after creation, whichever comes first. At a minimum, such works are guaranteed protection under the new law for a period of twenty-five years. Thus, most photographs in archival collections—registered or not, and whether or not the photographers are known—are copyrighted until 31 December 2002.

Under the Copyright Act of 1976, copyright registration is not mandatory for obtaining copyright protection, which begins at the point of creation, once the work is fixed in tangible form. Registration is encouraged, however, and does give the creator additional rights in the event of copyright infringement. To register a work, forms obtained from the Copyright Office must be filled out and submitted with a registration fee.[1] One copy of each unpublished photograph and two copies of published works must be submitted as part of the registration process. In instances where photographs have a high monetary value, as with fine art prints, it is not mandatory to submit copies.

The absence of a copyright notice does not mean that a photograph is not protected by copyright. The creator of a photograph has a right to protect his work from unauthorized use whether or not the copyright symbol is affixed, and with or without formal registration through the Copyright Office. The majority of photographs in historical collections are not marked with a copyright notice and never have been registered. Also, many, if not most, photographs in typical archival collections are anonymous, which further complicates the issue of copyright. However, such works are still protected under the law. The 1976 law guarantees protection of all unpublished, unregistered works for a minimum of twenty-five years, but at least until 31 December 2002.

Copyright protection exists from the moment the film is exposed in the camera, i.e., the photograph is original and exists in tangible form. The question of copyright ownership, however, varies depending upon the situation. A professional photographer who is working neither as an employee nor on a commission basis, or an individual taking photographs for pleasure, owns the copyright on photographs he takes. On the other hand, staff photographers—those working as employees of a corporation, university, or newspaper—create photographs as works for hire, and copyright resides with the employer, unless there is a written agreement to the contrary. Well-known newspaper photographers or photojournalists may negotiate such agreements with their newspapers, magazines, or agencies, and thus make their photographs available for a fee on a one-time-use basis. In such situations, when they sell the right to use a photograph, they are not giving up copyright.

Studio photographers who are producing photographs on a commission (or work for hire) basis do not own the rights to the photographs they take for a client. Thus, while they may retain a negative file (i.e., the physical objects), they cannot legally reproduce the photographs without written permission of the client or copyright owner. To get around this situation, many studio photographers request that customers sign forms that transfer rights to the photographer. When acquiring photographs, archival repositories must, to the degree possible, be aware of the conditions under which the photographs were made and must know who legally owns the rights to them. This is especially important in relation to studio collections, as these materials are increasingly being acquired by repositories and tend to raise a number of legal and ethical issues. The tension between custom or the traditional practices of many photographers and the actual provisions of the copyright law are also most apparent in this area. Archivists must take all factors into account when negotiating for such collections, not the least of which concerns are the rights of persons depicted in the photographs.

In order for archival agencies to function most easily as research institutions, it is important for repositories to obtain copyright as well as legal ownership of the physical items when acquiring collections. Just because an institution physically owns a group of photographs does not mean that it also owns the rights to them. As mentioned earlier, the legal transfer of copyright may be conveyed in a deed of gift or copyright transfer statement or form (see figure 6-4). The transfer must be in writing, using one of the following phrases: ''transfer of all copyrights'' or ''grant of exclusive rights.'' Copyright is divisible, which means the photographer or copyright holder can disperse or divide the privileges of copyright. Use of one of these phrases will avoid situations in which the repository jointly holds copyright with another individual or agency.

Publication may be defined as the distribution of copies of a work to the public by sale, rental, lease, or other transfer. The distribution of xerographic copies of photographic prints to researchers may be considered publication in this context, as may exhibitions or displays open to public viewing. Technically, without copyright, institutions do not have the right to distribute, reproduce, publish, or exhibit photographs in their collections. It is clear that most institutions do not hold copyright to the large majority of their photographic holdings. It is equally clear that few, if

---

[1] For registration forms and futher information, write: Copyright Office, Library of Congress, Washington, DC 20559. ''Publications of the Copyright Office,'' available free upon request, cites circulars and other materials that address various aspects of the copyright law.

Transfer of Copyright

I, _____ , hereby transfer all copyrights that I possess in the materials described below to the State Historical Society for its use in fulfilling its research, educational, publication, and exhibition goals.

Description of Materials:

Name of Collection:

Date Received: Accession Number:

Dated: _____   Signed: _____
                                                                        Donor

                                                           _____
                                                                        Address

                                                           _____

Accepted by: _____
                      State Historical Society   Date

Figure 6-4. A copyright transfer agreement can be executed to secure copyright on any collections or items that were accessioned without such a formal transfer. Since the donor can only transfer copyright that he or she actually owns, copyright also should be sought from all other individuals whose materials are significant and which are represented in the collection.

any, institutions are retroactively attempting to obtain copyright. Most repositories are thus theoretically open to lawsuits by the actual copyright holder for infringement. In practice, however, the possibility of such action seems remote because most holders of copyright are not aware that they own it, and if they are aware that they possess copyright to the material, they do not realize the potential monetary implications, which generally serve as an impetus to action. (Monetary gain would be a factor only in rare instances, however, For example, if the photographs were of high technical quality and contained unique information regarding important individuals or events, they might be of interest to a commercial publisher. In such cases the copyright holder might gain financially, especially if reproduction rights to an important print were sold repeatedly over time.) An archives or library in such a situation—that is, physically owning large masses of photographic materials but not owning the rights to them—may take a number of precautions while allowing the reproduction and use of the photographic collections. Warnings (see figure 6-5) should be posted and stated on forms to the effect that the user is responsible for copyright infringement. All copies supplied for study or research use should be stamped with similar disclaimers (see figure 6-6). Such disclaimers may not stand up in a court of law but will at least reinforce the good intentions of the institution.

Of special interest to archival institutions are provisions in Section 107 of the copyright law that define fair use provisions, according to which copyrighted material may be used and reproduced under what is termed fair use, or an equitable rule of reason. The following factors are considered when determining fair use:

—Purpose and character of use
—Nature of copyrighted work
—Use of entire work vs. portion of it
—Effect of use on value of work
—Whether the creator will lose money as a result of use

Under fair use provisions, repositories may make a security or preservation facsimile copy and reproduce and distribute copies for scholarship and research. An archives should not provide copies, however, if it is known that the user intends to infringe copyright. Libraries and not-for-profit institutions are not held responsible for copyright infringement for copies made on unsupervised photocopy machines.

Repositories have a number of obligations in making photographs available for public use responsibly and in conformity with the copyright law. First, transfer of copyright should be sought on new acquisitions. If the institution holds the copyright for materials in its possession, questions of use and publication are most easily resolved. To the degree possible, repositories should try to determine the

---

Warning Concerning Copyright Restrictions

☆ The Copyright law of the United States (Title 17 United States Code) governs the making of photocopies or other reproductions of copyrighted material.

☆ Under certain conditions specified in the law, libraries and archives are authorized to furnish a photocopy or other reproduction. One of these specified conditions is that the photocopy or reproduction is not to be "used for any purpose other than for private study, scholarship or research." If a user makes a request for, or later uses, a photocopy or reproduction for purposes in excess of "fair use", that user may be liable for copyright infringement.

☆ This institution reserves the right to refuse to accept a copying order if, in its judgment, fulfillment of the order would involve violation of copyright law.

Figure 6-5. This warning should be posted in reading rooms and at study tables.

---

copyright status of photographs for which this issue is not resolved or clarified by legal agreements or documentation. Records should be maintained on the copyright status of all photographs. These records should specifically indicate whether copyright is owned by the institution or by another individual or organization, or whether, after careful review, the copyright status is still unknown. Biographical data on photographers represented in the collection should be created as an aid in determining copyright expiration dates. This information should be made available to researchers and publishers, along with specific instructions regarding their responsibilities in meeting copyright obligations (see Chapter 7 for additional information on this topic).

Privacy Rights

Privacy may be defined as the right of each person to be left alone, free from unwanted publicity. No federal statutes cover privacy rights, although a number of states have privacy laws, with some variation among them. Because New York is the center of publishing in the United States and a large number of photographers, agencies, and publishers reside in the state, New York State law is often seen to set precedent in the area of publishing law, especially as it affects privacy rights.[2] The courts essentially strive to strike a balance between an individual's right to privacy, freedom

---

[2]As a case in point, see: Tim Malyon, "The Fateful Photograph," *Camera Arts* (October 1982): 26.

---

of the press, and the public's right to know. In practice, some people, including public figures and celebrities, have little right to privacy. The concept of privacy rights is applicable to photographs in several contexts.

Photographs that are commissioned and paid for (i.e., works for hire) cannot be used by the photographer for any commercial purpose without express permission. The purchaser, not the photographer, owns the copyright. Unless a written agreement or contract specifies otherwise, this can result in situations wherein the photographer owns or possesses the negatives as physical property but has no right to use or reproduce them except with the explicit permission of the copyright holder. Use of such photographs without permission would be a copyright violation and, depending upon the use, could also be seen as an infringement of privacy rights.

NOTICE

This material may be protected by copyright law (Title 17 U.S. Code).

Figure 6-6. All copy prints provided to researchers should be stamped with this notice.

Unsolicited photographs of recognizable individuals cannot be used for business or profit, as an illustration or advertisement, or in an offensive manner. Before photographs depicting recognizable individuals can be used, the photographer must have release forms signed to authorize use . Thus, noncommissioned photographs of recognizable individuals—whether of public figures or private citizens—taken on the street or in other public places cannot be used for any of the above purposes without the express written permission of the individuals. Traditionally, photographs of crowded streets, fans at sports events, and similar gatherings have been considered to depict news events and have therefore been used for publication. However, the manner and context in which such photographs are presented, along with accompanying captions, can lead to the charge that they are offensive or that they invade the privacy of the recognizable individuals they depict.

Within institutional settings, archivists must be aware that allowing publication of some images that depict recognizable individuals (either national or local figures) may constitute invasion of privacy. Generally, the dead are not considered to have privacy rights, although the sensibilities of relatives and heirs must be considered when making photographs available for various uses. Archivists must proceed judiciously and cautiously when permitting the use of photographs from their collections. They must evaluate the proposed use and determine copyright and other pertinent restrictions, as well as local sentiments of propriety.

7 Managing a Photographic Copy Service   *Mary Lynn Ritzenthaler*

Depending upon the character and use of the holdings, photographic archives require a variety of reproduction services to meet institutional goals and to fulfill the needs of researchers. When determining the range of services—and attendant policies and fees—to be offered by a copy service, the following needs must be considered.

Institutional Requirements

Repositories need copies of their photographic holdings to carry out a range of preservation actions, to enhance access to holdings, and to meet a variety of outreach activities, including the preparation of exhibitions, publications, and audiovisual presentations.

Preservation Copies

Preservation copies of photographic materials are often required to reduce handling of original items or to provide an archival replacement copy of photographs that are inherently unstable because of their chemical and/or physical composition. Preservation copies are intended to provide long-term access to the informational content of fragile or deteriorating images. The provision of preservation copies should be considered when the access requirements of viewing original photographs are such that the materials are endangered or likely to suffer loss. For example, under optimum conditions, negatives should never be handled by researchers. Not only are they a difficult medium to view and interpret, but, more importantly, they represent unique archival resources that are very susceptible to damage and loss. Glass negatives are very vulnerable to breaking or cracking, and film negatives can be readily scratched or marked with fingerprints, resulting in damage to emulsion surfaces. All negatives that exhibit chipping or flaking emulsions are endangered and should be kept rigid and handled as little as possible with no flexing; copying is therefore mandatory. When establishing use and access policies, special attention should be paid to negative images for which no prints exist, and suitable copying or duplicating should be undertaken. Positive prints that are affixed to brittle cardboard mounts or scrapbooks are also candidates for preservation copying.

Photographs that are inherently unstable should be copied for preservation purposes; these include cellulose nitrate and cellulose diacetate negatives. Prints and negatives that exhibit staining as a result of residual processing chemicals also should be copied, as the image may continue to deteriorate and the base may have been seriously weakened. Priorities for preservation copying must be established, based upon such criteria as condition, use or research potential, and value. Forms may be devised to aid in the evaluation process (see figure 7-1). Provision must also be made for periodic inspection of all unstable materials, as the rate of deterioration is so uncertain; evidence of increased activity (i.e., chemical breakdown) should alter the priority ranking as necessary.

Outreach Activities

Copies of photographs are often required for program activities that will enhance the reputation of the repository and further its position as a research and educational institution. Exhibition-quality copy prints are required when original photographs are not to be used in an exhibit. Photographs reproduced from the collection can add a great deal to the impact of institutional newsletters, catalogs, and brochures, and also help to carry the message that the archives maintains, and is interested in acquiring, photographic materials. Audiovisual programs (slide/tape, video, or motion-picture) that the repository may produce as research aids or for promotional purposes also require high-quality reproduction of photographic materials.

Research Use

Perhaps the greatest potential use for copies of photographs within archival institutions is to enhance research access to collections. Large collections can be microfilmed to increase access to the images and also to encourage off-site research use. Browsing files of commonly-sought images can be created to meet the needs of the general public or researchers who are not interested in searching entire collections for unique or seldom-used views. Finding aids or subject access files also may be enhanced by incorporating reproductions reduced in size (such as card files containing narrative descriptions along with small copy prints). All such copying may be considered in a broad sense to meet preservation needs as it reduces the handling of original photographs.

A copy service is also important in meeting the needs of researchers and other users of the collection. Photographic prints may be required for study purposes or publication in a variety of formats: print media, motion-picture films, videotapes, and other audiovisual presentations. As technology changes, the potential research and publication use of photographic images will change as well. It is certain, however, that scholars, writers, and other researchers are increasingly using photographs to help document and illustrate their publications. Repositories must be prepared to offer a range of copy services to meet these needs and, equally important, provide copies of the highest quality, since the images—as they appear in books and films—will reflect upon the reputation of an institution.

Needs of the print and television media also must be considered when establishing a copy service. Users from

---

PHOTOGRAPHS – PRESERVATION COPYING WORKSHEET

Collection: Accession Number:

Donor: Location:

(fill out one form for each process represented in collection)

Photographic Process   Number   Folder/Box

   Format

   Condition

   Level of use

Recommended copy method: Date of last examination_____

Priority ranking for copying: Archivist_____

☆ ☆

Copy method: Copying completed_____

Inspection completed:

Disposition of original photo-   Archivist_____
   graphs:

Figure 7–1. Such a form can be used to record information on unstable, fragile, or damaged photographic materials that require preservation copying. The completed forms can then serve as a reminder to undertake periodic inspection.

---

these media may have extensive needs and can be exacting and demanding customers; they generally require a great deal of the staff's attention while viewing and selecting images and often require same-day copy service. The repository must be able to meet their demands for quality reproductions and, when necessary, must resist when requested to alter or waive institutional policies on their behalf. However, since the reputation of the repository will very likely be enhanced by having its photographs appear in the news, efforts should be made to anticipate the specialized needs of such users without compromising the preservation or security of the collection. Use and reproduction policies should be established that balance the needs of the collection and the capabilities of the institution against the needs and requirements of researchers. Once agreed upon, these policies should be clearly stated in writing and adhered to consistently. Requests from the media to borrow original photographic materials or to have their own technicians undertake the copy work should be denied.

Establishing a Copy Service

When setting up a copy service, it is important to consider the above needs and other potential uses of such a program. The range of services offered and the decision

whether or not to invest in an in-house laboratory will relate in part to need, level of use, and cost. The framework for such decision making must include the acknowledgement that virtually every institution that maintains a collection of historical photographs has need of a copy service. Further, this service, whether it be in-house or provided contractually by an outside laboratory, must satisfy the preservation and security concerns of the institution.

Adoption of the policy that researchers will not be allowed to produce their own copies, either through borrowing original photographs or coming into the repository with their own copy equipment, will help to form the framework of the copy service. No matter how persuasive the arguments that may be presented, or how small the institution or limited in staff size, the archives must retain its position as sole producer and provider of all copies. This is important for obvious reasons of security and preservation, and also has legal implications. If researchers produce their own copies, the institution loses control of copy negatives and has no opportunity to stamp copy prints with ownership and copyright information. Before an institution undertakes any copy service the provisions of the copyright law must be fully understood, and the rights, limitations, and responsibilities accruing to the purchaser of the copies must be made perfectly clear. Legal requirements stated in the deed of gift or other conveyance that apply to the copying of individual collections because of agreements with donors must be known by all staff and adhered to uniformly when filling copy requests.

In-house vs. Commercial Photographic Laboratory

A number of factors should be considered when weighing the need for establishing an in-house laboratory against using a commercial firm. (Similar questions should be asked regarding an existing in-house laboratory to evaluate its range and quality of services.) The type of institution, size and nature of the photographic collection, and its anticipated use will greatly affect the determination of need for an in-house laboratory. For example, in many college, university, and business archives, the parent institution may maintain a photo lab to meet broad institutional goals, such as publication, promotional, and instructional programs. In such instances, the archives can take advantage of an existing service and work with the technical staff to meet specific archival needs. Repositories that are not within such institutional settings, or whose collections are so large that a separate copy service within the archives may be warranted, will need to weigh resources and costs for set-up, personnel, staff training, and maintenance against need and level of use in determining whether using an in-house lab is more cost effective than sending work to an outside commercial firm. Cost is not the only factor to be considered, however, when dealing with unique, irreplaceable images.

When evaluating both in-house and commercial photo labs, the security and safety of the photographs must be considered. Questions to be addressed include the following: What are the hours of the lab and who has access to it both during and after hours? Are technicians supervised? What is the training and technical expertise of lab personnel? Are they familiar with historical photographic processes, and do they have the requisite technical capabilities to deal with them? In this regard, attitude and orientation are very important. Lab personnel should be aware of the importance and value of historical photographs and of necessary preservation and security precautions. Institutional goals and policies in these areas should be understood and supported. Ideally, technical staff will be sympathetic to the special needs of historical photographs, aware of the technical characteristics of specific processes, and willing to gain new knowledge and work with the archivist to develop solutions to preservation problems. The lab should be able and willing to do tray (i.e., hand) processing to archival standards, which involves the individual attention of technical staff.

In addition to technical capabilities, the quality of work produced in the lab must be evaluated in terms of accuracy and clarity of copy work, and sympathy to the original intent of the photographer. Does the lab have the necessary equipment to undertake the range of services desired? The reputation of the lab and the integrity of the staff also should be considered; there should be no chance of photographs being lost or duplicate prints making their way into the market place. Costs, as well as the amount of time required for specific types of jobs to be completed, should be evaluated. Such questions must be answered satisfactorily before archival photographs are entrusted to either an in-house lab or a commercial firm; they also may serve as a checklist in developing standards for setting up an in-house lab. In general, the archives will be able to exert the greatest control over security and quality of work in an in-house lab.

An option midway between relying completely on either in-house or contractual services is to set up only a copy room in-house, rather than setting up both a copy room and a darkroom. This approach separates the functions of copying and processing and printing and may be a more feasible alternative for many institutions. The capabilities provided through an in-house copy service would ensure that all original materials remain in the repository, since only exposed copy film would be sent outside for processing and printing. A copy room also would be much less expensive to equip than both a copy room and a darkroom.

If it is necessary to send work to an outside lab, the lab's services should be carefully evaluated before entrusting it with valuable photographs. Recommendations may be sought from other local historical agencies and repositories. (If nearby archival institutions have their own in-house photo labs, it may even be possible to arrange to use their services on a contractual basis. The same sort of scrutiny as outlined above should be undertaken, however.) Several sample batches of similar work of limited value may be sent to local labs to compare cost, quality of work, and time required to complete it. The method of packaging the photographs and transporting them between the repository and the lab also must meet conservation and security requirements. A written agreement specifying the work to be done should be drawn up; this should adequately describe the number and type of images taken to the lab and can thus serve as both a work order and a receipt (see figure 7-2). Outside labs should be required to return all materials to the archives, including copy negatives, which many labs have traditionally believed belonged to them. This provision should be clearly stated in the contract or work order.

Work should be sent only to reputable professional custom laboratories; one-hour or overnight services should not be entrusted with valuable materials. Such labs are geared to process film quickly and are neither equipped to, nor, in most cases, able to, deal with unique images that require individual attention. Further, they usually are equipped only to do processing, not copy work. In small communities where no suitable professional labs exist, the most satisfactory approach will be to set up a limited in-house copy program that is capable of meeting basic preservation needs and patron requests for copy prints. In such instances, a staff member or friend of the repository who has some expertise in photography—or is interested in acquiring it—may be put to good use on behalf of the collection. However, it should be stressed that good copy work is exacting and is beyond the experience of most photographers, professional or amateur; it also can be expensive. Caution and care are thus required in selecting both personnel and the appropriate techniques.

Range of Services

The services to be offered will depend on the nature of the collection, research demands placed on it, and the availability of technical expertise. Among its basic functions however, the lab should be able to provide copy and duplicate negatives, transparencies, contact prints, and enlargements, all from a number of formats.

The requirements of researchers will generally be less esoteric or sophisticated than the preservation demands posed by the collection itself. Researchers will need prints that are suitable for publication and use in motion-picture films or video productions, as well as slides for audiovisual programs. Some commercial users may request enlargements of historical photographs; these are frequently used in decorating restaurants and offices, for example. In addition to determining whether it is feasible for an in-house lab to have the equipment necessary to meet such requests, the archives must consider whether such oversized formats alter the historical integrity of the photographs, and whether donors would be offended by particular commercial uses.

University of Alaska -Fairbanks

Alaska and Polar Regions Department Rasmuson Library

Photographic Work Order **Date:** ____________

☐ Patron Order ☐ In-House Processing ☐ Donor Obligation (copy project) ☐ Original Photo Assignment

Requested By: ____________ (staff member or patron)

For: ____________ (person or organization)

Contact By: ☐ Visit ☐ Letter ☐ Phone ☐ Internal

Subject/Collection(s)

General Instructions: ____________

Task Codes: ☐ (1)Research ☐ (2)Retrieval ☐ (3)Copying ☐ (4)Process Negatives ☐ (5)Number Negs & 'N' Originals ☐ (6)Printing & Toning ☐ (7)File Negs ☐ (8)Collate Order ☐ (9)Contact w/processing staff ☐ (10)Contact w/patron ☐ (11)Other____________

Task No.	Date:	Time in minutes:	By:	Additional Info:

S.W.

Figure 7–2. This photographic work order was devised for use by an in-house lab and encourages accurate record keeping of staff time spent on various tasks. In some situations, it would be important to allow space for a listing of photographs by image number or other identifier. *Reproduced courtesy of the Alaska and Polar Regions Department, University of Alaska-Fairbanks.*

In addition to basic copy work, special preservation projects may be required, such as copying cellulose nitrate or cellulose diacetate negatives, making a record copy of scrapbooks, or reproducing a collection in microformat. Such projects may be beyond the capability of a modest in-house copy service or local laboratory. If this is the case, it is important to wait until the necessary technical capability is available, rather than proceeding with the work and having it done poorly or improperly. It may be necessary to have such technically demanding work done at a regional conservation center or to hire a firm or a skilled technician to come to the repository to undertake the project.

Archival Copy

The concept of archival copy, which is applied somewhat differently in various situations, should be considered in the context of developing a copy program. The archival copy is the original photographic print or negative (or that closest to the original), which is intended to meet long-term preservation and information needs. In the case of preservation copying of unstable, deteriorating photographs, the reproduction replaces the original and becomes the archival copy. Thus, a copy service must be capable of producing archival copies as well as more expendable photographs to meet the needs of researchers, access files, and other short-term uses. To be considered archival, copies must be processed, stored, and handled according to precise specifications.[1]

The archival copy of every photograph should be protected against excessive use and handling; under optimum conditions it should only be accessed to create a second-generation copy for research and reproduction purposes, although in controlled instances it may be important to use the original for exhibition or publication purposes or to meet specialized needs of qualified researchers. For example, if the repository has negatives for which no prints exist, the lab should be able to make prints from various sizes of both glass and film negatives, which can then serve as the access point to the collection. In such instances, the negative is considered to be the archival copy, and it should be handled as little as possible. Copies also should be made of original prints for which no negatives exist. Such original prints are considered to be the archival copy and, optimally, should not be made available for browsing. These goals will not be completely attainable with a large photographic collection, however, and priorities for copying will have to be established based upon use, condition, and value of the photographs.

---

[1]The following specifications of the American National Standards Institute (ANSI) are pertinent: *Method for Evaluating the Processing of Black and White Photographic Papers with Respect to the Stability of the Resultant Image* (PH4.32-1980); *Methylene Blue Method for Measuring Thiosulfate and Silver Densitometric Method for Measuring Residual Chemicals in Films, Plates, and Papers* (PH4.8-1978); *Practice for Storage of Black and White Photographic Paper Prints* (PH1.48-1982); *Practice for Storage of Processed Safety Photographic Film* (PH1.43-1981); and *Practice for Storage of Processed Photographic Plates* (PH1.45-1981).

Formats

A number of copying options may be employed for various purposes. For preservation copying, the goal is to make an accurate reproduction of the original in order either to reduce handling of the original or to replace the original because it is unstable. In the former instance a xerographic (dry process) copy may suffice, while in the latter case a high-quality archivally processed photographic copy would be required. For exhibition purposes, photographic copies that are true to the original in detail, sharpness, tonal range, and contrast are required. For creating access systems, microreproductions or xerographic copies may be satisfactory. Researchers will most often require photographic reproductions with good contrast and tonal qualities that are suitable for publication. Thus, the specific type of reproduction will depend on use. Options to consider include the following.

Photocopying

Xerographic copies may be used satisfactorily to create access files and to aid off-site researchers in selecting images. Xerographic copies have long-term stability if the carbon image is properly fused onto the paper and if the paper used is permanent and durable. Bond paper with an alkaline reserve that meets conservation standards is available and can be accommodated by many copiers. Image quality varies depending upon the tonal range and contrast of the original print as well as the type of copy machine and its operational characteristics, but the quality of the copies is generally good enough to serve the needs of browsing files. Copying should be done only by trained staff, never by researchers, and some photographs should never be subjected to copying because of their format or physical condition. Prints mounted on boards that are curved or bowed, for example, would be damaged if forced to lie flat on the copy machine's platen. All copying should be undertaken carefully and cautiously.

Microphotography

Microreproduction, while offering the potential for enhancing access, saving space, and protecting original photographs from unnecessary handling, does have limitations. If it is to be done properly with all of the necessary controls and archival processing, it is time-consuming and costly. Collections must first be carefully organized and arranged; filming must be done with frame-by-frame adjustments to assure the best results; and processing must be done to archival standards. High-contrast film is usually used when filming printed matter, while continuous-tone film and appropriate processing is necessary when filming photographs. Frame-by-frame inspection must follow filming, and master negatives must be stored under precise environmental conditions if archival standards are to be met and maintained. Potential drawbacks with microfilm include the fact that it is not readily possible to compare images that are on a reel of film; further, any additions to the collection cannot be readily interfiled sequentially, and mistakes in arrangement are thus not easily corrected. Microfiche, on the other hand, can be updated or corrected fairly easily. If microreproduction is selected as the most desirable copying method for preservation purposes or access systems, qualified technical assistance should be sought, and applicable national standards and governmental specifications should be reviewed.[2]

Photography

Photographic copies comprise the largest category of copy work required, both for preservation activities when the copy is intended to replace the original, and for publication and exhibition purposes. Duplicate and copy negatives, prints and enlargements, as well as slides and transparencies are required most often. The specific range of services required depends on the condition of the photographic holdings as well as the formats and technical processes represented in the collection; research use and administrative requirements also must be considered. Minimally, a copy service should be able to provide the following:

—black-and-white prints, 8″ × 10″, 5″ × 7″, and 4″ × 5″

—copy negatives, 4″ × 5″ and 35-mm

—color transparencies, 4″ × 5″ and 35-mm.

Such capabilities will meet the needs of most researchers as well as administrative requirements for photographic copies to meet preservation, security, access, and outreach goals. Depending upon resources and technical capabilities, basic darkroom work could either be done in-house or sent to outside labs. Since the bulk of the work required is likely to fall within the areas of producing copy negatives and black-and-white prints for publication, it is feasible to set up in-house capabilities to meet these basic needs, while sending color work and enlargements to outside specialists. This approach will result in substantial savings, since the latter work is not only technically demanding but also requires the purchase of expensive darkroom equipment and chemicals that probably will not be used on a regular basis.

Technical Considerations

Factors to consider when selecting the photographic film and format for copy work include size, orientation of the image, stability, cost, and reproduction capabilities. When dealing with original negatives, it is always desirable to make a contact print (or an enlargement, depending upon the size of the negative) in addition to any other end-product

that is deemed necessary. Copy negatives produced from prints should be large enough to retain and reproduce the quality of the original prints. Negatives measuring 4″ × 5″ are the standard size used by most institutions for copy work; the film is exposed sheet by sheet, which can be an advantage for small copy orders. Also, 4″ × 5″ negatives can be contact printed, resulting in a usable print with no need for enlargement for most purposes. It is possible to acquire a good used 4″ × 5″ camera at a very moderate price, often for less than the cost of a 35-mm camera. A less expensive option for copy work is 2¼″ × 3¼″ film. Although image quality is not as good as that provided by 4″ × 5″ negatives, it greatly exceeds 35-mm negatives, and 2¼″ × 3¼″ negatives are acceptable for most requirements. Thirty-five-millimeter film is an acceptable copy film in some instances, although image quality will be poorer than with the other films mentioned. Both 2¼″ × 3¼″ and 35-mm films are roll rather than sheet films, which can be a disadvantage because it is necessary to wait for the entire roll to be shot before processing. However, roll film is more easily and quickly processed, especially by less experienced workers. Thirty-five-millimeter film is fine for certain applications (such as making 5″ × 7″ prints for halftone reproduction), while it is totally unsuitable for others (such as making exhibition quality prints). Of necessity, miniaturization results in some loss of image quality and integrity as a result of size reduction and alteration of original syntax.

Different films are used for copying continuous-tone materials (i.e., photographs) and line work (such as printed matter). The latter present no intermediate tones between the lines (i.e., the printed letters) and the background; such materials should be copied on high-contrast film that will show a sharp differentiation between the dense background and the lines. Handwritten manuscripts and some typewritten documents consist of uneven strokes and lights and darks, and thus must be copied using continuous-tone film such as that used for photographs. In general, Kodak Professional Copy Films and Kodak Commercial Films can be used for continuous-tone copying, but they demand precise exposures and processing. Slow speed, fine grain general purpose films (such as Panatomic X) are acceptable. Experimentation with various films and filters helps to determine what materials will best meet various situations.[3]

The quality of the camera lens used in copying is important. Unlike normal camera work where depth of field is a desirable asset, copy work requires a lens that is designed for a flat field and edge-to-edge definition. A suitable lens is a good investment, both in terms of the quality

[2]ANSI PH1.28-1976 and ANSI PH1.41-1976. Also see: Carolyn Hoover Sung, *Archives & Manuscripts: Reprography* (Chicago: Society of American Archivists, 1982), for a good discussion of technical and administrative aspects of microfilm programs.

[3]For technical information on films for copying, see *Kodak Films: Color and Black and White* (AF-1). Data sheets for each film discuss use, speed, exposure recommendations, and processing requirements. Also see: Robert Alter and Alan Newman, *Guidelines for the Duplication of Early Negatives* (Andover, Mass.: Northeast Document Conservation Center, forthcoming).

of the results and as an aid to efficient focusing by the camera operator.

Filters may be used to good advantage in copy work. Stained original prints may be copied with a panchromatic film, using a filter of approximately the same color as the stain, to remove or reduce stains on the copy print. Filters also can be used to enhance a copy of a faded photograph. Various colored filters should be tried, depending on the photographs to be copied, the film to be used, and the type of light source. For example, a yellow filter will often increase the contrast in copies of faded black-and-white photographs.

Archival processing employs procedures that will assure maximum permanence of photographic materials and relates to the purity of the chemicals used in processing, washing times, and subsequent testing for residual processing chemicals.[4] Archival processing is necessary when photographic copies are made that will replace unstable originals; copy photographs made for research purposes or finding aids, however, are considered to be expendable and do not have to meet such rigid processing specifications. When producing prints of archival quality, it is important to specify traditional fiber-based photographic paper rather than resin-coated (RC) paper.

Physical Condition and Format

To meet preservation concerns, special precautions are required when copying a number of photographic formats and processes. When copying daguerreotypes and other cased images, care must be taken to ensure that no pressure is exerted on fragile cases, causing hinges to break. It is often difficult to get good copies of daguerreotypes because of reflections from the shiny surface of the silvered copper plates; similar problems of reflection must be dealt with when copying dented and scratched tintypes, which offer numerous surfaces for reflecting light. The cover glass on all cased images poses problems with glare and reflection as well. Camera reflections can be controlled, and eliminated to a great degree, by hanging a black velvet or cardboard screen in front of the camera, with a hole cut in the screen to fit the lens barrel. Reflections also can be controlled by using polarizing filters over the light sources and/or the camera lens. Polarizing filters give reliable results and are thus a good investment.

Photographs mounted in scrapbooks and albums pose numerous problems in copying. As with cased images, care must be taken to protect the artifactual value of the albums, and efforts to get good clear copies of the photographs should not endanger the structure of scrapbooks and albums. Besides problems with the booklike structure, brittle paper and boards often must be contended with as well. Book cradles should be used when doing such copywork.

Prints mounted on boards that are bowed or curved must be handled carefully during copying procedures. Often such mounts are very brittle, and they will crack at the slightest exertion of pressure. In such instances, the physical format must be respected and not forced to conform to copy procedures that will cause damage. Such prints should be copied on a horizontal plane, and neither forced flat nor placed in a contact frame. It is unlikely that brittle mounts could bear the strain of being affixed flat to vertical copy boards. An increased depth of field will ensure the overall focus of the copy negatives.

Glass plate negatives, because of their fragility, must be handled very carefully during copying or printing. Cracked plates should be taped to a piece of clean glass to provide support during storage, handling, and copying; broken plates should be secured between two pieces of glass (see Chapter 5, Preservation of Photographic Materials, p.113). Because of the unevenness of much nineteenth-century glass, early glass plate negatives should not be placed in contact frames; the pressure of the frame on the uneven surface of the plate could result in breakage.

There are several options for duplicating cellulose nitrate, cellulose diacetate, and other unstable negatives. The preferred approach is through the interpositive method, whereby a film positive is made from the original negative by contact printing. The negative is placed in contact with a sheet of film, emulsion to emulsion, and exposed to a controlled light source. The film is then processed to archival specifications; the resulting image is a film positive that is exactly the same size as the original negative but laterally reversed. A duplicate negative can then be contact printed from the interpositive. The duplicate negative is thus the same size and has the same lateral orientation as the original negative. The interpositive should be handled as an archival copy and should be used only when another duplicate negative is required. If funds are limited, duplicate negatives can be produced from the interpositives on demand, rather than contact printing the entire collection of film positives en masse.

Copy negatives may be created by making contact prints from cellulose nitrate negatives and then making camera negatives from the prints using 4″ × 5″ or 2¼″ × 3¼″ film. This is a somewhat less desirable approach in terms of image quality, but it is certainly less expensive than the interpositive method. With careful controls, satisfactory results can be achieved.

Previously, many collections of unstable cellulose nitrate negatives were reproduced using Kodak Professional Direct Duplicating Film SO-015. This allows the creation of a negative image directly from the original negative; no interpositive is required. However, conservators are now questioning the stability of Kodak SO-015 both in dark storage and upon exposure to light. While some institutions are experimenting with various exposure times and process-

---

[4]Henry Wilhelm, *Procedures for Processing and Storing Black and White Photographs for Maximum Possible Permanence* (Grinnell, Ia.: East Street Gallery, 1970).

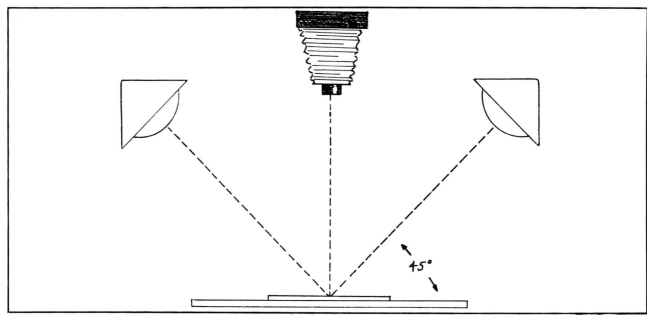

Figure 7–3. A vertical copy set-up, such as that illustrated, is good for copying photographs of a size up to about 20'' × 24''. Illumination is provided by two lights of equal intensity positioned at 45° angles to the axis of the camera. *Drawing by Pamela Spitzmueller.*

ing procedures, which may overcome the problems associated with this film, it is no longer generally recommended for duplicating historical negatives of value.[5]

Useful recommendations on copying techniques and procedures have been published by manufacturers of photographic equipment.[6] These recommendations are generally intended, however, for professional photographers who need practical, speedy, and economical results; they are not recommendations for the field of archival preservation. Thus, when reading the technical literature and implementing the suggested approaches, it is important to first evaluate them against sound archival and conservation practice. For example, the recommendation to dry-mount wrinkled or buckled prints to flatten them before copying is not acceptable in archival contexts. Further, if work is being sent to outside labs, it is likely that photographers and technicians there will proceed according to recommended industry practice, which may not be appropriate for archival materials. Archivists must function as advocates on behalf of the fragile photographic record; they must gain enough technical knowledge to work confidently with technical staff, and they must be able to suggest safe alternatives to standard procedures to protect valuable archival materials during copying and processing.

Setting Up a Copy Room

As noted previously, it is preferable to have an in-house copying facility so that original photographic materials do not have to leave the repository. In general, it is wise to purchase the best equipment possible, as this will prove to be the soundest investment over time. A separate secure area should be designated as the copy room. Security controls are important to protect both the equipment and irreplaceable photographs; access to the copy room should be strictly controlled, with separate keying to prevent casual entry or browsing. Researchers should not have access to the copy room, and only trained and qualified staff members should be allowed to undertake copy work. It is advisable to have the copy room set up on a permanent basis so that it will always be available when needed. The copy room does not have to be large, but it must have light sources that can be controlled. Specific requirements for equipment depend largely on the sizes of the original photographs to be copied and the sizes of requisite copy prints and negatives. A basic copy set-up consists of a camera, camera stand, copy board, and lights to illuminate the object; see figure 7-3 for a suitable arrangement.[7]

Use Policies and Fees

In making photographic collections available for public use, repositories have a number of rights and obligations. The archives should, to the degree possible, determine the copyright status of specific photographic collections and share this information with users. When acquiring new collections, institutions should try to receive copyright or re-

[5]Henry Wilhelm, "Problems With Long-Term Stability of Kodak Professional Direct Duplicating Film," *Picturescope* (Spring, 1982): 24-33.
[6]In particular, see *Copying,* Kodak Professional Data Book M-1 (Rochester, N.Y.: Eastman Kodak Company, 1971). This is no longer in print, but it is available in some public and private libraries.

[7]For further information, see James H. Conrad, *Copying Historical Photographs: Equipment and Methods.* Technical Leaflet 139. (Nashville: American Association for State and Local History, 1981).

Permission is granted for one-time use only. Photographs may not be re-used without the written permission of the State Historical Library. This material may be protected by copyright law (Title 17 U.S. Code).

Figure 7-4. In addition to the above information, prints provided to researchers can be stamped with the required credit line.

production rights from the creator in order to expedite use of the materials. Biographical files on photographers should be maintained to help document collections; birth and death dates and copyright status should be recorded. Ultimately, it is the responsibility of the user to fulfill copyright obligations, but the repository should provide as much data as is feasible to this end. All prints supplied to researchers and publishers should be stamped with copyright information (see figure 7-4), and photographic copy request forms should specify copyright obligations. In addition, it should be made very clear to researchers (and especially to publishers) that purchasing a photographic print does not transfer to them ownership or any rights other than the use specified in the purchase agreement; copyright status is not altered, and the institution neither gives up any rights nor implies that the same image will not be made available to other users. For further information on copyright, see Chapter 6, Legal Issues.

All prints made available to the public should also be stamped with the name of the institution, the name of the collection, the image or file number, and the photographer's name, if known. A statement specifying one-time-use only is also appropriate. Users should be provided with the specific wording of the citation as the institution wishes to see it in print. Once a photograph appears in print, it very likely will be requested again. Supplying the image number in a citation thus reduces the amount of search time required when the image is next requested. The assignment of image numbers, as well as accession numbers, is addressed in Chapter 4, Arrangement and Description.

The institution has the right to specify how its photographs may be used. For example, the archives may require full-frame printing and prohibit cropping or other alteration of the original image. The archives may insist on proper identification of the photograph; captions should accurately date and define the image in terms of event, place, location, persons, etc. If an author or publisher uses a photograph not for its own content but because it is evocative of a related event, this usage should be clearly stated; the cap-

tion should not be misleading. In making photographs available, especially for commercial use, the repository must consider whether the proposed use will offend or invade the privacy of the donor, the persons depicted in the photograph or their relatives, or the community at large.

Despite the fact that some requests to reproduce photographs must be denied because of copyright regulations, privacy rights, or donor-imposed restrictions, photographic collections should be open to all researchers on an equal basis. The practice of allowing preferred access or closing collections to benefit an individual researcher can open an institution to censure by other institutions and by the scholarly community. Repositories should resist pressure to participate in such actions that may be exerted by influential donors, board members, or scholars. The access policies adopted by the institution must be implemented uniformly; collections that are closed until they can be accessioned or until preservation copying can be undertaken should remain closed to all until the necessary work can be completed, and not opened under duress or at the whim of the curator.

Forms

Regulations governing the photographic copy service should be clearly spelled out on copy request forms. Two-sided forms are ideal: space for patron information and the copy order is on one side, and rules and regulations are on the other. Researchers should be required to read the regulations governing publication and use of photographic materials and to sign a statement to indicate their compliance. A request form with a carbon copy allows both the researcher and the institution to have a record of the transaction, including the specific images reproduced and their format. The researcher retains a signed copy of the request form and therefore has a reminder of the provisions agreed upon. (See figure 7-5 for a sample photographic copy request form.) Researchers should understand that on occasion requests for copies of photographs may be denied because of copyright regulations or physical condition of the images.

In addition to the request form, a specific list of available services should be prepared. This should indicate format and size as well as the reproduction fee. Most institutions do not release negatives to researchers or publishers, and if a copy negative must be created in order to make available a positive print, the researcher is charged for, but not given, the copy negative. This policy, while sometimes disputed by researchers, is a means of maintaining control over the collection and also helps to build the file of copy negatives. The cost of the copy negative may be listed as a service charge, but, however, the issue is resolved, researchers should be clearly informed that they will not be provided with negatives.

The archives must decide whether it will permit researchers to purchase and keep photographic copies, or whether

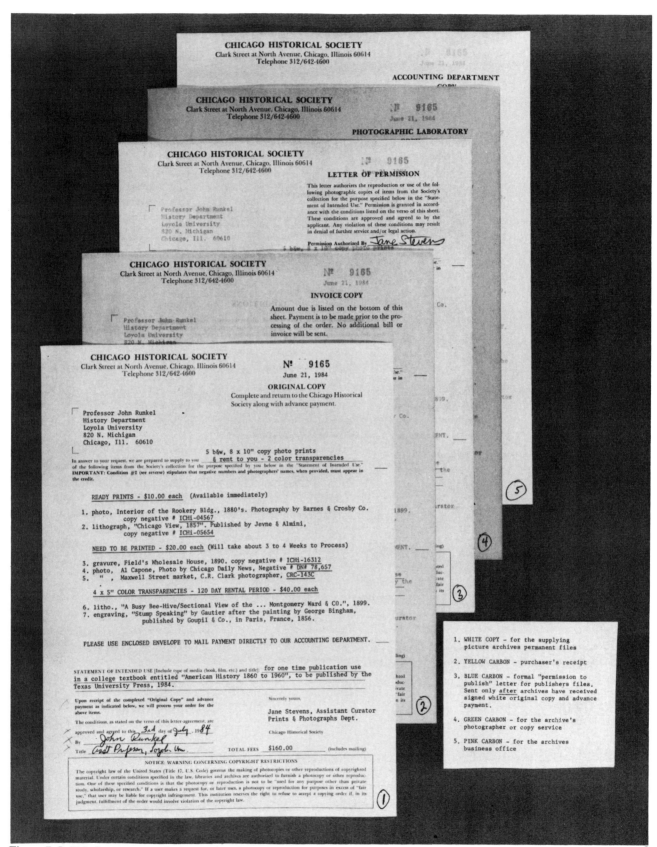

Figure 7–5. This form serves as both a work order and a contract. It is a permanent record of the transaction, meets accounting needs, conveys permission to publish the photographic materials, and specifies required captions. *Reproduced courtesy of the Chicago Historical Society.*

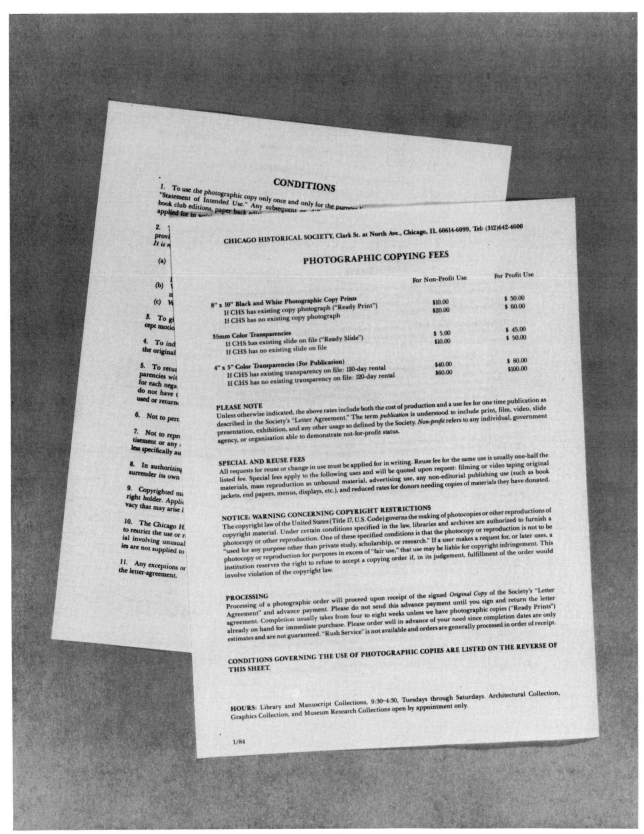

Figure 7–6. This schedule lists fees for both non-profit and for-profit users; conditions of use are printed on the verso. *Reproduced courtesy of the Chicago Historical Society.*

copies will be lent only for a specified purpose and time period. If the copy is sold, the fee charged is a copying fee; while if the copy is lent, the fee is a borrowing fee. In determining policy on this matter, the benefits of maintaining tight control over copies·of collection materials by requesting their return must be weighed against the amount of staff time and energy required to retrieve the materials. The goodwill of patrons also should be considered. Many patrons feel that they have a right to retain the copy in return for the fee paid, and other researchers will want the privilege of retaining the print for its study or association value. The policy's potential impact, beneficial or damaging, on the collecting program also should be considered.

Copy request forms should be kept by the institution as an aid to determining whether or not researchers have complied with appropriate use regulations, as well as for statistical purposes. Monitoring is time-consuming, but it is an important means of evaluating the use and the strengths of the collection. Compilation of an ongoing record of photographs used in specific publications, by the media, and in audiovisual presentations helps to convince administrators of the collection's value and use and of the contributions it makes to scholarship and public service. To assist in the process of monitoring use and record keeping, the institution should require that researchers and publishers submit one copy of every publication in which a photograph from the archives appears. As an alternative, a set of tear sheets showing how the photograph was used and the title page could be requested. Such provisions greatly simplify monitoring for correct citations, captions, and usage. If it is discovered that researchers have not properly complied with the regulations, the most feasible recourse is to deny future access to the collections. Most institutions do not wish to file lawsuits, except in the most flagrant cases of abuse when great treasures or large sums of money are involved.

Fees

The fee schedule established for reproductions should reflect laboratory and related costs. Specific fees vary depending upon the type of institution and whether copying services are provided in-house or contractually by an outside lab. Forms listing established fees and the range of services offered should be available for distribution (see figure 7-6). In addition to the actual copying fee, some institutions charge a service fee for staff time devoted to selecting pictures, making xerographic copies, etc. Generally, a modest amount of time is devoted without charge to filling researchers' requests, but search time beyond a thirty-minute limit is often billed at current research rates. This is not unrealistic, given the limited staff of most archival repositories, the numbers of researchers they must serve, and the generally massive backlog of archival tasks to be completed. Further, many of the patrons of major

photographic collections are paid picture researchers, and it is only fair that they (or their publishers) pay for special services rendered. Institutions should allow a realistic span of time between the date a copy order is placed and the promised date of completion. If rush orders are accepted, rush fees are commonly assessed. These may either be posted at a flat rate or figured as a percentage of the total order.

In addition to copying, service, and rush fees, many institutions charge use fees each time one of their photographs is used for publication or similar purpose. The issue of use fees in the context of archival collections is a thorny one that has not yet been fully resolved by the profession. The appropriateness of assessing use fees depends in large part on the nature of the institution, its mission, and its stated goals. Some public institutions by law cannot charge use fees. Collection of such fees, however, can in some instances accrue to the benefit of the photographic collection to meet preservation and related goals. The assessment and allotment of fees should be determined by the governing body of the institution. It is generally agreed that flexibility is important in assigning use fees so that the various categories of patrons—students, scholars, non-profit organizations, as well as commercial users—will all have equal access to the materials and pay a fair share of the expense of maintaining the collection in exchange for the privilege of using it.

Appendix A
Glossary

This brief glossary includes definitions of photographic terms as well as a number of archival concepts. Definitions of specific photographic processes are included in the text and may be reached by consulting the index. For further information, see Bernard Edward Jones, *Encyclopedia of Photography* (New York: Arno Press, 1974); and *A Glossary of Photographic Terms* (Rochester: Eastman Kodak Company, Publication No. AA-9, 1980). For definitions of archival terms, see Frank B. Evans, *et al., A Basic Glossary for Archivists, Manuscript Curators, and Records Managers* (Chicago: Society of American Archivists, 1974).

alkaline reserve Buffer or reserve of an alkaline substance added to paper to counteract acid. Usually 3 percent precipitated calcium or magnesium carbonate by weight of paper.

archival processing Photographic processing procedures designed to result in maximum permanence and stability of negatives and prints through a series of precise fixing, washing, and toning baths. Differs from ordinary processing by reducing the fixing time (and thus the retention of residual chemicals). Following thorough washing, photographs are treated with a gold solution or a toner, such as selenium. Archival processing requires the use of fiber-based rather than resin-coated papers. Archival processing alone will not insure archival quality; adherence to precise storage and handling procedures (as specified by the American National Standards Institute) is also required.

archives 1) The noncurrent records of an organization or institution preserved because of their continuing value; see also COLLECTION. 2) The agency responsible for selecting, preserving, and making available archival materials.

cellulose triacetate Safety film; used as a film base and also as a storage enclosure for photographic materials.

collection A group of photographs, manuscripts, or papers having a common source. A collection may also be formed artificially by accumulating photographs or other materials concerning particular events, people, or topics. See ARCHIVES.

contact print A print made by exposing photographic paper to a light source while it is in direct contact against the negative. Since there is no magnification, the print is the same size as the negative.

contrast Density range of a negative, print, or transparency. A photograph that has sharp blacks and whites with little gradation of gray tones in between has high contrast.

copy film Film used for copying photographic materials. Fine-grain, continuous-tone film is suitable for much copy work, although specific copying requirements must be matched against the capabilities of various copy films. Film data sheets that provide technical specifications are available from film manufacturers.

copy negative Negative made by rephotographing a photographic print for the purpose of reproduction or enlargement.

copy print Print made from a copy negative.

cropping Printing only part of the image that appears in the negative. During printing, the enlarger or the paper easel is adjusted so that only the desired part of the image is visible within the frame; the original photograph is not physically altered. Cropping is a technique often employed by publishers and editors to enhance the visual impact of photographs. Since cropping marks and instructions are often written directly on prints, original photographs should never be lent for publication purposes.

definition

Overall sharpness of image produced by lens and film. The impression of clarity of detail perceived when viewing a photograph.

density

Measure of the ability of a photograph to transmit light; determined by the density of the silver grains. The dark areas in a photograph are densest; thus, the dark areas in a negative transmit less light and the black areas in a print reflect less light.

direct positive

Unique photograph for which there is no negative; image is laterally reversed but tonal range correctly approximates object photographed. A tintype is an example of a direct positive image.

duplicate negative

Exact replica of a negative made via an optical system or contact printing using direct duplicating negative film or the interpositive method. See COPY NEGATIVE and INTERPOSITIVE.

emulsion

Liquid throughout which finely divided grains of a light-sensitive material (most often silver halides) are dispersed and in which they remain suspended without dissolving. For both prints and negatives, liquids commonly used as emulsions have been gelatin, collodion, and albumen.

enlargement

A photographic print that is larger than the negative; made by projecting an image of the negative through a lens onto a photographic paper.

ferrotype

Glazing, or the appearance of shiny patches, on the gelatin surface of photographs. Brought about by contact with smooth surface, particularly plastic enclosures or glass, under conditions of high relative humidity. If photographs are stored in plastic enclosures under pressure (i.e., in a stack), ferrotyping can occur at moderate levels of relative humidity.

fixer

Sodium thiosulphate, commonly called "hypo." Used in processing to cause photographic materials to lose their sensitivity to light by dissolving the silver halides. Image will continue to darken if not properly fixed.

glassine

A glazed, semi-transparent paper often used to make envelopes and sleeves for storing photographs. Usually acidic; hygroscopic.

grain

The clusters of light-sensitive silver halides in a negative that are changed into black metallic silver by development. The grain becomes more apparent in a print when the negative is enlarged. Generally, the more sensitive (i.e., faster) films have more grain than less sensitive (i.e., slower) films.

halftone

Photomechanical process for reproducing continuous-tone photographs. Printed with one color of ink, the halftone process gives the appearance of blacks, whites, and grays by converting the image into a pattern of clearly defined dots of varying sizes. The halftone process creates the illusion of tone gradation. The largest dots appear darkest and are in the shadow areas of the image, while the smallest dots seem lightest and represent the highlight areas. Intermediate sized dots reproduce the various middle tones of gray in a photograph.

hygroscopic

Able to absorb or emit moisture in response to changes in the relative humidity.

hypo

Sodium thiosulphate used for fixing photographic images. See FIXER.

interpositive

Film positive made from a negative by contact printing or through an optical system (i.e., camera or enlarger). Duplicate negatives can be made from the interpositive. See COPY NEGATIVE and DUPLICATE NEGATIVE.

latent image

An image contained on film or paper prior to development. A negative exposed to light in a camera or a print exposed under a negative contains an invisible image referred to as a latent image. The image is made visible by chemical development.

lateral reversal

An image that has been reversed from left to right, as in a mirror image. Many direct positive images, such as daguerreotypes and tintypes, are laterally reversed images. A camera negative is normally laterally reversed (as well as inverted) and is reoriented correctly in the printing process.

negative
Developed film that contains a reversed-tone image of the original object. Light areas of the image are represented by heavy or dark deposits of silver, and the dark portions are light or transparent. When negatives are printed on paper or film, positive images are produced in which the tone values are similar to what they were on the original object.

neutral pH
Exhibiting neither acid nor base (alkaline) qualities; 7.0 on the pH scale. Paper and board stock with a neutral pH are recommended as a storage material for photographic materials.

original negative
The negative exposed in the camera from which subsequent original prints are made. See COPY NEGATIVE and DUPLICATE NEGATIVE.

original print
Print made from an original negative and contemporary with the time the photograph was made. See COPY PRINT.

oxidation
Chemical reaction that converts an element into its oxide; to combine with oxygen. Image silver can react chemically with oxidizing agents, resulting in the discoloration of photographs.

polarity
The characteristic of being either a positive or negative image. Some photographic materials reverse polarity of the object photographed (a camera negative changes a positive image to negative, regular printing paper changes a negative image to a positive). Others will maintain polarity (slides produce a positive image from a positive, direct duplicating film normally is used to produce a negative from a negative but can also produce a positive from a positive). See NEGATIVE and POSITIVE.

polyester
Flexible transparent plastic sheeting made of polyethylene terephthlate. Sold under a variety of trade names, including Mylar®, Melinex®, and Scotchpar®. When formulated with no coatings or additives, it is inert and chemically stable. Used as a film base, to make storage sleeves for prints and negatives, and to encapsulate documents.

polyethylene
Chemically inert translucent thermoplastic that has a low melting point. Suitable as enclosures for photographs when made with no surface coatings or additives.

positive
The characteristic of having the same tonal values (either black-and-white or color) as the object originally photographed. See NEGATIVE.

syntax
Term used by William Ivins in his seminal work, *Prints and Visual Communication* (1953), to denote the physical and technical characteristics, and consequently the informational possibilities, of various print mediums, including photographs.

tonal range
Number of precisely measured gradients of gray that photographic materials (prints and negatives) are capable of producing between black and white.

transparency
Color or black-and-white film positive, viewed or projected by transmitted light (i.e., light shining through film). A slide is a transparency.

Appendix B
Bibliography

This selected bibliography is intended to serve as a basic introduction to the literature of photography for archivists, librarians, and curators of photographic materials. The articles, books, journals, and newsletters cited will provide useful information for planning programs to administer photographic collections. Subjects covered in the readings include preservation, legal issues, publication, exhibition, arrangement, description, and research use. The scope and character of the photographic record is treated in readings that discuss photographs from technological, historical, artistic, and sociological perspectives.

The literature on photography is broad and encompasses many disciplines. Once the basic literature, as represented by this bibliography, is mastered, further sources should be sought. Such fields as American studies, fine arts, sociology, anthropology, and museology all have potential and are well worth investigating.

Articles and Books

Achenbaum, W. Andrew, and Peggy Ann Kuznerz. *Images of Old Age in America, 1790 to the Present*. Ann Arbor: University of Michigan, Institute of Gerontology, 1977.

Albright, Gary. "Photographs." In *Conservation in the Library: A Handbook of Use and Care of Traditional and Nontraditional Materials*, edited by Susan Swartzburg, 79–102. Westport, Conn.: Greenwood Press, 1983.

Alter, Robert, and Alan Newman. *Guidelines for the Duplication of Early Negatives*. Andover, Mass.: Northeast Document Conservation Center, forthcoming.

American National Standards Institute. *Method for Evaluating the Processing of Black and White Photographic Papers with Respect to the Stability of the Resultant Image*. PH4.32-1980. New York: ANSI, 1980.

————. *Method for Manual Processing of Black and White Photographic Films, Plates, and Papers*. PH4.29-1975; reaffirmed 1980. New York: ANSI, 1975.

————. *Methylene Blue Method for Measuring Thiosulfate and Silver Densitometric Method for Measuring Residual Chemicals in Films, Plates, and Papers*. PH4.8-1978. New York: ANSI, 1978.

————. *Practice for Storage of Black and White Photographic Paper Prints*. PH1.48-1982. New York: ANSI, 1982.

————. *Practice for Storage of Processed Safety Photographic Film*. PH1.43-1981. New York: ANSI, 1981.

————. *Practice for Storage of Processed Photographic Plates*. PH1.45-1981. New York: ANSI, 1981.

————. *Requirements for Photographic Filing Enclosures for Storing Processed Photographic Films, Plates, and Papers*. PH1.53-1978. New York: ANSI, 1978.

————. *Specifications for Photographic Film for Archival Records, Silver-Gelatin Type, on Polyester Base*. PH1.41-1981. New York: ANSI, 1981.

Arnheim, Rudolf. *Visual Thinking*. Berkeley: University of California Press, 1969.

Askins, Barbara S., *et al.* "A Nuclear Chemistry Technique for Restoring Faded Photographic Images." *American Archivist* 41 (1978): 207–13.

Barger, M. Susan, comp. *Bibliography of Photographic Processes in Use Before 1880: Their Materials, Processing, and Conservation*. Rochester, N.Y.: Graphic Arts Research Center, Rochester Institute of Technology, 1980.

Barger, M. Susan. "Daguerreotype Care." *Picturescope* 31 (1983): 15–16.

Barger, M. Susan, S. V. Krishnaswamy, and R. Messier. "The Cleaning of Daguerreotypes: Comparison of Cleaning Methods." *The Journal of the American Institute for Conservation* 22 (1982): 13–24.

Betz, Elisabeth, comp. *Graphic Materials: Rules for Describing Original Items and Historical Collections*. Washington, D.C.: Library of Congress, 1982.

Betz, Elisabeth. *Subject Headings Used in the Library of Congress Prints and Photographs Division*. Washington, D.C.: Library of Congress, 1980.

Bohem, Hilda. "A Seam-Free Envelope for Archival Storage of Photographic Negatives." *American Archivist* 38 (1975): 403–05.

Brannan, Beverly W. "Copyright and Photography Collections." *Picturescope* 29 (1981): 14–19.

Browne, Turner, and Elaine Partnow. *Macmillan Biographical Encyclopedia of Photographic Artists and Innovators*. New York: Macmillan, 1984.

Calhoun, J. M. "Storage of Nitrate Amateur Still Camera Film Negatives." *Journal of the Biological Photographic Association* 21 (1953): 1–13.

Casterline, Gail Farr. *Archives and Manuscripts: Exhibits*. Chicago: Society of American Archivists, 1980.

Chernoff, George, and H. Sarbin. *Photography and the Law*. New York: Amphoto, 1977.

Coe, Brian. *Color Photography: The First Hundred Years, 1840–1940*. London: Ash & Grant, Ltd., 1978.

Conrad, James H. *Copying Historical Photographs: Equipment and Methods*. Technical Leaflet 139. Nashville: American Association for State and Local History, 1981.

Crawford, William. *Keepers of Light: A History and Working Guide to Early Photographic Processes*. Dobbs Ferry, N.Y.: Morgan and Morgan, 1979.

Croy, O. R. *Camera Copying and Reproduction*. London and New York: The Focal Press, 1964.

Darrah, William C. *Cartes de Visites in Nineteenth Century Photography*. Gettysburg, Pa.: William C. Darrah, 1981.

_____ . *Stereo Views. A History of Stereographs in America and Their Collection*. Gettysburg, Pa.: Times and News Publishing Co., 1964.

Eastman Kodak Company. *Preservation of Photographs*. Kodak Publication #F-30. Rochester, N.Y.: Eastman Kodak Company, 1979.

Eder, Josef Maria. *History of Photography*. Translated by Edward Epstean. New York: Columbia University Press, 1945. Reprint. Dover Publications, 1972.

Eskind, Andrew, and Deborah Barsel. "International Museum of Photography: Conventions for Cataloging Photographs." *Image* 21 (1978): 1–31.

Frassanito, William A. *Antietam: The Photographic Legacy of America's Bloodiest Day*. New York: Charles Scribner's Sons, 1978.

_____ . *Gettysburg: A Journey in Time*. New York: Charles Scribner's Sons, 1975.

_____ . *Grant and Lee: The Virginia Campaigns, 1864–1865*. New York: Charles Scribner's Sons, 1983.

Gear, James L., R. H. MacClaren, and M. McKiel. "Film Recovery of Some Deteriorated Black and White Negatives." *American Archivist* 40 (1977): 363–68.

Gernsheim, Helmut and Alison, *The History of Photography from the Camera Obscura to the Modern Era*. New York: McGraw-Hill, 1969.

Gill, Arthur T. *Photographic Processes: A Glossary and A Chart for Recognition*. Museums Association Information Sheet No. 21. London: Museums Association, 1978.

Hall, Edward T. *The Hidden Dimension*. Garden City, N.J.: Doubleday, 1966.

Haller, Margaret. *Collecting Old Photographs*. New York: Arco, 1978.

Haynes, Ric. "A Temporary Method to Stabilize Deteriorating Cellulose Nitrate Still Camera Negatives." *PhotographiConservation* 2 (1980): 1–3.

_____ . "Emergency Storage for Nitrate Films." *History News* 36 (January, 1981): 38–41.

Hendriks, Klaus B. "Archival Processing." *Canadian Photography* 7:12 (1977): 22–25, 32.

_____ . "The Conservation of Photographic Materials." *Picturescope* 30 (Spring, 1982): 4–11.

_____ . "The Preservation of Photographic Records." *Archivaria* 5 (Winter, 1977–78): 92–100.

_____ . *The Preservation and Restoration of Photographic Materials in Archives and Libraries: A RAMP Study with Guidelines*. Paris: UNESCO, 1984.

Hendriks, Klaus B., and Brian Lesser. "Disaster Preparedness and Recovery: Photographic Materials." *American Archivist* 46 (1983): 52–68.

Hurley, F. Jack. *Portrait of a Decade: Roy Stryker and the Development of Documentary Photography in the Thirties*. Baton Rouge: Louisiana State University Press, 1972.

Irvine, Betty Jo. *Slide Libraries: A Guide for Academic Institutions, Museums and Special Collections*. Littleton, Colo.: Libraries Unlimited, 1979.

Ivins, William. *Prints and Visual Communication*. Cambridge, Mass.: Harvard University Press, 1953.

Jammes, André, and Eugenia Perry Janis. *The Art of French Calotype: With a Critical Dictionary of Photographers, 1845–1870*. Princeton, N.J.: Princeton University Press, 1983.

Jenkins, Reese V. *Images and Enterprise Technology and the American Photographic Industry, 1839–1925*. Baltimore: Johns Hopkins University Press, 1975.

Jones, Bernard Edward, ed. *Encyclopedia of Photography*. New York: Arno Press, 1974. Reprint of 1911 edition of *Cassell's Cyclopaedia of Photography*.

Jussim, Estelle. *Visual Communication and the Graphic Arts*. New York: Bowker, 1974.

Kach, David. "Photographic Dilemma: Stability and Storage of Color Materials." *Industrial Photographer* 278 (August, 1978): 28–29, 46–50.

Keefe, Lawrence, E., Jr., and Dennis Inch. *The Life of a Photograph*. Boston: Butterworth, 1984.

Lessard, Elizabeth. *Cyanotypes: A Modern Use for an Old Technique*. Technical Leaflet 133. Nashville: American Association for State and Local History, 1980.

Lesy, Michael. *Wisconsin Death Trip*. New York: Pantheon, 1973.

Lewis, Karen R. *A Manual for the Visual Collections of the Harvard University Archives*. Cambridge: Harvard University Library, 1981.

Lyons, Nathan. *Photographers on Photography*. Englewood Cliffs, N.J.: Prentice-Hall, Inc., 1966.

Mathews, Oliver. *Early Photographs and Early Photographers*. New York: Pitman, 1973.

McQuaid, James, ed. *Index to American Photographic Collections*. Boston: G. K. Hall, 1982.

Moor, Ian. "The Ambrotype: Research into Its Restoration and Conservation, Part 1." *The Paper Conservator* 1 (1976): 22–25.

_____ . "The Ambrotype: Research into Its Restoration and Conservation, Part 2." *The Paper Conservator* 2 (1977): 36–43.

Munoff, Gerald J. "Dr. Robert Peter and Kentucky's Photographic Legacy." *The Register of the Kentucky Historical Society* 78 (1980): 208–18.

Naef, Weston, and James N. Wood. *Era of Exploration: The Rise of Landscape Photography in the American West, 1860–1885*. Boston: New York Graphic Society, 1975.

Newhall, Beaumont. *The Daguerreotype in America*. Greenwich, Conn.: New York Graphic Society, 1968 (revised edition).

———— . *The History of Photography from 1839 to the Present Day*. New York: Museum of Modern Art, 1982.

Norris, Debbie Hess. "The Proper Storage and Display of a Photographic Collection." *Picturescope* 31 (Spring, 1983): 4–10.

Orraca, José. "The Care of Glass Plate Negatives." *The Smith & Telfer Photographic Collection of the New York State Historical Association*. Cooperstown, N.Y.: New York State Historical Association, 1978.

Ostroff, Eugene. "Conserving and Restoring Photographic Collections." *Museum News* (May–December, 1974).

———— . "Rescuing Nitrate Negatives." *Museum News* 57 (September–October, 1978): 34–42.

———— . "Restoration of Photographs by Neutron Activation." *Science* 154 (October 7, 1966): 119–23.

Parker, William. "Everett A. Scholfield (1843–1930): A General Research Report." *Afterimage* 4 (1976): 22–23.

Peters, Marsha, and Bernard Mergen, "Doing the Rest: The Uses of Photographs in American Studies." *American Quarterly* 29 (1977): 280–303.

Picture Sources 4. Edited by Ernest H. Robl. New York: Special Libraries Association, 1983.

Porter, Mary Kay. "Filing Enclosures for Black and White Negatives." *Picturescope* 29 (Fall, 1981): 108.

Reilly, James. M. "Albumen Prints: A Summary of New Research." *Picturescope* 30 (Spring, 1982): 34–37.

———— . *Photographic Prints of the Nineteenth Century: Care and Identification*. Rochester, N.Y.: Eastman Kodak Company, forthcoming.

———— . *The Albumen and Salted Paper Book: The History and Practice of Photographic Printing, 1840–1895*. Rochester, N.Y.: Light Impressions Corp., 1980.

Rempel, Siegfried. *The Care of Black and White Photographic Collections: Cleaning and Stabilization*. Canadian Conservation Institute Technical Bulletin 9. Ottawa: Canadian Conservation Institute, 1980.

———— . *The Care of Black and White Photographic Collections: Identification of Processes*. Canadian Conservation Institute Technical Bulletin 6. Ottawa: Canadian Conservation Institute, 1979.

———— . "A Conservation Method for Nitrate Based Photographic Materials." *The Paper Conservator* 2 (1977): 44–46.

Rinhart, Floyd and Marion. *The American Daguerreotype*. Athens, Ga.: University of Georgia Press, 1981.

———— . *American Miniature Case Art*. New York: Barnes, 1969.

Ritzenthaler, Mary Lynn. *Archives & Manuscripts: Conservation: A Manual on Physical Care and Management*. Chicago: Society of American Archivists, 1983.

Rudisill, Richard. *Mirror Image: The Influence of the Daguerreotype on American Society*. Albuquerque, N.M.: University of New Mexico Press, 1971.

Shaw, Renata V. "Picture Organization: Practices and Procedures, Parts 1 and 2." *Special Libraries* 63: 10 and 11 (1972): 448–56, 502–06.

Storing, Handling, and Preserving Polaroid Photographs: A Guide. Cambridge, Mass.: Polaroid, 1983.

Swan, Alice. "Conservation of Photographic Print Collections." *Library Trends* 30 (Fall, 1981): 267–96.

———— . "Conservation Treatment for Photographs: A Review of Some of the Problems, Literature and Practices." *Image* 21 (June, 1978): 24–31.

Swedlund, Charles. *Photography: A Handbook of History, Materials, and Processes*. New York: Holt, Rinehart and Winston, 1974.

Szarkowski, John. *The Photographer's Eye*. New York: Museum of Modern Art, 1966.

Talbot, George. *At Home: Domestic Life in the Post-Centennial Era, 1876–1920*. Madison, Wis.: State Historical Society of Wisconsin, 1976.

Taft, Robert. *Photography and the American Scene: A Social History, 1839–1889*. New York: Macmillan, 1938. Reprint. Dover Publications, 1964.

Time-Life Books. *Caring for Photographs: Display, Storage, Restoration*. Rev. ed. Life Library of Photography. Alexandria, Va.: Time-Life Books, 1982.

———— . *Color*. Rev. ed. Life Library of Photography. Alexandria, Va.: Time-Life Books, 1983.

Vanderbilt, Paul. "On Photographic Archives." *Afterimage* 4 (September, 1976): 8–15.

Viskochil, Larry A. "The Elephant That Never Forgets." *Chicago at the Turn of the Century in Photographs*, ix-xv. New York: Dover Publications, Inc., 1984.

Wakeman, Geoffrey. *Victorian Book Illustration: The Technical Revolution*. Newton Abbot, England: David and Charles, Ltd., 1973.

Wall, E. J. *Dictionary of Photography*. London: Iliffe and Sons, n.d. (10th edition).

Weinstein, Robert A., and Larry Booth. *Collection, Use, and Care of Historical Photographs*. Nashville: American Association for State and Local History, 1977.

Welling, William. *Collector's Guide to Nineteenth Century Photographs*. New York: Collier Books, 1976.

———— . *Photography in America: The Formative Years, 1839–1900*. New York: Crowell, 1978.

Wilhelm, Henry. "Color Print Instability." *Modern Photography* 43 (February, 1979): 92 ff.

———— . "Color Print Instability: A Problem for Collectors and Photographers." *Afterimage* 6 (October, 1978): 11–13.

———— . "Problems with Long Term Stability of Kodak Professional Direct Duplicating Film." *Picturescope* 30 (Spring, 1982): 24–33.

———— . *Procedures for Processing and Storing Black and White Photographs for Maximum Possible Permanence*. Grinnell, Ia: East Street Gallery, 1970.

_____ . "Storing Color Materials: Frost-Free Refrigerators Offer a Low Cost Solution." *Industrial Photographer* 27 (October, 1978): 32–35.

Witkin, Lee D., and Barbara London. *The Photograph Collector's Guide*. Boston: New York Graphic Society, 1979.

Witteborg, Lothar P. *Good Show! A Practical Guide for Temporary Exhibitions*. Washington, D.C.: Smithsonian Institution, 1981.

Newsletters and Journals

The titles cited are either devoted entirely to photographs or contain pertinent articles on a regular basis, as well as notices of conferences, seminars, and new publications.

AIC Newsletter and *Journal of the AIC*. Publications of the American Institute for Conservation of Historic and Artistic Works, 3545 Williamsburg Lane, N.W., Washington, DC 20008.

ASPP Newsletter. American Society of Picture Professionals, Box 5283, Grand Central Station, New York, NY 10017.

The Abbey Newsletter: Bookbinding and Conservation. c/o Conservation Department, Brigham Young University Library, 6216 HBLL, Provo, Utah 84602.

Afterimage. Visual Studies Workshop, 4 Elton Street, Rochester, NY 14607.

The American Archivist. Quarterly journal of the Society of American Archivists, 600 S. Federal, Suite 504, Chicago, IL 60605.

Archivaria. The journal of the Association of Canadian Archivists. School of Librarianship, University of British Columbia, 1956 Main Hall, Vancouver, B.C. V6T 1W5, Canada. Volume 5 (Winter 1977–78) is a theme issue devoted to historical photographs.

Conservation Administration News (CAN). University of Tulsa, McFarlin Library, 600 South College Avenue, Tulsa, OK 74104.

History News. American Association for State and Local History, 708 Berry Road, Nashville, TN 37204.

Image. International Museum of Photography, George Eastman House, Rochester, NY 14607.

Picturescope. Quarterly Bulletin of the Picture Division, Special Libraries Association, P.O. Box 50119, F Street Station, Tariff Commission Bldg., Washington, DC 20004. The Spring 1982 issue is devoted to conservation of photographs.

PhotographiConservation. Graphic Arts Research Center, Rochester Institute of Technology, One Lomb Memorial Drive, Rochester, NY 14623.

Studies in Visual Communication. Annenberg School of Communications, University of Pennsylvania, 3620 Walnut Street, Philadelphia, PA 19104.

Technology and Conservation. The Technology Organization, Inc., One Emerson Place, Boston, MA 02114.

Appendix C
Supplies for the Care and Storage of Photographic Materials

This list contains basic supplies needed to examine and store photographic materials; use is briefly noted when necessary. Devices for monitoring environmental conditions are also included. Suppliers' and manufacturers' names and addresses are provided at the end of the list; please refer to the appropriate reference number. While the list of suppliers is extensive, it is not definitive. Inclusion in the list does not signify SAA endorsement, nor does exclusion indicate censure.

Item	Use	Source
Air bulb	surface dusting	21
Blotting paper, white (32″ × 40″, neutral pH)	work surface, flattening	17,24,31
Board		
Lig-free®	support for glass plates	5
Museum board (neutral pH) 2-ply and 4-ply	and brittle mounted prints, constructing mats	5,17,24,31
Boxes (polypropylene)	stereocard storage	17
Boxes (with an alkaline reserve) Document cases, clamshell, drop-front, etc.	print and negative storage	5,11,15,17,22 28,31
Brushes	surface dusting	
Camel's hair		17,21
Oriental		1,28
Cabinets, metal with baked enamel finish	lantern and 35-mm slide storage	17
Cellulose triacetate sleeves	print and negative storage	7,21
Environmental monitoring equipment		
Gas detector kits		3
Humidicator paper		4,17
Hydrogen sulfide indicator cards		19
Hygrometer		3,8,26
Hygrothermograph		3,8,26
Light meter		
Ultraviolet		18
Visible		21
Sling Psychrometer		17,26,29
Sulfur dioxide test papers		10
Thermometer		8,26
Water Alert®		31
Erasers, Magic Rub®, vinyl	cleaning mounts	2,28
Filmoplast® tape	rebinding lantern slides, adhering glass plate negatives to supports	17,28
Folders (with an alkaline reserve)	print and negative storage	5,11,15,17, 22,28,31

Item	Use	Source
Garbage cans, plastic (one large and one small in one of the following combinations: 45 gal. and 20 gal. or 32 gal. and 10 gal.)	humidity chamber	14
Glass Window, clear white (various sizes)	replacing cover glass, support for glass plate negatives	12
Plate (32″ × 40″ × ½″, smoothed edges)	work surface	
Gloves, white cotton	handling photographs	17,21,28
Light table	examining negatives and transparencies	17,21
Magnifiers hand-held (3x to 10x), linen tester (5x), loupe (8x to 10x)	examination	4,17,28
Map cases	oversized storage	13,31
Microspatula (stainless steel)	disassembly of cased photographs	4,28
Paper enclosures (neutral pH) Envelopes, sleeves, folders	print and negative storage	5,17,28,31
Paper, Japanese (Kozo)	rebinding lantern slides	1,24,28
Photo corners, polyester	mounting	17,31
Pliers, nipping	frame disassembly	14
Polyester Sleeves and folders Sheets	print and negative storage interleaving	5,6,11,15,16, 17,20,28,30,31
Polyethylene sleeves and pockets	print, negative, and slide storage	17,23
Polypropylene sleeves and pockets	print, negative, and slide storage	9,17
Syringe	surface dusting	21
Tissue paper (neutral pH)	interleaving, wrapping	24,28,31
Tubes, wide diameter (neutral pH)	rolling oversized prints	31
Ultraviolet (UV) filtering shields Filtering sleeves for fluorescent tubes		5,17,27
Low UV emission fluorescent tubes		32
Plexiglas® UF3, sheets		17,25

1. Aiko's Art Materials Import
   714 North Wabash
   Chicago, Illinois 60611
   (312-943-0475)

2. Art supply store

3. Bendix Corporation
   National Environment Instruments Division
   P.O. Box 520, Pilgrim Station
   Warwick, Rhode Island 02888

4. Conservation Materials, Ltd.
   340 Freeport Boulevard
   Box 2884
   Sparks, Nevada 89431
   (702-331-0582)

5. Conservation Resources International, Inc.
   8000 H Forbes Place
   Springfield, Virginia 22151
   (703-321-7730)

6. E. I. DuPont de Nemours & Co., Inc.
   Fabrics and Finishes Department
   Industrial Products Division
   Wilmington, Delaware 19898

7. Eastman Kodak Company
   Rochester, New York 14650

8. Fisher Scientific Company
   711 Forbes Avenue
   Pittsburgh, Pennsylvania 15219
   (412-562-8300)
   (check telephone directory for local distributors)

9. Franklin Distributors Corporation
   P.O. Box 320
   Denville, New Jersey 07834

10. Gallard-Schlesinger
    584 Mineola Avenue
    Carle Place
    Long Island, New York 11514
    (516-333-5600)

11. Gaylord Bros., Inc.
    Box 4901
    Syracuse, New York 13221
    (800-448-6160)

12. Glass distributor

13. Hamilton Industries
    1316 18th Street
    Two Rivers, Wisconsin 54241

14. Hardware store

15. Hollinger Corporation
    P.O. Box 6185
    3810 South Four Mile Run Drive
    Arlington, Virginia 22206
    (703-671-6600)

16. I.C.I. America Inc.
    Plastics Division
    Wilmington, Delaware 19897

17. Light Impressions Corporation
    439 Monroe Avenue
    P.O. Box 940
    Rochester, New York 14603
    (800-828-6216)

18. Littlemore Scientific Engineering
       Company
    Railway Lane, Littlemore
    Oxford, England

19. Metronics Associates, Inc.
    3201 Porter Drive
    Palo Alto, California 94304

20. Photofile
    2000 Lewis Avenue
    P.O. Box 123
    Zion, Illinois 60099
    (312-872-7557)

21. Photographic supply store

22. Pohlig Bros., Inc.
    P.O. Box 8069
    Richmond, Virginia 23223
    (404-644-7824)

23. Printfile, Inc.
    Box 100
    Schenectady, New York 12304

24. Process Materials Corporation
    301 Veterans Boulevard
    Rutherford, New Jersey 07070
    (201-935-2900)

25. Rohm and Haas, Plastics Division
    Independence Mall West
    Philadelphia, Pennsylvania 19105
    (check telephone directory for local distributors)

26. Science Associates, Inc.
    Box 230, 230 Nassau Street
    Princeton, New Jersey 08540
    (609-924-4470)

27. Solar-Screen Company
    53-11 105th Street
    Corona, New York 11368
    (212-592-8223)

28. TALAS
    Technical Library Service, Inc.
    213 West 35th Street
    New York, New York 10001-1996
    (212-736-7744)

29. Taylor Instrument Company
    Consumer Products Division
    Sybron Corporation
    Arden, North Carolina 28704

30. 3M
    Film and Allied Products Division
    3M Center
    St. Paul, Minnesota 55101

31. University Products
    P.O. Box 101
    South Canal Street
    Holyoke, Massachusetts 01041
    (413-532-9431)

32. Verd-A-Ray Corporation
    615 Front Street
    Toledo, Ohio 43605
    (419-691-5751)

An excellent source of new photographic equipment and supplies for setting up a copy room and a darkroom is VWR Scientific Inc., P.O. Box 7900, San Francisco, CA 94120 (415-468-7150). VWR issues an extensive catalog containing darkroom equipment, cameras, film, and furnishings. The firm's international headquarters is in San Francisco, although there are more than twenty-five regional offices across the United States. *Shutterbug Ads* (P.O. Box F, 407 S. Washington Avenue, Titusville, FL 32796) is a national monthly tabloid offering used cameras and darkroom equipment for sale. While used equipment must be evaluated to assure that it is in good working order, purchasing used rather than new equipment can result in great savings. Local sources of used equipment, such as camera and photographic supply stores, also should be explored.

Appendix D
Funding Sources for Photographic Collections

Many local, state, and national agencies and foundations, in both the public and private sectors, support photographic projects. Funding guidelines and requirements vary from grantor to grantor, and emphases on types of projects change over time. In the past, monies have been granted to support printing and copying of negative collections, conservation research and treatments, arranging and describing collections; photographic exhibits, and similar activities that have made photographic materials more readily available for research use.

A brief list follows of public and private funding sources that operate on a national scale and have been known to grant monies for photographic projects. Inquiries regarding specific areas of interest, funding priorities, and application procedures should be directed to the individual agencies.

The Ford Foundation
320 East 43rd Street
New York, NY 10017
212-573-5000

The Andrew W. Mellon Foundation
140 East 62nd Street
New York, NY 10021
212-838-8400

National Endowment for the Arts
Museums Program
Visual Arts Program
2401 E Street NW
Washington, DC 20506
202-634-6369

National Endowment for the Humanities
Research Resources Program
Museums and Historical Organizations Program
Old Post Office
1100 Pennsylvania Avenue, NW
Washington, DC 20506
202-786-0200

National Historical Publications and Records Commission
National Archives and Records Service
Washington, DC 20408
202-523-5384

National Museum Act
Arts and Industries Building
Smithsonian Institution
Washington, DC 20560
202-357-2257

National Science Foundation
1800 G Street NW
Washington, DC 20550
202-357-2257

Rockefeller Foundation
1133 Avenue of the Americas
New York, NY 10036
212-869-8500

Information on grant-giving agencies is available from a number of organizations and publications, including the following:

The Foundation Center, a national service organization with four regional offices, provides information on foundation funding, helps locate appropriate grant sources, and publishes *National Data Book* (annual), *Foundation Directory* (biannual), *Source Book Profiles* (quarterly), and *Grants Index* (annual). Toll-free number: 800-424-9836.

The Foundation Center
79 Fifth Avenue
New York, NY 10003
212-957-1120

The Foundation Center
1001 Connecticut Avenue, NW
Washington, DC 20036
202-331-1400

The Foundation Center
312 Sutter Street
San Francisco, CA 94108
415-397-0902

The Foundation Center
1442 Hanna Building
Cleveland, OH 44115
216-861-1933

Grants Magazine
The Journal of Sponsored Research and Other Programs
Plenum Publishing Corporation
233 Spring Street
New York, NY 10013

Cultural Directory to Federal Funds and Services for the Arts and Humanities
Federal Council on the Arts and Humanities
Smithsonian Institution Press
Washington, DC 20560

Funding Sources and Technical Assistance for Museums and Historical Agencies. A Guide to Public Programs
American Association for State and Local History
708 Berry Road
Nashville, TN 37204

Index

Index compiled by Laura K. Saegert

Acknowledgements

The primary focus of the Basic Archival Conservation Program over the past two years has been activities directed toward administering photographic collections. Program elements have included a series of workshops, a consultant service, and preparation of this manual. Members of the Advisory Committee have been consistently supportive and helpful. Thanks are extended to Shonnie Finnegan, Mary Todd Glaser, Edward R. Gilbert, Sue E. Holbert, Howard P. Lowell, William L. McDowell, Jr., George Talbot, and Larry A. Viskochil.

Edward R. Gilbert, Technical Advisor to the Program, read the entire manuscript and offered many helpful suggestions. His counsel through all phases of the project has been much appreciated.

We are also grateful to our colleagues who read the manual in its various stages and offered helpful criticism and advice: Nancy Malan, Anne P. Diffendal, Philip P. Mason, Larry A. Viskochil, George Talbot, Carol Turchan, Andrew Raymond, James Reilly, and Terry Abraham. SAA staff members also provided support during the preparation of the manual. Special thanks are due Ann Morgan Campbell, as well as to Deborah Risteen who designed the layout and coordinated production of the manual. Linda Ziemer assisted in the preparation of illustrative material and also managed many phases of the workshop program.

Special thanks are due Larry A. Viskochil and his colleagues Jane Stevens, Maureen O'Brien Will, and Walter Krutz of the Prints and Photographs Collection of the Chicago Historical Society for their efforts in providing photographs for the manual. We are very grateful for their work on our behalf. James C. Anderson of the Photographic Archives, University of Louisville also provided many photographs both for the manual as well as to meet instructional needs in the workshops. His assistance is much appreciated. Thanks are also extended to the following institutions for making photographs available to us: Prints and Photographs Division, Library of Congress; Archives of Labor and Urban Affairs, Wayne State University; State Historical Society of Wisconsin; Special Collections Department, University of Illinois at Chicago; Special Collections, University of Kentucky; Minnesota Historical Society; Alaska and Polar Regions Department, University of Alaska, Fairbanks; and the George Eastman House.

Pamela Spitzmueller's drawings add greatly to the manual, not only for the information they provide but because they convey it in such a pleasing way. We are also grateful to Laura K. Saegert for compiling the index, which greatly increases the usefulness of the manual.

Finally, and certainly not least, thanks are extended to our colleagues who attended the photo workshops. Their enthusiastic response helped to move us forward, and always made it a pleasure to share the wonder of the photographic record!

Mary Lynn Ritzenthaler
Gerald J. Munoff
Margery S. Long

About the Authors

Mary Lynn Ritzenthaler is Director, Basic Archival Conservation Program, Society of American Archivists. She was formerly Assistant Manuscript Librarian/Associate Professor at the University of Illinois-Chicago. She is author of *Archives & Manuscripts: Conservation* (SAA, 1983).

Gerald J. Munoff is Director of Administrative Services, Kentucky Department for Libraries & Archives, and was formerly Curator of the Photographic Archives, University of Kentucky. He is chairman of SAA's Aural and Graphic Records Section.

Margery S. Long is Audio Visual Curator, Archives of Labor and Urban Affairs, Wayne State University, where she teaches a course entitled Administration of Photographic Collections.